Reader praise for *Bulimia: A Guide to Recovery*

"This is essential reading for clinicians, but perhaps its greatest strength is the encouragement it gives to patients and families to understand and work through this disorder free of guilt or shame, and endowed with knowledge and effective strategies. I recommend it for all my patients."

—Arnold E. Andersen, MD
University of Iowa, Professor Emeritus

"If I had only one book to give someone with bulimia it would be this 25th anniversary edition of *Bulimia: A Guide to Recovery.* Lindsey and Leigh offer their experience: through the darkness of an eating disorder to the light of recovery and a life of love and service."

— Carolyn Costin, MA, MEd, MFCC
Monte Nido Treatment Center, Malibu, CA
author of *The Eating Disorder Sourcebook*

"Everyone whose life is touched by eating disorders can gain insight, inspiration, and practical tools from this comprehensive and compassionate text. Bravo, Lindsey and Leigh—and thank you once again from the bottom of our hearts!"

—Shannon Cutts
author of *Beating Ana* and founder of MentorCONNECT

"This invaluable book combines practical, 'how-to' information with Lindsey's honest, intimate story. It is an excellent resource for understanding the whole spectrum of eating disorders and offers sound, empowering strategies for recovery. Wise, respectful, and thorough."

—Judi Goldstein
Vice President, The Renfrew Center Foundation

"This groundbreaking book is as relevant today as it was when it first offered hope. Thank you, Lindsey and Leigh, for shining light on the path towards recovery and for continuing to lead the way with such courage and grace!"

—Anita Johnston, PhD
author of *Eating in the Light of the Moon*

"Superb! The best book written on battling bulimia, with new sections on mindfulness, healthy eating, and balanced exercise. A must have for anyone affected by bulimia."

—Diane Keddy, MS, RD
Nutrition Consultant, Newport Beach, CA

"I've recommended *Bulimia* to many of my clients over the decades and know it has helped each of them. Your story has inspired troubled eaters all over the world to take heart and follow in your footsteps. How fortunate for us all—clients and clinicians—that you had the courage and wisdom to write it."

—Karen R. Koenig, LCSW, M.ED
author of *The Rules of "Normal" Eating* and *Food & Feelings Workbook*

"Lindsey and Leigh combine all the elements essential to a seminal book about bulimia: a deep and thorough understanding of the subject from both personal and professional viewpoints, profound compassion for those who suffer from the illness, and inspiration and hope about the possibilities for recovery."

—Johanna Marie McShane, PhD
author of *Why She Feels Fat*

"Lindsey Hall and Leigh Cohn have done more for the eating disorders field than the rest of us put together. They have educated treatment professionals, individuals with eating disorders, and loved ones across the globe. Lindsey published her story before most people had even heard about bulimia."

—Dianne Neumark-Sztainer, PhD, MPH, RD
Professor, University of Minnesota

"This revision, filled with warmth and wisdom, clearly establishes *Bulimia: A Guide to Recovery* as a classic in the field. Lindsey and Leigh are an unbeatable team, offering practical tools, day-to-day strategies, and compelling insights into the inner struggles of all who suffer. A must for anyone—patient, family member, or therapist—committed to learning about the journey to recovery."

—Judith Ruskay Rabinor, PhD
author of *A Starving Madness*

"A rare eating disorder book—essential information and contagious inspiration, in equal measure. There is no doubt that I have recommended this book to more of my eating disorder clients than any other, and I don't see that changing any time soon."

—Thom Rutledge, LCSW
co-author of *Life Without Ed,* and author of *Embracing Fear*

"*Bulimia: A Guide to Recovery* remains a truly heartfelt and sensitively drawn account of an illness that although far better understood today is no less painful to endure."

—Michael Strober, PhD
Director, Eating Disorders Program at UCLA

"In this updated and revised 25th anniversary edition, Lindsey and Leigh have added a considerable amount of new material while keeping the pearls of wisdom and insights that made this book vitally meaningful and invaluable to so many readers over the years."

—Joel Yager, M.D.
Editor-in-Chief, *Eating Disorders Review*
Professor, University of Colorado School of Medicine

From readers of prior editions:

"It wasn't until I read your book that I was able to walk through the steps of recovery. It was truly the first time I had felt hope in more than 16 years."

"When I finished the first day of the two-week program, the words 'sleep well' brought tears to my eyes. I felt like someone out there really understands and cares. Thank you from the bottom of my heart!"

"Please forgive my personal disclosure of struggles with emotions or relationships. I just would like to appreciate your generous treatments in this letter. Today I am peaceful because you really touched my thirsty soul like a warm spring wind." (from Japan)

"There are no words that would aptly describe just how much my life has changed, and how much your shared wisdom helped me along the way."

"I just wanted you to know that I read your book every night when I go to bed, and it keeps inspiring me more and more. I am not going back!"

"I can't believe I've finished the course, and have not had one single binge. But the most precious thing I found in the course is an inner peace with myself, and a realization that it *is* possible to recover completely."
(from Switzerland)

"Every thought I'd ever had concerning my bulimia was in your book. It became one of my closest friends and began to replace the 'friend' that bulimia had been."

"When I look in the mirror now, my eyes don't look hollow and empty. They are once again sparkling with life."

"The book has brought my niece spirit food." (from China)

"I have been carrying your book in my backpack for four months now, since I stumbled upon it in a bookstore in Madras, India. I find something on every page that speaks to me."

"I want to tell you that you touched my soul. You are real. You are empathetic and honest. I have recommended your book to everyone who has or is in danger of suffering from an eating disorder."

"Whenever I feel like giving up or like there is no hope, I remember how difficult it was for you, too, and I remind myself that I can do it."

Bulimia: A Guide to Recovery
25th Anniversary Edition

25th Anniversary Edition

Bulimia

A GUIDE TO RECOVERY

Completely Revised & Updated

Lindsey Hall
&
Leigh Cohn

gürze books

Bulimia: A Guide to Recovery
25th Anniversary Edition

Gürze Books
P.O. Box 2238
Carlsbad, CA 92018
(760) 434-7533
www.bulimia.com

Cover design by Abacus Graphics, Oceanside, CA
Original Fabric art by Dorothy Turk
Photos on page 277 by David Hall, PhD

Publishing History:

This 25th Anniversary Edition has been fully revised and updated but includes some information from the following, previously published editions: *Bulimia: A Guide to Recovery "Fifth Edition"* (Gürze Books, 1999); *Bulimia: A Guide to Recovery "Revised Edition"* (Gürze Books, 1992); *Eating Without Fear* (Bantam Books, 1990); *Bulimia: A Guide to Recovery* (Gürze Books, 1986); Set of three booklets (Gürze Books, 1980-83).

Library of Congress
Cataloging-in-Publication Data

Hall, Lindsey, 1949-
Bulimia: a guide to recovery / Lindsey Hall and Leigh Cohn. -- 25th anniversary ed.
p. cm.
Includes bibliographical references and index.
ISBN 978-0-936077-51-2
1. Bulimia--Popular works. 2. Self-care, Health--Popular works.
I. Cohn, Leigh. II. Title.
RC552.B84H35 2011
616.85'263--dc22
2010038041

Disclaimer:
The authors and publisher of this book intend for it to provide accurate information. It is meant to complement, not substitute for, professional medical and/or psychological services.

2 4 6 8 0 9 7 5 3 1

Let us all
love and respect
ourselves
and
each other.

Table of Contents

CHAPTER 2. *Eat Without Fear: A True Story of Recovery from Bulimia*

PART ONE: OVERCOMING BULIMIA

CHAPTER 3. *Getting Started*

CHAPTER 4. *Professional Treatment*

CHAPTER 5. *Tools for Recovery: What Has Worked for Many*

Acknowledgments

Past editions of *Bulimia: A Guide to Recovery* have included various acknowledgments. We've thanked each other; our parents, who have now passed away; Leigh's late sister, Ellen; Lindsey's brother, Ben Hall; and our sons, Neil and Charlie, who grew up with Gürze Books.

Now, we'd like to thank the eating disorders community—the individuals suffering from these disorders, their loved ones, therapists, educators, and researchers—all of whom have been our teachers. Most of the authors listed in the bibliography are people we know, some of whom are friends. Two in particular, Diane Mickley, MD and Kathryn Zerbe, MD, were sensitive, intelligent, and generous with their feedback about earlier drafts.

Introduction

I am wide-awake and immediately out of bed. I think back to the night before when I made a new list of what I wanted to get done. My husband is not far behind me on his way into the bathroom to get ready for work. Maybe I can sneak onto the scale before he notices me. I am already in my private world. I am overjoyed when the scale says that I am the same weight as I was the night before, and I can feel that slightly hungry feeling. Maybe IT will stop today, maybe today everything will change. What were the projects I wanted to do?

We eat the same breakfast, except that I take no butter on my toast, no cream in my coffee, and never take seconds (until he gets out the door). Today, I am going to be really good, which means eating certain predetermined portions of food and not taking one more bite than I think I am allowed. I am careful to see that I don't take more than he does. I can feel the tension building. I wish he'd hurry up and leave, so I can get going!

As soon as he shuts the door, I try to involve myself with one of the myriad of responsibilities on my list. But I hate them all! I just want to crawl into a hole. I don't want to do anything. I'd rather eat. I am alone, I am nervous, I am no good, I always do everything wrong anyway. I am not in control, I can't make it through the day—I know it. It has been the same for so long.

I remember the starchy cereal I ate for breakfast. I am back into the bathroom and onto the scale. It measures the same, BUT I DON'T WANT TO STAY THE SAME! I want to be thinner! I look in the mirror. I think my thighs are ugly and deformed looking. I see a lumpy, clumsy, pear-shaped wimp. I feel frustrated, trapped in this body, and I don't know what to do about it.

I float to the refrigerator knowing exactly what is inside. I begin with last night's brownies. I always begin with the sweets. At first I try to make it look like nothing is missing, but my appetite is huge and I resolve to make another batch of brownies to replace the one I'm devouring. I know there is half of a bag of cookies in the trash, thrown out the night before, and I dig them out and polish them off. I drink some milk so my vomiting will be smoother. I like the full feeling I get after downing a big glass. I get out six pieces of bread and toast one side in the broiler, turn them over and cover them with butter and put them under the broiler again till they are bubbling. I take all six pieces on a plate to the television and go back for a bowl of cereal and a banana. Before the last toast is finished, I am already preparing the next batch of six more pieces. I might have another brownie or five from the new batch, and a couple large bowlfuls of ice cream, yogurt, or cottage cheese. My stomach is stretched into a huge ball below my rib cage. I know I'll have to go into the bathroom soon, but I want to postpone it. I am in never-never land. I am waiting, feeling the pressure, pacing the floor in and out of rooms. Time is passing. Time is passing. It is almost time.

I wander aimlessly through the living room and kitchen once more, tidying, making the whole house neat and put back together. Finally, I make the turn into the bathroom. I brace my feet, pull my hair back and stick my finger down my throat, stroking twice. I get up a huge gush of food. Three times, four, and another stream of partially digested food. I can see everything come back. I am glad to see those brownies, because they are SO fattening. The rhythm of the emptying is broken and my head is beginning to hurt. I stand up feeling dizzy, empty, and weak.

The whole episode has taken about an hour.

For nine years, I binged and vomited up to five times daily. Although there were a few days without a binge, the thoughts were always there, even in my dreams. It was painful and frightening. No one knew about my bulimia, because I kept it safely hidden behind a facade of competence, happiness, and average body weight. When my health and marriage began to fail, however, a series of coincidences brought me face-to-face with recovery, and I soon became devoted to freeing myself from my obsession with food.

I worked hard and willingly, and underwent an amazing transformation. As the bulimic thoughts and behavior subsided, I was able to see how it had served me all those years—an effective tool for survival when I knew no other. It had been a friend, lover, hiding place, voice, and a quest for meaning and love. It was a way to cope with growing up in what felt like a distant family and a frightening and uncertain world. But what had started as an innocent diet became a monster, which threatened to devour my entire life.

My healing was not an overnight thing. I spent over a year gradually letting go of the bulimic behavior, examining every binge for its meaning and purpose. Along the way, I learned to eat without fear by taking one step at a time. I continually exposed myself to more than just my "safe" foods, so I could learn to eat *anything*, and do it intuitively. Out of that healing sprang a relationship with my body, which I began to treat with newfound respect and caring. Feelings of inadequacy, isolation, and judgment transformed into feelings of peace, connectedness, and acceptance. I naturally became accepting of other people's bodies, too—no matter what their shape or size—and an advocate for the beauty of diversity.

One of the most profound revelations I had during recovery was that I didn't know who I was or would be without the bulimia. So, in order to know myself at a deeper level, I purposefully shifted my focus from what I looked like on the outside to what I thought and felt on the inside. I did this through meditation, journal and letter writing, long walks, and deep conversations. I discovered that I was a good and loving person with ups and downs like everyone else, and once I made the connection to this inner life, everything began to change. I am now healthy, happy, and completely free from bulimia, and have been for over 30 years.

In 1980 when my husband, Leigh Cohn, and I wrote my story in a booklet titled, *Eat Without Fear,* there were no other publications available solely on bulimia. In fact, the term "bulimia" hadn't become standard yet; it was sometimes called "bulimarexia" then. The response was tremendous! Our little booklet motivated many others who were trying to quit; and, as we learned more about the binge-purge syndrome, we realized there was more to say.

Over the next few years, we gave many talks around the country, and I became the first person to share her story of bulimia on national television. We wrote several books, including *BULIMIA: A Guide to Recovery*, of which there are now more than 150,000 copies in print in various forms. We also created a niche publishing company, Gürze Books, which specializes in books on eating disorders written by a variety of respected authors and has long been considered a leading resource for information on eating disorders.

This 25th anniversary edition of *BULIMIA: A Guide to Recovery* has been completely expanded and updated. The eating disorders field has grown since we started over three decades ago, and new research has emerged in areas of treatment, prevention, genetics, brain research, and education. During that time, we have collected nearly every book published on the subject, and for this edition, we have utilized the newest and most authoritative sources from that library. We've also added a chapter on treatment and removed the "Guide for Support Groups" (now posted under "Support Groups" at *bulimia.com*).

The book is divided into two main parts. The first, "Understanding Bulimia," answers questions often asked about bulimia and recovery, and includes my own story, *Eat Without Fear.* The second part, "Overcoming Bulimia," offers motivation, support, inspiration, specific recovery suggestions, things to do instead of bingeing, and advice for loved-ones.

Also in part two is "A Two-Week Program to Stop Bingeing." This is just what it says, two weeks of activities, exercises, and written assignments to focus on *instead of bulimia*. It is not intended to be an instant cure, (although that would be great!), but rather an initial experience of self-awareness and confidence to motivate readers to pursue their recovery further. Written in a personal, informal style, the instructions are direct and specific, and demand attention and dedication. It has successfully been used by thousands of individuals in recovery.

Throughout the book are quotes in italics from anonymous readers who have written us to share their experiences of recovery or thank us for our support. These individuals come from diverse backgrounds; the only apparent element common to all of them is that they have an understanding of bulimia because of their direct experiences with it.

Much of this book is addressed to "you," the reader with bulimia. Although past editions relied upon the use of feminine pronouns, we have attempted to make this version primarily gender-neutral because of the increased incidence of males with eating disorders. Consequently, the information and practical self-help tools are equally useful for women and men. Additionally, although "I" am the "speaker," Leigh equally contributed to the writing, ideas, and publishing of this effort, and sometimes "we" both speak in the text.

When I first wrote *Eat Without Fear*, I did so as a way to bring closure to my recovery from bulimia. But I've been blessed to have spent over 30 years working side-by-side with my husband in a fascinating field, with sensitive, intelligent colleagues, helping as many people as I could. For all of it, I feel deeply honored and grateful.

Sharing my experience has remained an integral part of my life because of the effect it has had on others. In the pages of this book, I hope you find the inspiration and motivation you need for your journey to wholeness, fulfillment, and joy.

PART ONE

Understanding Bulimia

Chapter One

Questions Most Often Asked About Bulimia

What is bulimia?

Bulimia is an obsession with food and weight characterized by repeated overeating binges followed by compensatory behavior, such as self-induced vomiting or excessive exercise. This book primarily uses the term "bulimia," but "bulimia nervosa" is also correct, though more formal. In my first publication in 1980 I used "bulimarexia," which is rarely used today.

In 1980, the American Psychiatric Association formally recognized "bulimia nervosa" in *Diagnostic and Statistical Manual of Mental Disorders (DSM)*, a publication that has been updated various times. The diagnostic criteria for bulimia have been only slightly revised in subsequent *DSM* editions. They include:

A. Recurrent episodes of binge eating, with an episode characterized by (1) eating in a discrete period of time, usually less than two hours, an amount of food that is significantly larger than most people would eat during a similar period of time and under similar circumstances; and, (2)

*At the time of this writing, the DSM-IV-TR was in use, and we also consulted the proposed DSM-V.

a sense of lack of control over eating during the episode, such as a feeling that one cannot stop eating.

B. Recurrent inappropriate compensatory behavior in order to prevent weight gain, such as self-induced vomiting, misuse of laxatives, diuretics, enemas, fasting, or excessive exercise.

C. Behaviors occur at least once a week for at least three months.

D. Self-evaluation unduly influenced by body shape and weight.

E. Behavior occurs separate from anorexia nervosa.

The above list was created to help clinicians diagnose and treat this complex disorder, and there are other, similar definitions used internationally. Also, there are many individuals with "subclinical" bulimia, who fulfill only some of the criteria. Whether these people technically have bulimia or another classification (see the next question on other eating disorders) their behaviors are also life damaging and need to be taken seriously. For example, someone may binge and purge less often than once a week, but still have all the concerns as someone who exhibits this behavior daily.

Although the overt symptoms of bulimia revolve around food behaviors and a fear of gaining weight, bulimia is actually a way to cope with personal distress, emotional pain, and chemical imbalance. An eating disorder takes time and focus away from painful feelings such as anxiety, fear, depression, inferiority, etc. Binges can be a form of self-medication that satisfies cravings for particular nutrients or neurochemicals that are lacking. A purge is an effective way to regain the control and feelings of safety lost during the binge and to prevent dreaded weight gain.

While bulimic behavior may start as a seemingly quick way to lose weight, it soon becomes addictive. Dieting behaviors naturally lead to hunger, which is followed by eating, guilt, bingeing, purging, relief, and then the cycle begins again. Additionally, there is a physical "high" that accompanies the whole act. This vicious cycle becomes a diversion from all kinds of other problems.

Most individuals with bulimia are ashamed and secretive, sometimes going to great lengths to maintain the appearance of normal eating around other people. Many describe feeling like two people—one who wants to give it up and be healthy, and another who constantly sabotages. Lying and sneaking are common traits. Many people describe stealing food that they know belongs to other people or digging through the trash during particularly desperate episodes.

Although a typical binge represents a tremendously large quantity of food, a binge is uniquely defined by the person who is eating. Even a "normal" meal might feel like "too much" to someone who is terrified of getting fat, and a single bite of something "bad" might be too much for some individuals. I once spoke to a woman who felt compelled to throw up after drinking one can of diet cola.

Binges can be triggered by a number of things: a high number on a scale, eating something that is normally "forbidden," taking one bite more than "allowed," a traumatic event, or something as innocuous as thinking about food. Many people describe their feelings during binges as completely out of control, driven by a desperate desire to escape or numb out. While they might feel ugly, unworthy, hopeless, and helpless before and during a binge-purge episode, after, they might feel a mix of control, shame, relief, disgust, high, dizziness, exhaustion, and resolution. Part of the cycle often includes the promise that each incidence will be the last.

How many people have bulimia?

It is difficult to say how many people have bulimia, as researchers are not in agreement. Statistics may not truly reflect the total numbers because, as we previously stated, bulimics generally hide their behavior. In fact, one study showed that college students answered questionnaires more truthfully only when told to put a dab of their saliva on the survey paper, because they believed their sample could be chemically analyzed to determine if they were bulimic! Also, conflicting criteria for bulimia may have been used in various studies.

Of the research done on the prevalence of eating disorders, one reliable review of many studies showed that 1.0 to 1.8% of college women meet the strict clinical criteria for bulimia, and 2.6 to 3.3% have subclinical levels (Crowther, 2008). Another well-respected survey found that 1.5% of adult females and 0.5% of adult males had a lifetime prevalence of bulimia (Hudson, 2007). However, some studies offer much higher numbers. For example, one study of female high school and college students reported that 15% met the criteria for bulimia (Cavanaugh, 1999), although these figures seem abnormally high. There was a notable, temporary increase in prevalence in the early '80s (Russell, 1997), when the public first became aware of bulimia, otherwise rates among women have remained fairly constant since that time.

Historically, men were determined to account for about 10% of cases, but in recent years this number has substantially increased to one male for every three females. Whatever the actual figures, it is undeniable that a substantial number of both women and men are engaging in this self-destructive behavior.

How is bulimia related to other eating disorders?

Eating disorders can be conceptualized as existing on a continuum—with anorexia nervosa on one end, binge eating on the other, and bulimia somewhere in between the two. Some people move along the continuum, perhaps restricting their eating for years and later becoming binge eaters. I've known women who have had anorexia for a period of time, and then bulimia, and visa versa.

The most common eating disorders are (with prevalence for adult women from the Hudson study): anorexia nervosa (0.9%), bulimia nervosa (1.5%), and binge eating (3.5%). Another category, "Eating Disorders Not Otherwise Specified" (usually referred to as EDNOS), refers to subclinical levels of anorexia or bulimia. However, this is an emerging field of study and these categories have shifted in various editions of the *DSM*. For instance, binge eating started as a subcategory of EDNOS, and bulimia was also considered to be one type of anorexic behavior.

Bulimia has also been grouped with binge eating disorder, for obvious reasons. Certainly, in all cases, the relationship with food is a symptom of other serious problems, and many other similarities do exist.

These disorders overlap so much that labeling them can be limiting. For example, an anorexic might occasionally binge or purge. However, the distinctions between types of eating disorders are convenient for clinical approaches to treatment and insurance company classifications.

Anorexia Nervosa

Anorexia nervosa is characterized by self-starvation. The *DSM* criteria for anorexia nervosa continue to evolve, but they can be generalized as follows:

A. The individual maintains a body weight that is about 15% below normal for age, height, and body type.

B. The individual has an intense fear of gaining weight or becoming fat, even though he or she is underweight. Paradoxically, losing weight can make this fear of gaining pounds even worse.

C. The individual has a distorted body image. Some may feel fat all over, others recognize that they are generally thin but see specific body parts (particularly the stomach and thighs) as being too fat. Their self-worth is based on their body size and shape. They deny that their low body weight is serious cause for concern.

A requirement for an absence of at least three consecutive menstrual cycles in women has been debated. However, the trend is to eliminate the amenorrhea prerequisite, because sometimes women meet all of the other criteria for anorexia nervosa and still continue to menstruate. Also, some experts questioned whether males were being ignored, especially when many have lowered testosterone levels.

There are two specific types of anorexia nervosa. The "restricting type" denotes individuals who lose weight primarily by reducing their overall food intake through dieting, fasting and/or exercising excessively. The "binge-eating/purging type" describes those who occasionally binge (consume large amounts of food in short periods of time), and purge through self-induced vomiting, excessive exercise, fasting, the abuse of diuretics, laxatives, and enemas, or any combination of these measures. There seems to be little difference between this type of anorexia and bulimia, other than the frequency of bingeing and purging.

In general, anorexics restrict food in the extreme, have lower body weight, are not socially outgoing, and usually begin their disorder in childhood or adolescence, although there are mature women who develop anorexia later in life. In contrast, the majority of bulimics maintain a weight that appears normal, began purging in their late teens or early twenties (many anorexics turn to bulimia when they get older), and are more socially outgoing.

There are also similarities between anorexics and bulimics, such as a preoccupation with the size of their bodies and what they have or have not eaten. Both groups are focused on an inner, empty place, which can be viewed in physical, emotional, social or spiritual terms. Both use the control of food to handle intense feelings and to avoid situations where there is a potential for conflict, disapproval, or failure. Both use food as a form of self-expression. However, while a binge and purge can give a bulimic the courage to face the world, restriction is empowering to an anorexic. The bottom line in recovery means being able and willing to care for one's self with appropriate amounts of food (not starving or stuffing) in a healthy, self-nurturing way.

Binge Eating Disorder

The diagnostic criteria for Binge Eating Disorder (BED) are modeled after those for bulimia, but without compensatory behaviors or a preoccupation with weight and shape. Additionally, the binge eating episodes are more defined for BED, including some, but not necessarily all, of the following: eating rapidly, eating when not physically hungry or until uncomfortably full, eating alone due to being embarrassed about how much is eaten, and feelings of self-disgust, depression, and guilt after a binge. These behaviors are all common amongst those with bulimia, but they are not included in that clinical diagnosis. Similarly, most binge eaters dislike their bodies even though that's not a criterion of BED.

Purging is the main difference between these two eating disorders, which otherwise share few differences. Much more common than the other eating disorders, BED includes a higher percentage of men, with Hudson showing 57% of cases being males. Also, BED does not have a weight criterion and should not be confused with obesity, which is a medical condition rather than an eating disorder. For example, obesity can be caused by excessive cortisol or abnormal hormones, not just by overeating.

Virtually all of the suggestions in this book apply to individuals with or in recovery from BED.

Other Eating Disorders

EDNOS, or Eating Disorder Not Otherwise Specified is a DSM catch-all category for individuals who don't meet all of the criteria necessary for a diagnosis of a specific eating disorder. For example, someone might not qualify for bulimia or BED because they binge less often than the required once a week for three months, or might have all of the symptoms of anorexia nervosa except the required 15% weight loss. These kinds of details prevent individuals from getting insurance coverage for therapy. The EDNOS diagnosis was created, in part, to get managed care to pay for all levels of eating disorders treatment.

Other types of disordered eating and related issues include Night Eating Syndrome, pica, rumination, childhood feeding problems, orthorexia, and body dysmorphic disorder that are beyond the scope of this book.

Also, although dieting is not considered an eating disorder, per se, people who yo-yo diet share many similarities with those described in this section. What's more, the current obesity epidemic in the Western world has a lot in common with some aspects of EDNOS.

Why do people become bulimic?

There is no easy answer to this question, because bulimia is a multidimensional disorder. It is caused by a combination of factors including, but not limited to, culture, family, personality, genetics, biology, and trauma. Although there is evidence that every one of these factors can play a significant role, none singly is a predictor of who will be afflicted.

The Culture of Dieting

In the first sentence of her book, *The Religion of Thinness*, Michelle Lelwica writes, "We live in a culture that worships thinness." She exposes the intersection between the all-pervasive media and $60 billion per year weight-loss industry. We are constantly bombarded with digitally enhanced images of models selling concepts of happiness, success, and intimacy. Whether the product is a diamond ring or diet, the message is the same: Your life would be better if you were thinner.

A widely published study of Fiji Islanders illustrates this point. Prior to the introduction of television in 1995, the island had no reported cases of anorexia nervosa, bulimia, or weight concerns; but, within three years of American and British TV programming, more than two-thirds of Fijian girls had attempted dieting, and three-quarters of them felt "too fat." The thin ideal had crept into their lives.

Dieting, so normalized in our culture, is often referred to as a "gateway" to eating disorders. Most people with bulimia began restricting or purging as the result of a failed diet. However, 95% of diet attempts end in failure, and clearly not *all* of those people develop serious eating disorders. So, while dieting is a risk factor, it alone does not "cause" bulimia.

While bulimia was a secretive disease 30 years ago, it is now a well-publicized, almost glorified, condition. Descriptions of binges and purges can easily be found on the web, as can encouragement for the eating-disordered "lifestyle." Celebrities with anorexia nervosa are sensationalized throughout popular culture, and eating disorders are essentially "taught" to innocent teens. College residence assistants have complained that serial vomiting damages dormitory plumbing, and some students binge and purge in groups. When I started telling my story, few people had ever heard of bulimia, but now everyone knows someone who has had some kind of eating disorder. Sadly, public awareness focuses on the symptoms rather than the devastating consequences, so large numbers of people continue to experiment with bulimia with the hope of getting thinner.

Family

In the '80s, people believed that bulimia primarily affected white, upper middle class girls whose mothers were controlling. However, we now know that eating disorders do not discriminate by race, age, gender, or socio-economic class, and are global problems. The tendency to blame parents is also outdated, because all types of families are susceptible.

That said, bulimia often manifests in families where the emotional, physical, or spiritual needs of its members are not met and attachments are tenuous. In some of these households, feelings are not verbally expressed, and communication skills are lacking. There may be a history of depression, substance abuse, or eating disorders; the child might unconsciously recognize that escape is an appropriate, and necessary, thing to do.

Oftentimes, parents are unaware of problems. For example, a girl who hides her bulimia might appear to be an "ideal" child, presenting an acceptable facade—outgoing, confident, and independent—while anxious feelings bubble underneath. She may be valued for not needing to be nurtured, for taking care of herself, and for growing up early, all the while feeling guilty and unlovable. Bulimia is a way of expressing what cannot be said directly in words, in this case something like, "I want to be taken care of" or, "Would you love me if you really knew me?"

Sometimes, young people use bulimia to postpone growing up, and parents—especially those who don't want to let go—can be unaware of how they reinforce their child's insecurities. A "perfect little girl" who always looks to her parents for validation might be ill equipped to trust herself and face the outside world alone. This may explain why college students away from home for the first time are prime candidates for developing bulimia.

Families that emphasize weight and appearance, or have rigid rules about food, can also promote eating disorders. Kids who grow up watching their mothers and fathers go on diets and over-exercise are likely to do the same. If parents are judgmental and gossip about how so-and-so has gained a few pounds, their children will learn that body size is a measure of worth and will themselves feel judged and be prone to a poor body image.

Furthermore, parents who do not communicate openly and honestly foster poor relationship skills in their children. Also, daughters whose fathers are physically and emotionally absent experience "father hunger," which can contribute to problems with body image, self-esteem, and food (Maine, 2004). Finally, emotional, physical, or sexual abuses by family members are obvious risk factors.

Compared to the general population, the risk of developing bulimia is 4.4 times greater for women with a female relative who has experienced an eating disorder (Crow, 2010). Whether that is a result of nature or nurture is unclear, and, regardless, families are only part of the equation.

Personality

The complex relationship between personality and susceptibility to eating disorders has been of interest to researchers and clinicians for a long time. Certain personality traits—perfectionism, sensitivity, compulsivity, impulsivity, and inflexibility—appear to predispose a person to developing an eating disorder. Some may be genetically hard-wired into our biology, some the result of co-occurring conditions, and others shaped by individual experience.

In general, people with bulimia are attempting to avoid painful feelings, which may be the result of these personality traits, such as a naturally sensitive person feeling unloved and anxious, or a perfectionist feeling overwhelmed. Most devastating of all are the feelings associated with low self-esteem—that we have no worth, that our lives have no value or purpose, and that we will never be fulfilled or happy. These kinds of feelings, no matter what their source, often lead to eating disorders.

Genetics and Biology

Genes, hormones, and biochemistry influence personality and behavior. Researchers are just beginning to uncover the genes—or groups of genes—involved with depression, anxiety, and other mental disorders. Twenty years ago, the conventional wisdom was that culture and dysfunctional families caused eating disorders, but in recent years, genetics has been recognized as a substantial factor. Some experts attribute 50 to 80% of a person's risk being due to genetic predisposition (Bulik, 2007).

Genetic research for eating disorders is only emerging and, thus far, has concentrated more on anorexia nervosa. However, it is already widely accepted that there is a genetic component to bulimia, the exact nature of which is still unknown. If a specific bulimia gene exists, then why has bulimia only been known for the past 30 years? The way researchers explain this contradiction is that someone may be born with a genetic predisposition for an eating disorder, but that the behaviors only develop as a result of cultural and environmental triggers—for example, mass media, the diet mentality, and increased availability of food.

Research advances are also finding connections between eating disorders and biochemistry. For example, abnormal levels of the brain chemical serotonin are common in individuals with bulimia. Also, evidence suggests that changes in sex gland hormone status, both in puberty and adulthood, may impact eating behavior (Crow, 2010). Studies in this area indicate that biology may play a greater role than previously thought and deserve further inquiry.

The consequences of malnutrition have long been studied, and the harmful effects of disordered eating are well established. Subjecting the body to the nutritional toll of restricting or purging has significant physical and mental repercussions. The medical complications of bulimia are described later in this chapter, but for our purposes here, suffice it to say that starving your brain can cause psychological problems—including misguided thinking. After all, why else might someone who has been dieting think it would be a good idea to try bingeing and purging?

Finally, normal, biological weight gain during puberty, a time when body image becomes so important to both boys and girls, is often interpreted negatively. Especially in today's society, when tremendous emphasis is placed on the "obesity epidemic," teens feel the pressure to be thin. Large kids are often teased for their size or put on diets by well-meaning parents, which can alienate them from their bodies for the rest of their lives.

Trauma

Most individuals with bulimia have been preoccupied with food and dieting for years, but the onset of binge-purge episodes may be triggered by trauma (abuse, an accident, extreme stress) or major life events, such as: moving away from home or beginning college, graduation or career change, rejection by a lover or wished-for lover, marriage, or death of a loved one. (The link between bulimia and sexual abuse is addressed on page 43.)

One reason that trauma causes the onset of bulimia might be that severe or prolonged stress creates alterations in the brain and neuroendocrine system, including abnormalities of neurotransmitter levels and cortisol production. This can disrupt crucial physiological functions, contributing to depression and fatigue, both risk factors for an eating disorder (Woolsey, 2002).

Summary

Individuals with bulimia identify various causes for their disorder. Many remember specific reasons for their initial binges, as well as how the behavior subsequently served them. Few thought it would become addictive. Once the binge-purge cycle is begun, the original causes—which still exist—are blanketed with guilt, secrecy, physical side-effects, and an increasing number of reasons to want to escape.

Regardless of the underlying reasons, bulimia "works" on many different levels. Binge eating provides instant relief. It replaces all other actions, thoughts, and emotions. The mind ceases to dwell on anything but food and how to get it down. Feelings are on hold. Even vomiting can be pleasurable when it is the most intimate contact allowed with the body. When the whole binge-purge episode is over, for a brief moment, the bulimic regains control. No longer feeling guilty for having eaten so many calories, she is drained, relaxed, and high. Soon, these feelings are replaced by negative ones, and the cycle of this painful, debilitating, exhausting illness begins again.

No two people are the same, so everyone's reason for developing bulimia is unique. Here are some quotes from actual sufferers:

I started because I was rejected by a boy at age 15. I thought the main thing wrong with me was my weight.

I developed my eating disorder the night before my first college finals. My father had passed away a month earlier, and I was nervous about my tests and about returning home and having him not there.

I started throwing up during my fourth month of pregnancy when I could not handle my changing body, and dieting away the calories became impossible.

One of my friends showed me how to do it when we were in junior high. Looking back, she didn't do me any favors!

Why are bulimics mainly women?

In simple terms, we live in a society that is fundamentally unsatisfying to many women. Their sexuality is exploited, their intelligence is questioned, their safety put at risk, and their roles are often limited and confusing. They are bombarded with promises of a "better self" through the dieting, fashion, cosmetics and anti-aging industries. Most feel unsupported by a culture with such shallow values. Their role within this society, which is at different times limiting, confusing, frightening, and unfulfilling, propels enormous numbers of women into the security and numbness of food problems.

Here are a few of the main reasons why specifically women are vulnerable to eating disorders:

• ***Women are socialized in ways that increase their risk of getting eating disorders.***

In the course of growing up, girls are socialized to relate and behave in ways specific to our culture. At increasingly early ages, they are bombarded with images of female bodies as objects to be scrutinized unmercifully. They are also made hyper-aware of stereotypical "feminine" traits, such as cleanliness, docility, unselfishness, politeness, and sometimes being a temptress. By the time sexual game-playing starts, most of them already know that their bodies are tools for popularity and power, and that there is appropriate and inappropriate behavior associated with being a girl.

Also, a strange thing happens to girls when they reach adolescence. Their sure sense of self, strong opinions, and unabashed involvement give way to feelings of powerlessness, insecurity, and doubts about their appearance. They are no longer cute little girls, they are budding sexual women. From a girl's perspective, this puts her in a vulnerable position with regard to men, and a competitive one with other females. At a time when she is forging an identity, altering her body to fit cultural expectations seems to be a reasonable way to fit in with everyone. Many young women develop eating disorders when their initial attempts at dieting fail, and they are faced with the fear of never being an "ideal" woman.

Although strides have been made, many archaic ideas remain, such as women should put the needs of others ahead of their own, they should mistrust their spontaneity and leadership skills, or their bodies are objects to be judged, objectified, and sexualized. These lessons teach women their social and cultural "limitations." They become afraid to express themselves freely and deny their unique needs, strengths, opinions, and inherent beauty. Bulimia can be a reaction to, and distraction from, feeling disconnected from both body and soul.

• *Having a female body in this society can be frightening.*

Statistics of sexual abuse and violence against women are staggeringly high. Women are often fearful and feel unsafe in the world. An eating disorder is a way of coping with their vulnerability.

In the case of abuse, an eating disorder is a form of self-harm: an unconscious reenactment of the original act, or a way to punish the body that was "to blame" for the assault. It can also be a way to distance one's self from the body, numb the feelings associated with abuse, and regain control that was lost: "My body is my own. I am in control of what goes in and out of it." Ultimately, an eating disorder is a safe place to hide from pain and fear.

• *Our society denies the natural variety and function of women's bodies.*

Women come in all shapes and sizes, but rather than embracing the natural diversity of bodies, society only places a value on thinness. "Becoming a woman" in contemporary Western culture is for many an embarrassing, self-conscious affair, requiring daily self-scrutiny. Most women feel pressured to shave their legs and underarms, hide their periods, control body odors, and obliterate signs of the aging process. That's in addition to the cultural pressure to be thin. Even women who have experienced the miracle of giving birth are driven to quickly flatten their stomachs afterwards, as though it had never happened. An eating disorder is a misguided effort to achieve the "perfect" body, even though that is a superficial and unattainable goal.

Also, few young women are prepared for the normal weight gain that accompanies puberty. During this time, girls gain about a third of their adult body weight in preparation for childbirth. Rather than celebrating this miraculous maturation, our society denigrates it.

- ***Women are expected to control their emotions.***

Many women with bulimia fear the intensity of their bottled-up feelings. Few have experience with emotions or appetites for sex, food, or a meaningful life. They are expected to keep their anger in check, deny their fears, not even talk "too" much! Some say that they have reached a point where they cannot distinguish one feeling from another. Letting out their emotions might mean being engulfed by them, or engulfing others. Controlling their bodies, specifically food intake, becomes a concrete way to feel in control of this inner instability.

- ***Women are frustrated in the workplace.***

Although the women's movement has provided opportunities for a fortunate minority, women continue to be underrepresented in the upper-echelon marketplace and political arena. Those who are able to land jobs in the areas of their interest and expertise are often paid less than men and are under tremendous pressure to perform. Also, many of our institutions, corporations, and systems have a more patriarchal, hierarchical structure. This type of environment, which favors independence and competition, can be unsatisfying for those who are more apt to thrive in cooperative, interdependent settings. Bulimia can be a symptom of a life devoid of meaning, creativity, or rewarding work. It can also help let off steam or be a way to self-sabotage in order to avoid risk or failure.

• ***The media and money perpetuate the status quo.***

The extensive influence of the media on each and every one of us is unquestionable. Billion-dollar businesses depend on women (and men) feeling insecure about their appearance, and they accomplish that goal with impossibly thin and sexualized images.

While a cover girl's photo or cosmetics advertisement does not cause a binge, constant reminders that thinner equals better establishes values that lead to distorted ways of viewing food and the self. How can a woman feel good about who she is on the inside if everyone else seems to focus on the outside? How can she accept her natural size and shape when she is urged to take up less space at every turn? Ironically, many of the thin actresses and models, who are paid enormous sums for their "look" and skinny bodies, are themselves struggling with eating disorders in an effort to remain marketable.

Do men have bulimia?

While the actual numbers of men with eating disorders are unknown and are certainly less than for women, more men have bulimia than anyone thought in the early '80s, or even just a few years ago. While the incidence of bulimia in women has stayed fairly constant over the years, male eating disorders have noticeably risen. Historically it was believed that about 10% of individuals with eating disorders were male, however recent figures put the prevalence around 33% (Hudson, 2007). Also, unlike women, some men become obsessed with getting larger and more muscular—a condition called "reverse anorexia" or "body dysmorphic disorder" which can also become addictive.

The stigma of having a "women's disease" prevents many men from seeking professional help, which is one reason why the male prevalence rate is sketchy. It also means that men often don't realize they have an eating disorder, nor do the people closest to them. Further, the purge of choice for a lot of men seems to be overexercise, which can masquerade as a healthy escape instead of eating-disordered behavior. Incidentally, some men do binge and vomit.

There are far more similarities than differences when comparing men and women with bulimia. Men are equally influenced by culture, family, genetics, etc., and the diagnosis and behaviors are the same, regardless of gender, as are the approaches to treatment. Men are under pressure to appear strong, in control, and independent, and as such, their roles in our culture have limitations and drawbacks, just like women's. Many have difficulty expressing feelings and have had little experience in emotionally intimate relationships. Most feel tremendous pressure to be in charge, to shoulder financial worries and be the foundation for their families. Few would want to be labeled as obsessed with their appearance. All these situations might make them more susceptible to using bulimia as a coping mechanism, as well as extremely reluctant to seek help.

When comparing scores on clinical assessments, men and women with eating disorders have similar ratings in areas such as drive for thinness, body dissatisfaction, perfectionism, and fear of growing up, although women tend to have slightly higher degrees of severity. At any given time, about 80% of women would like to lose weight, and likewise, 80% of men would like to *change* their weight, as well. However, here's one of the differences: Only half of those men would like to be thinner; the others want to be more muscular, even if it means putting on a few pounds (Andersen, 2000).

Men are even more affected in certain areas than women. The media deluges them with idealized standards of muscularity and advertisements for improving sexual competence, losing love handles, and adding or removing hair. They are also more susceptible to developing eating disorders and overzealous attitudes about exercise as a result of a father's health problems. Furthermore, the very act of binge eating—so impermissible for women—is often viewed as "typical guy behavior."

Some male athletes, such as jockeys and gymnasts, use bulimia to maintain or lose weight and become hooked on it, just as is the case for many female athletes. Purging behaviors among wrestlers became so commonplace that the NCAA wrote guidelines to outlaw severe weight-loss methods like self-induced vomiting, diuretics, and exercising in saunas.

Homosexual men—as compared to heterosexuals—are at particularly high risk for developing eating disorders because of their preference for a thin, muscular appearance, as well as greater body dissatisfaction, higher levels of depression, lower self esteem, and discomfort with sexual orientation. However, eating disorders are not exculsive to the gay community and the likelihood exists that (due to the vastly higher numbers of heterosexuals in the general population) more straight men may have eating disorders than those who are gay.

As you know, the language of this book primarily addresses women, but most of the underlying messages and suggested activities are equally worthwhile for men. Moreover, I want to raise awareness of the problem for those who suspect that a man they know or love has an eating disorder. This might even be the father, son, or partner of a person with bulimia.

How is bulimia related to sexual trauma?

Clinical studies are inconsistent in reporting the numbers of eating disorder patients who have been sexually abused, and there is some controversy about this. Figures for bulimics with a history of sexual abuse range from an astounding 7% to 70%. Regardless of the exact frequency, there is a subset of bulimic patients who have this kind of trauma in their background, and it is obviously of crucial significance to the development and treatment of their eating disorder.

This is an extremely sensitive topic, and a self-help book alone is not adequate for healing these issues. With the understanding that victims need to work with a mental health professional who has experience treating individuals suffering with both eating disorders and sexual trauma, I will present an overview on this subject. Also, although I am using feminine pronouns, incest and sexual abuse occur with startlingly high incidence among males, with similar consequences.

Being sexually assaulted, especially by a "trusted" adult, parent, or sibling, is a terrifying, confusing, horrific experience for anyone. It is an act of violence and betrayal so intense that just remembering it is agonizingly painful. In order to survive not only the trauma itself but also the memory of it, a victim might dissociate from the event and from those parts of herself that were present at that time. She may even consider the person being violated to be separate from herself, because the pain is too much to bear. Her emotional and physical survival depend on her not remembering the events or the associated feelings.

An eating disorder works to protect, repress, complete, divert, numb, or confuse these feelings and memories. Certainly it is not within a child's realm of possibility to blame the abuser for what happened, but even an adult will tend to blame herself for such an attack, making her body the focus of hatred and control. Stuffing down food will stuff down the anger and silence the voice that cries out, "Don't do this to me!" Planning and executing a binge will numb anxieties and deny physical needs, such as for hunger or affection. Being in charge of what does, and does not, go into the body is a way to symbolically regain that control which was lost during the original trauma.

The relationship with food makes it difficult to have full relationships with others, thus eliminating the risk of another betrayal. Depending on the individual's internal survival tools, being extremely large or thin, or even perceiving one's self as too large or too thin, is a way of keeping potential abusers at a distance. Finally, the painful and violent act of vomiting is a way of expressing and releasing feelings of rage and self-loathing.

Although we are defining sexual abuse here in terms of more extreme behaviors, practically every woman has suffered sexual humiliation in some form or another. Their breasts have been "accidentally" brushed up against, their virginity has been the subject of male gossip, and they have been whistled or jeered at by strangers.

Sexual trauma must be treated in a safe, trusted environment. Coming to terms with the experience, repressed or not, and returning the individual to an experience of unconditional love and acceptance is a tremendous undertaking. It requires gentle understanding and patience by therapist and patient alike. Keep in mind that eliminating the binge-purge behavior without introducing healthy coping skills can result in a retraumatization. Making some kind of peace with the nightmare that lies beneath the bulimic surface is best achieved with the guidance of a trained and skilled professional (Schwartz, 1996).

Working and uncovering the truth about my family, and the fact that I was a victim of incest, helped everything make sense. I saw how wounded I was, and how much pain and anger I worked dutifully to deny.

After reading a blog on sexual abuse, I realized that my bulimia was a way to keep the abuse secret. I was trying to protect my family.

When I was 12, my brother began sexually abusing me. I was overwhelmed with confusion and believed if I became fat, he might leave me alone. I think gaining 40 pounds in three months was also my way of saying, "Hey, there's something wrong here," without having to verbalize it.

My physical and sexual abuse began at an early age. Much of the abuse centered around food, with my father demanding favors for desserts. Some days, it was all right to leave food on my plate, others it wasn't. Food became my lasting enemy.

I had a swallowing problem due to being forced into oral sex. I would spit out all of my food, even liquids. I had been through every medical test in the book because the doctors thought there was something wrong with my throat. After four years of therapy, that problem is finally gone; but, it comes back at times of high stress or when memories surface.

It's important for parents, therapists, doctors, and the public to know that women who were sexually abused are in a lot of pain. Their eating disorder is a way of dealing with all of the feelings—rage, anger, secrecy, fear, betrayal, powerlessness, and many others. An eating disorder is a feeling disorder because it helps you handle your feelings.

How does bulimia affect my relationships?

Bulimia is sometimes referred to as a "relationship disorder" because it disrupts normal, healthy connections with other people. Individuals with bulimia gradually withdraw from social interaction until their obsession with food becomes an overriding focus.

Relationships are the foundation for our feelings of significance, competence, and ability to be loved. Children without healthy attachments often do not feel loved or safe and look outside themselves for cues on how to behave. As a result, their relationships will be "other-directed" and founded in fear and low self-esteem.

Bulimia, which often begins as a misguided attempt to gain thinness and thereby please people, is an example of this other-directed behavior. The person with bulimia is not following her heart; instead she is reacting to external circumstances. While the bulimia appears to be protecting her by preserving a false front, it also keeps people at a distance. She interacts with others knowing she can withdraw at any time to her familiar, repetitive behaviors. Even when she appears to be present in conversation, her mind can be light years away, preoccupied with the last or next binge.

Certain aspects of bulimia are particularly detrimental to honest, fulfilling relationships. Obviously, maintaining a happy, competent façade on the outside, while feeling anxious or depressed on the inside, takes effort and is a distraction. The binge and purge behaviors are done secretly, usually shrouded by feelings of guilt and shame. Mood swings and lying are common characteristics. Focusing on thinness encourages competition between women instead of support, and emphasizes the sexual nature of relationships with men instead of affection or respect. Over time, a bulimic's relationship with food will come to supersede all others.

Although some women think that bulimia is a friend who does not criticize, judge, compete, or reject, in fact it does all those things. It does not nurture, support, or fulfill us at the deepest inner level, as anyone who has repeatedly gorged and purged (and recovered) will testify. Jenni

Schaefer, author of the book *Life Without Ed*, conceptualized her eating disorder as a distinct being with unique thoughts and a personality separate from her own. "He was abusive, controlling, and never once hesitated to tell me what he thought, how I was doing it wrong, and what I should be doing instead." She needed to divorce Ed and "make room for the real me to exist."

Giving up bulimic behavior is extremely frightening for someone who has little experience being close to others. But the payoffs are obvious—honesty, trust, enjoyment, intimacy, and love. As the section in this book on getting support emphasizes, an open, trusting relationship with even one person can be a crucial factor in recovery. Many people found this trust in therapy or counseling of some kind; others found it with parents, lovers, spouses, and friends.

How could I have a relationship with someone based on honesty and truth if I was constantly lying about how much I ate, didn't eat, exercised, or purged?

When I have no close relationships or involvement with others, I feel like I am starving. Food reduces the anxiety and masks the feelings. Only working on intimacy stops this pattern. For me, relationship building is essential to recovery.

Basically, my life became a massive cover-up. Any lie or deception that protected my freedom to binge-purge was okay, and I'd always placed a high value on honesty prior to this!

My relationships with my family members deteriorated as they caught me in numerous lies. They couldn't trust most of what I said. I actually believed that the reason my sisters were tracking me around the house, in an attempt to stop my vomiting, was because they were jealous that I was finally thinner than they were!

When I went out with friends, I was so detached from what was going on that all I could do was calculate how fast I needed to get to the bathroom to vomit. I had no real interest in the people around me; but, through therapy, that's all changing now.

I recall on many occasions turning on my answering machine, settling down to plates of my favorite binge foods, and listening to friends leave messages, while I frantically shoveled in food. Food had become more important than my friends. Food was my BEST friend.

As I became more comfortable with myself, I saw my life change in many ways. I found myself surrounded by friends who really liked me. And they were happy people, not miserable and depressed like my old friends.

In recovery, I have learned how to say "no" to people, and earned a lot of respect for doing so. I was always afraid of what would happen if I disagreed or wanted something to be different. Now I feel worth having an opinion.

What is a typical binge?

"Typical" depends entirely on the individual. According to the *DSM*, binges are defined as, "eating, in a discrete period of time (e.g., within any two-hour period) an amount of food that is definitely larger than most people would eat during a similar period of time and under similar circumstances," and a sense of lack of control while eating.

I've corresponded with lots of people who have had bulimia and have observed that the size and frequency of binges can vary, as can the type of purge and the length of time between sessions. A binge is really whatever causes a person to feel guilty, and even a small amount of "forbidden" food might be too much. Most bulimics describe a typical binge in the same terms. Driving the behaviors are overwhelming feelings, particularly low self-esteem, anxiety, disconnection, fear, and hopelessness. Then a "letting go" into eating occurs, which is a distraction from those painful feelings. Although the pace of eating is usually frantic, there is a certain peace about losing one's self in the "doing" of the binge. This is, for many, a safe, familiar, numb place. Eventually, whatever is eaten is purged, and the person is left mentally, physically, and emotionally drained. This, too, can feel like a relief, and is sometimes referred to as a "high."

The fact that this cycle is a form of self-harm is given only minor attention, mainly because it feels to the person like an act of survival. The pain inflicted on the body has alleviated the pain of the psyche—until the feelings come up again, and the next cycle begins.

Many bulimics have said that they can relate to my former binges, one of which I've described in the introduction to this book. Usually I would start a binge while in the course of eating what I thought to be a "good" or "safe" meal. For example, I may have gone to a salad bar and carefully allowed myself a moderate portion. As I ate, I would begin to feel guilty about the calories in the salad dressing or the fact that I had taken croutons. At one point in the meal, I would decide I had eaten one bite too many. Rather than stop eating, I'd think, "What's the difference. I've already gone too far. I'll do a binge, and none of the calories will matter after I vomit." It never occurred to me that there were "issues" driving this bizarre food behavior, or that my cavernous appetite might have been due to the restricting I was doing between episodes.

If I had my choice, I would devour sweets and refined carbohydrates. A single binge might include: a quart of ice cream, a bag of cookies, a couple of batches of brownies, a dozen donuts, and a few candy bars. When I was desperate, I would binge on anything: oatmeal, cottage cheese, carrots, or day-old rolls that I fished out of the trash from what was to be my last-ever binge. (After being recovered for 30 years, I can hardly believe I ate all that!)

I would move at a frenzied pace, sometimes doing mindless tasks here and there until I felt stuffed. My stomach stretched so much that I looked pregnant, yet I usually postponed vomiting for about 30 minutes of numbness. Then I'd force myself to bring up every last bite. The whole episode would last about an hour, and I was weak and dizzy afterwards.

This doesn't describe the many other scenarios that occurred during those nine years, like eating in a restaurant and trying to find a bathroom away from friends or family. Or eating breakfast in a dorm kitchen and vomiting in a public bathroom on the way to class. I had many opportunities and I took them. I was a scared young woman with few life skills, a family history of chemical imbalance, and no close relationships. Somehow, the bulimia was helping me get through the days.

Friends and loved-ones need to understand that vomiting from a binge is not the same thing as vomiting when you are sick. The person with bulimia doesn't feel nauseous, she feels desperate and driven. Bingeing and purging temporarily removes stress, much like a drug. After a vomiting purge, there is also a physical high from the pressure of being upside down and exhausting physical effort. Feelings of cleanliness, renewal, relaxation, mindlessness, and emotional numbness are common. There may also be sexual satisfaction from the emerging, private excitement, complete involvement, fullness, stroking, and sudden release.

What are the medical dangers?

Bulimia can be a fatal disease. Mortality rates for eating disorders vary widely between studies, with sources listing anorexia nervosa deaths from .3% to 10%. One fairly new study compared the records of individuals who had been treated at specialized eating disorders clinics with the National Death Index. Their findings for crude mortality rates were: 4% for anorexia, 3.9% for bulimia, and 5.2% for EDNOS (Crow, 2009).

The most common causes of sudden death in bulimia are cardiac or respiratory arrest, the result of electrolyte imbalances from excessive purging. Electrolytes, which are minerals in the blood—like potassium, chloride and sodium—help maintain a regular heart rhythm, as well as the function of the muscles that enable the heart to pump and the lungs to breathe. When these chemicals are depleted due to purging—often made worse by weight loss and excessive water drinking—heart arrhythmia (irregular heartbeat) can occur. Since this can lead to sudden death, it is important to have blood tests to monitor electrolytes, and medical treatment if they are amiss. This danger resolves when proper health and nutrition are restored.

Less common causes of death in bulimia include choking, rupture of the esophagus or stomach, and suicide. Kidney failure is another possible life-threatening side-effect of prolonged low potassium (Mehler, 2010).

Gastrointestinal symptoms may result from vomiting or laxative abuse. Severe acid reflux causing inflammation of the esophagus and heartburn, spontaneous regurgitations, and chest pain are the more common GI symptoms from vomiting. Constipation or diarrhea (or both), gas, bloating, abdominal cramping, dehydration, and blood in feces occur from laxative use. Also, the lower bowel can lose muscle tone, becoming limp and unable to produce contractions.

Oral and dental problems frequently occur due to vomiting. These include erosion of tooth enamel and subsequent cavities or loss of teeth, gum inflamation, sore throat, dry mouth, and difficulty swallowing.

Individuals with bulimia may also experience cold hands and feet, and develop calluses on the back of the hand from rubbing against teeth when inducing vomiting (called "Russell's sign" after Gerald Russell, a British psychiatrist who wrote the first academic article on bulimia nervosa in 1979). Other potentially serious complications include internal bleeding, pancreatitis, irregular or absent menstrual periods, impaired fertility, bone loss leading to osteoporosis, muscle loss, and brain changes.

Some bulimics use syrup of ipecac, detergents, or foreign objects to induce vomiting—all of which are extremely dangerous. Ipecac, a horrible tasting liquid, is used to treat poison victims, and its abuse can result in both muscle weakness and cardiac arrest (Mickley, 1999; Mitchell, 1997).

Some medical conditions have been documented as risk factors for eating disorders, although we can only speculate about the mechanism. These include: diabetes mellitus, cystic fibrosis, inflammatory bowel diseases such as Crohn's disease, and mononucleosis. Incidentally, as many as one in three teenaged girls and young women with type 1 diabetes mellitus purposely manipulate doses of insulin to lose weight, a practice shared on the Internet and called "diabulimia." This leads to poor control of blood sugars associated with the development of diabetic complications, such as blindness and kidney failure, within just a few years (Bock, 1999; Yager, 2007a; Zerbe, 1995).

It is difficult, if not impossible, to know which bulimics are at greatest risk for developing any of these specific conditions. Certainly, the longer the bulimia continues, the greater the risk of cumulative damage. However, even someone who has only started to purge faces the possibility of serious physical consequences, even death.

Pregnancy and Postpartum Issues

Many bulimics have concerns about getting or being pregnant. Some fear that their vomiting will harm the child or that they will get too fat. Although information on pregnancy and eating disorders is limited, what we do know is:

- An eating disorder can impact fertility as a result of hormonal disturbances, sexual dysfunction or lack of desire, related polycystic ovarian syndrome (PCOS), and ambivalence about having a family.
- An eating disorder may start or worsen during pregnancy, but some women experience complete remission for the sake of their child.
- Women with eating disorders are at risk to deliver low-weight babies and have a significantly increased incidence of birth defects, Caesarean sections, and miscarriages.
- Since pregnant women have separate digestive systems from their fetuses, purging by vomiting while pregnant does not necessarily harm the child. However, poor nutrition, restricting, and a mother's negative frame of mind are unhealthy for both.
- For pregnant women in recovery, some antidepressants can be used, but others should be avoided. In any case, they should check with their doctors about specific medications.

- New mothers often return to their bulimia, especially when faced with added weight. They are also at high risk for postpartum depression and anxiety.
- The birth of a child can awaken emotions about a wide range of issues including: mother/child relationships, parenting, marriage, sexuality, separation conflicts, worries over proper feeding for baby, and preoccupation with the baby's appearance.

Obviously, recovery from an eating disorder is important for the welfare of both mother and child (Yager, 2007b; Zerbe, 2008).

What thoughts and feelings are associated with bulimia?

This is a tricky question, because some of the thought patterns and feelings associated with bulimia may be the result of chemical imbalances in the body. Depression, which is a co-occurring condition for many bulimics, creates a cloud of negativity that feels real and should be honored, but that can be alleviated by certain medications or missing nutrients. Also it's difficult to determine whether the negative thoughts and feelings are the cause or the effect of the eating disorder.

That said, eating disorders are "*feeling* disorders" in that the rigid rules and rituals of bulimic behavior are a concrete way to distance one's self from feelings that seem unmanageable, overwhelming, or just plain terrifying. These range from the nightmarish fear of memories of abuse, or the quiet pain of being unloved or considered unimportant, to unnamed feelings that are buried in past events or freshly raw from current life. A binge can push away loneliness, fear, guilt, shame, and a host of other emotions by providing another focus.

Paradoxically, in the early stages, an eating disorder can "raise" self-esteem and feelings of confidence when it provides someone with a sense of success—in this case by achieving the cultural ideal of thinness.

However, once the bingeing and purging cycle begins, the resulting metabolic imbalances and habitual escape become an ever-deepening hole, eventually eroding any initial sense of self-worth.

As time goes on, the binge-purge cycle becomes the preferred way for individuals with bulimia to handle *all* their feelings, leaving them powerless and without choices. What's more, the illness brings with it a whole new set of complications that mask and amplify the original problems. For example, a person who is afraid of others may use bulimia to keep her distance by hiding her embarrassing thoughts and rituals. Or someone who feels incompetent may perfect the art of throwing up, while attempting little else. In this way, whatever precipitated the binge-purge behavior is effectively denied, and in the long run, buried beneath fresh shame and guilt.

Most individuals suffering with bulimia have trouble even identifying and talking about their feelings, or they feel the need to purposely censor themselves. Often this is because they were raised in families that did not know how to express or allow a full range of emotions, especially "negative" ones, like anger, disappointment, or even disagreement. Some families have unwritten rules for controlling which emotions can be expressed and what modes of expression are permitted. The end result is that everyone monitors and protects whatever is going on for them, and in many situations, the truth is denied altogether.

A bulimic may not even know exactly *what* she is feeling, or might assume that her feelings are bad and she is bad for having them. She might fear other people's feelings, as well, and work hard to ensure that no one is ever upset. She will also have cut herself off from her experience of the "felt" sensations of the body, no longer attuned to the physical experiences of hunger or fullness. She may not even know what feeds her soul, because she is disconnected from her own joy and purpose in life. Separated from a sense of *self*—physical, emotional, or spiritual—she feels adrift with no anchor.

In general, individuals suffering with bulimia say that they feel depressed, empty, unmotivated, and powerless a lot of the time, which drives them into their binge-purge cycle. During an episode, feelings can also repeat, moving from: *worthlessness* (low self-esteem), to *powerlessness* (I have no control over my life), *effectiveness* (I can get rid of these feelings), *high* (from the release of the purge), *hope* (that this binge might be the last), and finally back to *worthlessness*.

Bulimia is also a "*thinking* disorder" in that sufferers are trapped in harmful thought patterns. One example is black-and-white thinking, where everything is divided into extreme categories: foods are either "good" or "bad," bodies are either "fat" or "thin," and not being in-control means being completely out-of-control. Other patterns are magnifying problems, magical and dramatic thinking, constantly comparing one's self to others, and taking remarks or situations too personally. Some bulimics also seem to hold a generally negative attitude towards life, which influences all aspects of their human experience. Most think that they are worthless and unlovable, as evidenced by the size of their bodies.

Individuals with bulimia typically harbor a set of deeply held, core ideas upon which other harmful conclusions are drawn. For instance, the belief that being fat is bad will also mean that food is bad, that having a large body is a sign of failure, and that self-indulgence is a sign of weakness. Believing that "I am a bad person," which many bulimics think is true, makes possible the thoughts, "There is no reason to take care of myself," and, "No one can love me." This sets up an entire system of values and ideals upon which they are constantly monitoring and judging themselves—and sometimes others. Their minds do what is referred to as "spinning," or going over and over the same negative thoughts. These endless, automatic loops in the mind make it impossible for bulimics to hear anything else, much less their own inner wisdom.

All these negative feelings and thought patterns must be brought to light and challenged in recovery. This can be at once a frightening, rejuvenating, enlightening, exhausting, and rewarding experience, which is why it is best done with the guidance of a mental health professional.

Before I started therapy, I never associated my desire to binge with my emotions. I always felt it was an uncontrollable desire for huge amounts of food. Now I understand the binge takes the place of allowing myself to feel.

When I feel sad, troubled, panic, anger, or loneliness, this disease jumps out on me like a Jack-in-the-box. I find it scary because I also feel helpless and not in control. Then again, the mental "numbness" blocks out all the emotions and makes me forget about my problems. It's not worth it, though.

What other behaviors do bulimics share?

People with eating disorders have compulsive personalities; the rituals they create are safe and familiar places to reside. Many of the rituals revolve around food and body image, such as arranging food on their plates, excessive exercise, eating systematically, looking in the mirror, and obsessive calorie counting. Some behaviors are not related to food, such as always knowing where the nearest bathroom is, avoiding people, lying, keeping secrets, stealing, and compulsive shopping.

Most bulimics take exhaustive steps to cover up their symptoms. During the five years of my first marriage, my husband never discovered my secret bingeing and purging. No one knew! Covering my tracks was part of my daily routine. Lying about food was second nature to me. For example, if I went to the same grocery two days in a row to buy large quantities of binge food, I would tell the checker that I was a nursery school teacher buying snacks for the children. My rituals included a preoccupation with scales, mirrors, and trying on clothes. I used to weigh myself before and after binges to be sure that I gained no weight. (At one point in my recovery, I took a hammer to the scale!) I could not pass a mirror without judging every slight bulge or hair out of place.

Some individuals with bulimia also have other psychiatric conditions, such as mood disorders (depression, bipolar), anxiety disorders (obsessive compulsive disorder, panic disorders, social phobia), substance-related disorders (drugs or alcohol abuse), borderline personality disorder (impulsivity which may include self-harm, bingeing, promiscuity, etc.), and attention deficit hyperactivty disorder. Unfortunately, research on eating disorders and comorbidity is contradictory, and generalizations about prevalence are not helpful. Experts do not even agree about whether anxiety or depression is more common in patients with bulimia. More study about comorbidity is being done, and more needs to be done (Crow, 2010; Yager, 2008).

When a person is in recovery from bulimia, they may have to face the burden of addressing some of these other behaviors, as well. For this reason, professional help is highly recommended for more complex situations. In many cases, regardless of the symptoms, the same issues must be examined, and that is usually best accomplished in therapy.

When I first tried to give up my bulimic behaviors, I began to drink more alcohol. I was substituting one escape for another. I would get so depressed over my drinking that I would finally binge. I joined Alcoholics Anonymous, have been sober five months, and find my bulimia much more manageable. Until I quit drinking, I kept having recurrent episodes of my old bulimic behavior.

I stopped stealing after I got caught with a chicken in my purse!

How do I know if I have bulimia?

Have we been talking about you? I binged and vomited daily for nine years without thinking I had a problem, although that was before bulimia had been given a name. I came across the very first magazine article about "bulimarexia" and was shocked to discover that there were other people who had the same eating behavior as I did. Identifying my behavior as a coping mechanism, not a diet gone awry, compelled me to get help.

Whether you binge and purge daily or only occasionally, overeat and exercise compulsively, or just engage in yo-yo dieting behaviors, you are abusing your body in a bulimic manner. Even if you are only obsessive in your thoughts about weight, diet, and food, you *still* have a problem, even if you do not meet the clinical definition for an eating disorder.

Just about everyone enjoys an occasional large meal (holiday indulgences!), but an obsession is an escape. If you have constant negative thoughts about food and your body, you have a problem regardless of its clinical classification, and I urge you to face it.

How long does it take to get better?

The time it takes to stop the bingeing and purging behavior varies with each individual. I have heard of people who have gone "cold turkey," quitting instantly, and of others who have decreased the number of binges slowly over a period of months or years. No matter what the case, though, stopping the behavior is a bit like opening Pandora's box. Within are the reasons why the bulimia began and took hold, as well as those it created anew—all of which need to be resolved.

Remember, bulimia serves a purpose, meaning it takes care of the person in some way, perhaps by helping them manage anxiety or repress frightening memories. To force the recovery process by taking away that option would be like expecting a drowning man to give up his life jacket and swim to shore. Most people are better equipped to fully let go of their bulimia once they have learned new life skills in therapy.

I am often asked how long it took me to recover. I love this question because it raises the corresponding question, "What is recovery?" Over the past 25 years, there have been hundreds of outcome studies done on recovery (measuring length of time with the illness, improvement of symptoms, crossover to another eating disorder, etc.). The findings are too varied to be meaningful, but a couple of generalizations can be made. First, recovery requires treatment of some kind. Second, in most studies, various treatment approaches resulted in improvement in bingeing and purging behavior. Studies of self-help, both guided and self-directed were also positive. (Richards, 2000; Sánchez-Ortiz, 2010; Yager, 2010).

Recovery means different things to different people. I like to look at it as a process that begins by stopping the behaviors, moves through an examination of the underlying mental, emotional, and spiritual issues, and evolves into feelings of integration, connection, and purpose. First, though, must come the motivation and readiness to change.

During my recovery, I took a close look at every binge I did to discover what it had to teach me. I pledged never to lie to anyone again. And in the process of slowly letting go of my "security blanket," I learned about other ways to take care of myself. I did everything I could think of to help free myself from the prison of bulimia. Over a period of about a year and a half, I completely stopped the binge-purge behaviors, and I had begun to confront the issues that led me to become bulimic in the first place.

Over the next few years, I continued to work at improving different areas of my life: the relationship with my parents, making more friends, being able to handle conflicts, and understanding my emotional needs and being able to articulate them. Yes, I had thoughts about wanting to be thinner, but I was able to look at those thoughts, but not act on them. I worked on my body image, too, because I wanted to be able to love the body I was in, no matter what its size or shape, and I wanted to stop judging other people's bodies, too. It was several years before I considered myself able to do that. Most wondrous of all, I eventually moved from being a basically negative person to a basically happy one. At that point, I felt completely free. I called myself fully recovered, and have been for the past two and a half decades.

Recovered vs. In Recovery

Not everyone agrees that full recovery from an eating disorder is possible. Some believe that bulimia is an addiction and that practicing the "abstinence approach" from certain foods as well as behaviors, is a lifelong way to prevent future relapse. They stress adherence to food plans devoid of "addictive substances," and working through various "steps" of recovery with the help of a sponsor. Like an alcoholic, a complete cure is not possible for someone with bulimia, because it will always be an option for dealing with life's pain. These folks would use the terms "in recovery" or "recovering" when referring to someone who has had bulimia, no matter when their last episode occurred.

This abstinence approach works for many people, especially those new to recovery where it can provide a sense of safety and structure. But I personally wanted to *lessen* my focus on food, so I could be completely free to eat anything I wanted. And so, my recovery focused on what is called the "legalized food" approach. Instead of restricting, advocates of this approach stress differentiating stomach hunger from emotional hunger, and fulfilling both appropriately. They emphasize getting satisfaction from eating what the body wants and needs, and not labeling food as "good" or "bad." They would be more inclined to use terms like "full recovery" or "recovered."

People often ask whether I believe in full recovery. I say I do, because that term works for me. I haven't binged in over thirty years, and don't expect to ever again. Is this a guarantee? No, it's not. What's more, people who have practiced the abstinence approach might have the *same* successful track record, yet still call themselves, "recovering." Perhaps this is just a case of semantics. If someone believes in their heart that they have made peace with food, that they love and appreciate their body, and they are comfortable with the hard-won "freedom" from obsession they have earned by whatever method, then they can call themselves anything they want!

I personally recommend therapists and facilities that use either the abstinence or the legalized food approach. The information in this book applies to bulimics interested in recovery regardless of their stance on this issue. I do not advocate any specific modality of treatment—whatever works for you, do it!

Can medication help in recovery?

Even the strongest proponents of pharmacotherapy do not recommend treatment based entirely on medication. No "magic pill" can fully resolve the emotional and spiritual issues underlying bulimic behavior; therapeutic drugs should be just one part of a multidisciplinary treatment approach. Still, antidepressants—particularly fluoxetine (brand name Prozac®)—are often used in the treatment of select patients with bulimia.

Although these drugs are termed "antidepressants," they are just as useful for bulimics who are not depressed. Medication may enable a patient to benefit from the other components of treatment. For example, medication and Cognitive Behavioral Therapy (CBT) are mutually reinforcing. It is important to note that many patients who have taken these medicines, but not in the high doses required for bulimia, mistakenly feel they can't be helped by them.

Currently, fluoxetine is the only FDA-approved drug for treating bulimia, but not the only one routinely prescribed. It is in the class of selective serotonin reuptake inhibitors (SSRIs), which increase levels of serotonin in the brain. The side-effects of fluoxetine are relatively benign compared to other antidepressants, anticonvulsants, or monoamine oxidase inhibitors (MAO's). While the course of drug treatment usually begins with fluoxetine, when the patient has concurrent symptoms of other psychiatric disorders or does not respond well to fluoxetine, other remedies are considered (Broft, 2010). Primarily physicians, such as psychiatrists—or in some jurisdictions Master Level Nurse Practioners—who are also knowledgeable about eating disorders should prescribe these medications.

In many cases, bulimics respond well to non-pharmaceutical treatment as an alternative to drug therapy. In fact, the American Psychiatric Association guidelines for treating bulimia recommends delaying the initiation of medications to see if therapeutic approaches—particularly CBT—are successful (APA, 2006). However, when patients prefer a pharmaceutical approach, it is appropriate to begin at the same time as talk therapy. Other reasons to include medications initially would be severe bulimic symptoms or significant comorbidity, such as being so depressed, anxious, or obsessional that a patient can't get the full benefit of therapy.

Some bulimics respond well to drug treatment and reduce their cravings to binge within weeks. Many of these people have a history of depression, although being caught in the cycle of bulimic behavior can certainly cause depression, as well. Some bulimics benefit from medications because the chemical changes in their bodies increase their ability to feel hunger and fullness. I've also heard from many women who indicated that drug therapy decreased their cravings to binge, allowing the issues that fueled the binge-purge behavior to surface and be resolved.

Recognizing that food is medicine and a bulimic's body is lacking key nutrients, dietitians on a treatment team will provide well-balanced menu plans, and some practitioners recommend nutritional supplements and amino acids. Although select people respond well to supplements, they are not "evidence-based" treatments, meaning their efficacy has not been proven by clinical trials.

Two of many psychiatrists I tried were biochemically oriented, and willing to modify pharmaceutical rules based on their own experience. We kept trying different doses and medicines until something worked.

I started using Prozac, and it really helped me. My urge to binge lessened practically overnight. It made me feel more ready for therapy.

I am being treated with Zoloft, which has changed my life. It offers a "normal" mood, as well as freedom from binges. Of course, therapy in conjunction with medication is the ideal situation, and I'm trying that too. I don't think one without the other would do.

How do I learn to eat normally?

Just as there is not one road to recovery, there is not one way to eat. Every body is different, and deciding what and how much food is right for *your* body is a personal decision. In the early stages of recovery, though, when emotions are high and thoughts are spinning, food decisions are extremely difficult, sometimes immobilizing. It is helpful to have a plan you feel comfortable with, as you learn how to eat in a new way. A qualified dietitian or nutritionist, perhaps one who is working in conjunction with your therapist, can help you with this. (See Chapter Six, "Healthy Weight, Eating, and Exercise.")

In her book *The Rules of "Normal" Eating*, Karen Koenig identifies four basic rules that "normal" eaters follow: eating when hungry, choosing satisfying foods, eating with awareness and enjoyment, and stopping when satisfied. For individuals in recovery from an eating disorder, this is like making peace with the enemy—a monumental, but extremely worthwhile, undertaking.

As I indicated earlier, there are two main approaches to food in recovery from bulimia. The abstinence approach encourages a varied, nutritious diet, but advocates the elimination of certain trigger foods, such as white flour and sugar, and the use of a food plan. This avoids fears about weight gain or eating a food that might set off a binge. One common practice is to have three, structured meals each day and up to three healthy snacks. Some formal abstinence approach programs use a sponsor to mentor new members.

The legalized approach encourages people to eat whatever food they want, in moderate portions when they are physically hungry, and stop when they are full. This is a more spontaneous approach, and for this reason can be extremely difficult for someone new to recovery. It requires an awareness of hunger cues and permission to eat food that was previously considered "bad," without guilt or loss of control. Most therapists recommend a more externally structured eating plan at first, with a slow introduction to more a intuitive, internally-guided plan.

Food is fuel for the body and brain. A body without fuel has no energy, a compromised immune system, and a malnourished brain that does not think clearly, make good decisions, or think happy thoughts. Recovery from bulimia requires a basic understanding of healthy nutrition that includes a balance of complex carbohydrates, protein, fat, vitamins, and minerals, which is covered in Chapter Six.

Eating normally means enjoying what I eat. It also means loving myself enough to nourish my body with healthy, adequate nutrition.

To normal eaters, food is just food; it's not a substitute for something missing in your life, or a way to stuff feelings.

There are no more "good" or "bad" foods. I eat when I'm physically hungry, and stop when I'm comfortably satisfied. I can eat the foods I enjoy whenever I am hungry for them, and I am more aware of the taste and texture. I no longer binge as a result of deprivation.

I no longer binge or purge, but I also have to watch how much I eat, and I abstain from certain foods such as wheat, flour, hard cheese, and crispy, salty things like potato chips or rice cakes.

Eating normally is being able to eat anything I want, in moderation, with anyone I want. Now, I enjoy going out to eat with my husband and friends.

If I quit purging, will I gain weight?

Obviously, this issue is a concern for most people with bulimia, but there is no single answer that is true for everyone. While you might expect to gain weight in recovery, that won't necessarily happen, because in many cases more calories are retained after bingeing and purging than by eating moderately. So, you might actually lose weight. However, many bulimics—especially laxative abusers—who resume normal eating do gain some weight while their metabolism adjusts to new eating patterns and they replenish their cellular water supply. So, some people gain weight when they stop purging, others lose or stay the same.

The fact is that Mother Nature didn't design us all the same. Bodies come in all shapes and sizes and what is healthy for one person might not be for another. Everyone has a "natural" weight (or weight range) that is most healthy for them at every age. This is the weight at which they feel best, are neither eating too much or too little, are getting regular, moderate exercise, and have a balanced metabolism. Taking genetics into account, this "ideal" weight can be a lot different than the one that is found on a standardized table.

Let's face it: You can find your body on your family tree and there is not much you can do about it. Whether you gain or lose weight is really not as important as whether you are healthy and have a life filled with meaning, satisfying relationships, inspiration, and purpose. This is a revolutionary thought, and you need to be a revolutionary! (See Chapter Six, "Healthy Weight, Eating, and Exercise.")

So the question then becomes, "Can I love my body at any size or shape?" And the answer is yes. The people I talk to, who have worked hard to *change their goal from thin* to *healthy*, feel that their bodies have come to rest at weights that are comfortable, beautiful, and unique.

I used to weigh myself at least 25 times a day. Now, I have not been on a scale for over two years. What should count is how you feel, not a number on the scale. It's hard to break the scale habit, but my advice to anyone is, don't weigh yourself at all!

I'm content with myself and realize I don't have to be skinny any longer. My health is more important to me than the image of "model thin."

Nothing could hurt me as much as being called "fat." It's only now, with definite steps toward recovery, that I'm able to understand how I used food and weight problems to hide from the real issues: relationship problems, loneliness, and shyness.

My weight stays within a five-pound range. I will admit that I would like to weigh about five pounds less, but I consider stopping bulimia much more important than being "thin."

This increase (eight pounds) was right after I stopped vomiting every day, but I have stayed at that weight ever since.

How do I choose a therapist?

Most bulimics should consider professional therapy. First and foremost, find someone who specializes in eating disorders. These are complex and multidimensional problems, and particular knowledge and experience is needed—not all professionals are trained in this field. Professional organizations, such as the International Association of Eating Disorders Professionals and Academy for Eating Disorders, as well as helpful websites, are excellent places for qualified referrals. Local health agencies may also be able to provide names of people in your area. (Sources for eating disorders specialists can be found in the "Resources" section at the end of this book.)

When I use the word "therapist," I am referring to psychiatrists, psychologists, marriage and family counselors, licensed clinical social workers, and other professionals who have training and experience doing individual psychotherapy integrating cognitive behavioral, motivational, family, psychodynamic or other therapies. Also some registered nurses, clergymen, life coaches, acupuncturists, chiropractors, or those who practice therapeutic touch can be helpful adjuncts to treatment. A multidisciplinary approach combines several professionals as a treatment team, of which dietitians and nutritionists are an essential part. If drug therapy is a consideration, a professional who is qualified to prescribe medication *must* be part of that team, as well.

Put in time and effort to find a therapist who is a good fit for you. Call their office and perhaps schedule an initial session or phone interview. Be prepared with a list of questions, and if you feel good about their answers and you communicated well with each other, that's a good indication. When you investigate therapy options, consider the following:

QUESTIONS FOR CHOOSING A THERAPIST

- How much experience do they have treating eating disorders?
- What is their clinical approach? (See Chapter 4)
- Do they focus on changing thought patterns and expressing feelings?

- Do they give homework to keep clients engaged between sessions?
- Do they work with other members of a treatment team?
- How will the team members be coordinated, and who will be the leader or point person for questions?
- What if you need medication?
- How often will we have a session?
- Will there be a support group?
- How soon does the therapist expect to see results?
- How long would they expect therapy to last?
- What will the charges be, and will they accept your insurance?
- Do they have a comfortable office?
- Does the therapist seem kind and nonjudgmental?
- Does the therapist answer you directly and invite you to express yourself?

Interviewing someone doesn't mean you have to work with them, especially if you have other options. Once you've made a choice, though, try at least a few sessions. You might decide together on a reasonable time period before evaluating your progress. Give therapy a chance. If your first choice proves unsatisfactory, find someone else!

You may need a higher level of care, and the same questions apply. There are many treatment centers that specialize in eating disorders, offering inpatient, residential, outpatient, or day treatment programs, as well as groups open to the public. (Referral sources can also be found in the "Resources" section.)

What can I do to help someone who has bulimia?

The support of a spouse, parent, sibling, or friend is one of the most valuable tools a person with an eating disorder can have. In my case, Leigh was available to brainstorm, listen, be a punching bag, and love me unconditionally; and, that help was invaluable.

If someone close to you has bulimia, you can be there for her (or him), but remember *she* is the one with the problem. Loved ones can research treatment options, read appropriate books, attend lectures, talk to experts, and lend a supportive ear, but only the bulimic herself can do the work.

What you would do depends on your relationship. An adult's needs are different than those of a child. In any case, the first step is to let them know that you care about them and want to help. Keep in mind that bulimia is a protective device used to handle pain. If it were easy to give up, the person would have done so already. Someone who uses food as a coping mechanism needs understanding and compassion. The reality of bulimia may shock or disgust you, but you need to separate the individual from her binge-purge behavior. She deserves love and appreciation for who she is apart from the bulimia, and compassion for the pain that has driven her to it. If a loved one became disabled or injured, you would still be there for her—bulimia is also disabling and life-threatening.

At the same time, do not be manipulated or lied to for the sake of binges. Do not enable the disorder by looking the other way or pretending that the problem is not serious. If you stock the refrigerator with food only to have it disappear, be honest and assertive about your rights and needs. Bulimics should not be allowed to abuse your trust or pocketbook; having bulimia is not justification for treating loved ones poorly. Also, don't turn meals into battles—food is not the central issue.

Parents of bulimics especially need to be aware of their limitations—for example, when the child is not living at home or doesn't want their help, they cannot force the issue. Otherwise, family-based treatment can be particularly effective in monitoring and encouraging healthy eating behaviors. Also, family therapy has been shown to be a worthwhile part of treatment. With better communication, increased self-knowledge, and mutual acceptance of what has happened in the past, parents and children can focus on the important task of recovery in the present.

All caregivers, whether they are parents or life partners, need to take care of themselves, as well as the sufferer. This might mean taking time away from the problem or seeking professional advice. They also have to explore their own values, such as preconceived notions about weight and thinness, and should be open to changing their ways of communicating, family rules about food, ways of handling feelings, parenting roles, and the family's decision-making process.

In severe situations, when the bulimic behavior is life-threatening and the person is unwilling to confront it, an intervention would be appropriate. This could take the form of a frank, one-on-one discussion, a family meeting, or a conversation involving other family members, friends, and even a professional, such as a school counselor or therapist. In the most dire circumstances, a person can be legally committed for treatment against their will, although that is rarely the approach of choice.

Ultimately, the process of recovery is a singular, internal process, but it can be greatly assisted with outside support.

What can be done to prevent eating disorders?

In the past 30 years, since I wrote the first publication in print about bulimia (Hall, 1980) and began working to increase education about eating disorders, I've come across hundreds of books written on the subject, as well as countless newspaper, magazine, and Internet articles, television programs, movies, radio talk shows, and public lectures. Numerous eating disorders organizations and treatment facilities have come in and out of existence, there have been informative conferences and workshops, and a whole new specialty has developed for health-care professionals. My efforts and those of other writers, speakers, organizers, therapists, administrators, and educators have helped real people. Also, due to increased public awareness, individuals with eating disorders are today able to find help more easily and know that they are not alone with their problem.

Sadly, there are still millions of people who suffer from eating disorders and countless others who are preoccupied with weight and body dissatisfaction. In fact, after a brief rise and decline in the incidence of bulimia in the early '80s, which may have been due to initial public awareness, the prevalence of this eating disorder has not diminished despite our efforts. Further compounding the problem are harmful "pro-ana" and "pro-mia" websites that promote eating disordered behaviors. It is apparent that although we have developed a variety of successful treatment programs, our long-term goal must be to prevent these disorders altogether.

Healthy eating and the dangers of dieting must be incorporated into every elementary, middle, and high school curriculum. We should further educate parents, prospective parents, teachers, the medical community, fitness instructors, physical educators, clergy, the media at large, and others who interact or mentor young people about the symptoms, causes, and consequences of eating disorders, with early detection and intervention in mind. However, in order to be successful, prevention programs must go beyond the presentation of basic information, which has shown to be largely ineffective (Piran, 1998). Despite our best intentions, a one-hour lecture about bulimia, for example, may only teach listeners how to become bulimic!

For prevention to truly work, the approach must be participatory, systemic, and consistent. The most successful programs emphasize media literacy, gender and teasing as risk factors, positive body image, and positive relationships (Piran, 2010). It is ineffective to solely teach a student about the hazards of eating disorders without also educating her teachers, parents, and peers. Too frequently, a health instructor will offer information on healthy eating and the futility of dieting, only to have the student attend another class with a teacher who is on a diet, then have lunch with friends who only eat carrots and celery, return home to a family that is weight prejudiced, and be exposed to media that advocate the false promise of thinness. To actualize prevention, the message must permeate an individual's whole life and be integrated into all areas of our culture.

In a perfect world, free from eating disorders, all people would appreciate that love and self-esteem are their birthright regardless of shape or weight. Families, aware of the causes and consequences of eating disorders, would be a constant source of communication and sharing. Women would be safe from victimization in their homes, in the work place, on public streets, and in the media. Inner beauty and competence would be recognized and rewarded without regards to age, color, or body shape. Food would be a symbol of life rather than a tool for abuse. In other words, people would be allowed to be themselves without conforming to tight-fitting roles based on artificial limits.

So many different factors contribute to an eating disorder that *all* must be addressed, whether they are cultural, social, biological, familial, emotional, sexual, or other. This is a lofty goal that would require a revolution of contemporary thought. But I believe that every person who recovers from an eating disorder, every person who even embarks on recovery or who refuses to diet, is just that—a revolutionary. And the repercussions of that person's actions can be far-reaching.

Obviously, we have a long way to go, but we must each move in the right direction. Striving for far-reaching goals means that we must first face weight prejudice in our own lives and learn to embrace ourselves and others, regardless of differences. It is only within an atmosphere of mutual love and respect that we will fully realize eating disorders prevention on an individual, and ultimately a societal, level.

Chapter Two

Eat Without Fear
A True Story of Recovery from Bulimia

I finished writing the story of my bulimia and recovery on my 31st birthday in 1980. I printed 100 copies of the 32-page booklet, which I titled, *Eat Without Fear,* and finally felt completely free from bulimia. Getting it all down on paper was the final purge for me. What's more, I felt that I had accomplished something that could help others because, at that time, there were no other books solely about bulimia.

My bingeing and vomiting days may have been over, but my involvement with eating disorders as a "field" was just beginning. Those first 100 copies disappeared in a hurry, and I didn't even give them all to my family! The booklet was reprinted 14 times, making apparent the need for information and education about eating disorders. In partnership with my husband, Leigh Cohn, who co-wrote *Eat Without Fear,* I began to write and speak about eating disorder recovery, and we have been doing so ever since.

This chapter, "Eat Without Fear" is a version of that original booklet. In various editions, more than 150,000 copies have now been published. I've heard from thousands of people that my story has inspired them, and this edition seems as vital to me now as it did 30 years ago when I first wrote it. I hope it speaks to you.

Me in the kitchen (age 3)

Beginning

I grew up in an affluent family that lived in a three-story colonial house an hour north of New York City. My father, an investment banker, commuted to Manhattan, and my mother ran the household. I had three much older siblings who paid little attention to me—except for one who teased me unmercifully. Each was sent to a boarding school around the age of fourteen, after which I saw them primarily on vacations. I was seven when the fifth child was born, and my parents hired a live-in Dutch couple, Margaret and Jack, to take care of my baby brother and me.

The overall impression I have of my childhood is of being alone, whether wandering around our 14-acre property or sitting at the dinner table. I remember often feeling afraid that I had done something wrong. I didn't mean to get in trouble; on the contrary, I always tried to be the perfect little girl. Nevertheless, I had the perception that I was constantly screwing up, like the time I put my sister's toy animals in a pillowcase to show to someone, not realizing they were delicate china and would all break. Fifty years later, I can still feel the terror at the memory of my father spanking me in a total rage—he couldn't stop—while my mother watched from the library door begging for it to be over.

One of my biggest goof-ups was accidentally locking myself in my mother's clothes closet when she went to New York City, and I stayed in there all day, crying and afraid of the shoes which felt like snakes under me. No one heard my screams, and I wasn't found until my mother came home late that afternoon. I felt like life in that house could go on without me and no one would notice. I was not the smartest, prettiest, oldest, youngest, or a boy, any of which I believed would have given me some importance in the household.

I also clearly remember the atmosphere in our house as being filled with fear and anxiety. My father was easily angered and we all did our best to stay out of his way. At the dinner table, we listened to him tell stories of his day at work or joke about people he had met in the city, and wondered why he always sounded so much happier to be away from us. He sometimes put down my mother for not being interested enough in his work or smart enough to understand it. The older I got, the more this infuriated me, and I often stepped between them to deflect his verbal attacks.

My mother was a soft-spoken, well-educated woman who came from a large Catholic family. She was active in environmental causes, weekly tennis matches, and amateur photography. She had a darkroom built in the basement of the house, and I can remember spending time with her in the dim light, watching the images emerge from the stinky pans of chemicals. I don't remember her ever standing up to my father, but then again, very few problems were ever discussed around me. From the time Margaret and Jack were hired, I spent less and less time with either of them.

Mostly I retreated alone to my room, attic playroom, or the empty barns. I had a few friends who lived nearby, but I avoided going to their houses for fear of their parents. One of the mothers used to laugh or yell at me when I didn't want to eat. Another threatened to hit me with a wooden spoon if I didn't sit at the table and finish my lunch. I was terrified of going there again—she made me eat tomatoes!

When I was ten and at an annual physical exam, I overheard the doctor tell my mother that I weighed too much. They said nothing to me directly, but after that I was conscious of my imperfect size. Salesgirls in the clothing store where my mother and I shopped for dancing-school dresses always sympathized with my "figure problem" and recommended "A-line" skirts. Despite my nickname "Thunder Thighs," at grammar school, I wasn't ugly or misshapen. By the age of 13, I weighed 135 pounds and was 5'5" tall. I was active, athletic, and actually had a shape similar to the one I have now.

In the backyard, wearing my school uniform (age 12)

I was sent away to a prestigious East Coast boarding school just before I turned 14. Everyone else from my grammar school class went away to private schools too, because the local public school was considered "lower class." Without realizing how afraid I was or how to communicate my apprehensions, I left home in tears. For months I cried at the slightest provocation. I had never shared emotional issues with my parents or confided in friends. I didn't even know what was bothering me, really. All I knew was that I was desperately unhappy and felt terribly alone.

The other girls at school all seemed distant, yet beautiful: long fingernails, neat clothes, curly hair, and *thin* bodies. It was obvious that "thin was in" right from the start. Having a pear-shaped body was an unspoken sin. I had heavy legs, which to me was the most repellant form of being "overweight," and a small chest, which was equally undesirable. From that point onward, I began to focus on my body as the source of my unhappiness, making every bite that went into my mouth an undisciplined and selfish indulgence, and becoming more and more disgusted with myself every day.

There were a few other girls whom I suspected had problems with food, although nothing was ever said. The girl living in the next room was always buying quarts of ice cream and hiding in her room. Then she would proudly announce that she was starting a diet that required fasting for two days. Another girl lost so much weight that her muscles could no longer hold up her 5'10" frame, and she walked bent over, her emaciated pelvis tucked forward for balance. She was taken out of school, rumored to have been throwing up to get skinny. That rumor was the first knowledge I had of someone forcibly vomiting. Even a childhood friend from my hometown who also attended the school pulled a "crazy" act by eating hardly anything but oranges for several months. I visited her in the infirmary where she had been sent for blood sugar tests because her weight was so low, and I didn't know what to say. I secretly envied her willpower and her protruding ribs and could feel our friendship slipping away.

By the time I reached my senior year, my crying in public had stopped, and I was no longer outwardly unhappy. I played sports, sang in the choir, and had one good friend. She knew I thought of myself as ugly, and often reassured me that looks didn't matter, but I honestly thought she was humoring me. I avoided situations that would make me feel like a failure. I begged to be let out of honors math, refused to be nominated for any student-body offices, rarely went to dances, and was afraid to talk in class. I was happy to get menstrual cramps once a month and retreat to the safety of the infirmary. I didn't seek out other friends, opting to spend my time alone or taking care of animals in the biology lab. I began to hoard food in the dorm refrigerator and sometimes hid in my closet during dinner hour, indulging in my private stash of coffee yogurt. I kept a five-pound can of peanut butter from which I sneaked teaspoonfuls when no one was around. Obsessive thoughts of food were often with me although I had not yet binged and purged.

I repeatedly tried on clothes in front of a full-length mirror to see if they had gotten looser or tighter. I compared my body to the models in magazines and the girls on diets at school. I feared I would never be thin enough. Who would want me? I took up smoking cigarettes in private, which in my mind was a bad thing to do, but it was better than eating. I chewed gum, sometimes up to five packs a day. Through all this, my weight held steady.

While home on vacation at the end of my senior year, a grade-school friend told me about a doctor put her on a diet that caused her to lose ten pounds in one week. Feeling desperate, I got my mother to take me to him. He gave me a pamphlet outlining the diet, and I returned to boarding school thinking that my life was really going to change; I was going to lose the extra 20 pounds that sat between happiness and me. I would be off to college, a new person, thin, confident, lovable. But the diet was horrible.

I was instructed to drink two tablespoonfuls of vegetable oil before breakfast and dinner, eat only high protein foods, and drink 64 ounces of water daily. I lost eight pounds in one week, but felt bloated, nervous, and depressed. Weak and sick, I went off the diet, feeling like a failure, certain that I would never be able to achieve what I thought was so important for a woman—a thin appearance. At that time I had a "boyfriend" at a nearby school, but when the diet failed, I quit seeing him. I also had the word "CHANGE" in two-foot letters cut out and pasted on one wall of my room, but I no longer expected that to happen.

I started snooping in other girls' rooms to look at their belongings. Kept on a small clothing allowance, I could not afford anything but essentials. I sometimes "stole" clothes, hoarding them for a few days or weeks until the newness wore off, and then I would try to return them, unnoticed. Often an item was reported lost and there was a big to-do about how low a person the thief must be, and I would have to maneuver the circumstances so it looked as if the victim had just misplaced the missing item. I didn't want to be thought of as a thief; I just wanted to be like everyone else for a short time.

The most devastating thought, though, was that other people could eat and I couldn't. I would watch the skinniest, most gorgeous girl spread brown sugar and butter on her toast every morning and never get fat, never even seem to feel guilty! What would it be like to live in a world like that, where you *didn't* think you were ugly? I began to withdraw from people and became jealous of everyone who was thinner.

Before bulimia, at my "coming out" (age 18)

The first time I thought of sticking my fingers down my throat was during the last week of school, after I saw a girl come out of the bathroom with her face all red and her eyes puffy. Even though her body was very shapely, she had always talked about her weight and how she should be dieting. I instinctively knew what she had just done, and I graduated knowing that throwing up might be the solution to my "weight problem."

I tried it three weeks later at a Wimpy's burger stand in Oslo, Norway, at the beginning of a summer exchange program. I still remember the secrecy, physical distress, and hope that I had indeed found the answer to my prayers. I could be thin. I could be a success. I could be in control.

I spent that summer living with a Swedish farming family. They were loving people, but I was unable to speak their language and, as usual, felt isolated and unsure of myself. I was embarrassed to decline food at any of their *five* daily meals! I tried to throw up at least once a day, but, still experimenting with this dangerous behavior, I couldn't always get the food to come back up. My weight got higher and higher, and I returned to the States larger than I had ever been.

I shocked everyone—including myself—by being accepted to Stanford University, 3,000 miles from home, and I left in a blatant show of independence and bravery. Once alone in my single dorm room, however, faced with familiar feelings of loneliness and self-loathing, I retreated into eating to numb my anxiety and learned to perfect the act of throwing up.

I began with breakfasts, which were served buffet-style on the main floor of the dorm, quickly learning which foods came up easily. When I woke in the morning, I often stuffed myself for half an hour and threw up before class. There were four stalls in the dorm bathroom, and I had to make sure no one caught me in the process. If it was too busy, I knew which restrooms on the way to class were likely to be empty. Sometimes one meal did not satisfy the cravings, so I began to buy extra food. I could eat an entire bag of cookies, half a dozen candy bars, and a quart of milk on top of a huge meal. Once a binge was under way, I did not stop until my stomach looked pregnant and I couldn't swallow one more thing.

That was the beginning of nine years of obsessive eating and throwing up. I didn't tell anyone what I was doing and I didn't try to stop. I was more attached to being numb than I was to anything else, and, although lovers, schoolwork, and my job were distractions from the cravings, I always returned to food.

I was convinced that bingeing was just a way to diet. Also, I didn't think there was anything wrong with it, even if I did it every day. I didn't connect my bizarre behavior with underlying issues, nor did I consider myself addicted, because I was sure I could stop anytime. Many times I promised myself that, "this binge will be the last" and that I would magically, and with ease, metamorphose into a "normal" person as soon as I threw up this "one last time."

My letters home fluctuated between questioning why I was at college and vague complaints about my health. Letter after letter said the same things: *I'm afraid, but don't worry about me. I'm sick, but I'm being brave and getting better. I'm probably going through some phase.* With every plea for attention, there was quick reassurance that I didn't need it; and, as much as I wanted them to ask me how it felt to be alone and scared, I would have denied those feelings. I know it. I was a smart girl, had been to the best schools, came from a family of bankers, lawyers, and PhDs. I was athletic, seemingly independent, and "together." How could I admit that I was throwing up to be thin?

Living with a Habit

I moved off campus my sophomore year because I couldn't stand the pressure of constantly being around people. I thought it looked like the kind of thing a "liberated woman" would do, and no one questioned me. I arranged my life to accommodate my habit, pretending to everyone, including myself, that I was being more of an adult. I vowed that when I got to a new place I would stop the eating and vomiting because I wouldn't have people around to make me nervous. I'd start an exercise program, become infused with willpower, get thin, and the world would be mine. The only hitch was that as soon as I was alone, the bingeing and purging took over once again.

I decided that what I really needed was a specific weight goal. I chose 110 pounds because I thought I'd look like a model at that weight. This goal stayed with me as an eight-year obsession, and I only reached it one day when I was completely dehydrated from vomiting. Even then, at 110 pounds, my body image remained unchanged; I thought I looked the same—and that was fat. I felt the same disgust when I looked at myself in the mirror, too. Had I felt this kind of self-loathing when I was younger? What had happened to me?

If I bicycled home from school, I usually carried cookies and doughnuts to eat as I pedaled. Sometimes I got home and threw up that batch only to be overwhelmed with anxiety an hour later, when I would set off again for a frantic, uphill ride to the grocery store. Then I could glide home downhill, cramming cookies into my mouth the entire way, knowing that there would be full release once I got home.

Given a choice, I bought the same foods: one package of English muffins, a pound of butter, usually a package of frozen doughnuts, a bag of Vienna Finger cookies, and always milk (preferably chocolate) or ice cream—and maybe five or six candy bars to start off the binge. Already eating in line, I told the checkers I was buying for a nursery school so they wouldn't suspect it was all for me. I could eat that much food in about an hour. If there was anything that I just couldn't finish, I threw it away, convinced and promising myself that this was the last time. If I hadn't bought enough food at the store, or if I were unable to get back there, I would eat anything: a couple of omelets, a batch of sugar cookie dough, a loaf of toast, or bowlfuls of Cream of Wheat. It didn't matter.

Things were different now that I was living alone off-campus. There was no worrying if the bathroom would be empty or if anyone would think it strange that I came into my room with a grocery bag full of the same foods every day. The addiction was now in control.

I began to run out of money. My parents sent me tuition, but only a small allowance, so I was in a work/study program testing mentally disabled children. I was happy about the work because I felt good helping others and the job kept me away from food for a few hours, but I always spent as much money as I earned.

It was at this point that I started stealing food. I felt a tremendous rush of success when I got away with a bag of cookies or pound of butter. It was similar to how I felt stealing at boarding school; I wanted what wasn't mine and what I felt was denied me. But there was one major difference: I did not plan on returning the goods. About six months later I was caught in a supermarket with a pint of substitute sugar in my purse, and the manager threatened me with jail. I promised to "go straight" and did, but the binges continued full force.

Marriage with a Secret Life

I had many short relationships that year, which were fun, but not what I thought was the real thing. Then I met a man whose name was Doug. I liked being with him. As we spent more time together, I could tell that he was truly a good person. Talented, enthusiastic, smart, safe. Ashamed, I decided not to tell him about my eating habits because I was sure that they would be changing "tomorrow" anyway. I was 20 and it felt nice to be in love. Due to his military obligation, our two-year courtship was spent apart much of the time. When we were together for weekends, I would often be free from my food behaviors.

My parents loved Doug immediately, which made me feel that I had made the right choice. Picking him was at least one thing that I had done right! During visits home, however, the more my family included him, the more I retreated. They seemed to like him more than me. Used to feeling unnoticed, but not knowing how to deal with that feeling, I would eat and throw up. I felt and behaved like an outsider, sneaking my sandwiches and cookies, and throwing up in a bathroom with a fan so loud that no one could hear what I was doing.

When we left, it was always with the same feelings of disconnection that I had felt leaving years before. Clinging to the stability and safety of my relationship with Doug, marriage seemed like the logical next step. I didn't think it would matter that my mind was often elsewhere, dreaming about food, because I felt loved and in love.

In my wedding dress, after five years of bulimia (age 23)

For the five years we were married, the daily rituals and idiosyncrasies of my food problems became more and more rigid. I learned to put face powder on my eyes to hide the redness from the force of vomiting over a toilet, and on my knuckles where they became raw from rubbing against my teeth. I routinely ran water in the sink to drown out the sounds of throwing up. I stepped on the scale every time I passed the bathroom, as well as before and after every binge. I continued my habit of trying on clothes in front of a full-length mirror, hoping they would hang looser than the time before. I became a meticulous housekeeper, especially when I did not have a job and was "working" at home. Sometimes I delayed vomiting while I vacuumed and washed dishes, eating all the while, setting the stage for the "cleaning" of my body.

I was averaging three to five binges every day, which necessitated covering my tracks. Between binges, I ran to the store to restock the food. There were days when I had to re-bake batches of brownies a couple of times. I washed dishes constantly, and was careful to clean the toilet to be sure I'd left no traces. I wanted everything to be orderly and clean. The only thing that was not just perfect was me! And I was caught in a nightmare that I could tell no one.

Although we ate out a lot, I was nervous and preoccupied in restaurants. In nine years, I never ordered an entree because I was afraid I'd lose control. Instead, I would order side dishes, and suggest we get ice cream after dinner so that I would be able to get rid of anything I had eaten. I always ordered whole milk, because it was thick and smooth and made the food come up easier. I even knew which restaurants had private bathrooms.

To others I seemed like a health food freak. In public, I made sure that I ate only low-calorie, low-fat foods. I read books on nutrition and health, thinking they would be a positive influence. I took a course in Anatomy & Physiology because I thought that if I could see what I was doing to myself physically, maybe I would stop bingeing. At one point, I even took a course called "Lucid Dreaming" by a woman named Patricia Garfield because I thought that maybe my dreams would reveal the key to my unhappiness. Little did I know.

I was surprisingly productive during those five years that my bulimia worsened. I got my bachelor's degree from Stanford, held two challenging jobs, and produced creative projects on my own. I started a business that is still running, and I maintained relationships with family and friends, albeit from a distance. But even though I was able to make my external life appear normal, internally I was walking an emotional tightrope.

After nine years of bingeing and vomiting up to five times practically every day, some physical side effects became worrisome. My vision was often blurry and I endured intense headaches. What used to be passing dizziness and weakness after purging became walking into doorjambs and exhaustion. My complexion deteriorated, and I was often constipated. I was usually dehydrated but didn't like to drink water because it made me feel bloated. Large blood blisters appeared in the back of my mouth from my fingernails. My teeth were a mess. Still, I refused to see that I had a serious problem even though the signs were obvious: a raving addiction, deteriorating health, an increasingly distant marriage, isolation, low self-esteem, fits of depression, and shameful secrets.

Shift in Focus

In spite of the intensity and secrecy of my bulimia, Doug and I did have many happy and loving times. We never openly questioned being together, but he was committed to many outside activities, and I had my food. When Doug got an offer for a fellowship at Cornell University, we moved back East together, but he was often gone, and I was alone to "do my thing."

As a surprise, in the middle of that winter, my father invited me to go with him to a small island in the West Indies for two weeks. Even though the idea made me extremely nervous, I jumped at the chance. Maybe chaining myself to a bathroom for nine years was beginning to get old. I don't exactly know. But I do know that I took a trip with my father, of whom I was deathly afraid, which began the journey of recovery for me. For the entire time I was there, I was completely bulimia free.

That in itself was a miracle, but on that trip something even more unexpected happened. In the middle of one night, I woke up and recorded in my dream journal, "I met a woman whose name was Gürze. She had mink hair and was inhabited by seven animals." In the morning, I reread this statement and looked at a drawing I had sketched of a funny little woman with long legs, a big head, and red, heart-shaped lips. I didn't dwell on it at the time, and I spent the last few days of my trip learning an unusual batik process taught by local artists.

When I came home, I began to experiment with batik designs, hammering together eight-foot frames for the fabric and spending hours over barrels of hot wax and dye. On a whim, though, I also created a five-foot-tall soft-sculpture doll, modeled after my dream woman, Gürze, and dressed her in my colorful batik fabrics. Then I made her a boyfriend, Dash, and eventually a whole group of friends, all the same large size and dressed as funny characters.

For a year I crammed my art between binges, and when I had accumulated a large enough body of work, I took my fabrics and two of the dolls to New York City to sell. I planned to stay with relatives whom I didn't know very well, but I was determined to give it my best and scheduled appointments with designers. I tried to have enough confidence to accept criticism willingly, but the pressure felt overwhelming. Going back to the apartment was scary. On most evenings, I stopped at a market on the way to pick up stashes of food that I devoured in my room after everyone had gone to bed. One night, preoccupied by a binge, I left some important papers where I had stopped for pizza and ice cream. I ran back through dark, unfamiliar streets, oblivious to the danger. My obsession with food had robbed me of rational thinking.

It was during this trip, though, that I happened upon an article in *Psychology Today* about people who "gorged and purged." This may have been the very first exposé written about what we now call bulimia. The lead author, Marlene Boskind-Lodahl, considered what she termed "bulimarexia" to be related to anorexia nervosa, an illness characterized by self-starvation, but different because of the repetition of binges and purges. I was shocked! She was at Cornell, conducting therapy groups three miles from where I lived!

Also, incredible as it seemed to me at the time, on a Manhattan street corner, a gentleman inquired about the two dolls that were hanging out of my backpack. He subsequently bought them both. There was little interest in the batiks, but wherever I went people asked about the dolls.

My world suddenly shifted. Not only did my work feel turned upside down because people liked the dolls, but I couldn't get that article about bulimarexia out of my mind. When I returned home, I spent a week bingeing heavily and then called Dr. Boskind-Lodahl, who told me to come right over. On my way, I stopped to stick my finger down my throat for what I was afraid would be the last time. What if she cured me today? I wasn't ready!

During the interview, I downplayed my lack of control and the severity of the problem. This was the first time I had told anyone about my behavior! I don't know if she guessed that I was holding back, but she invited me to join one of her ongoing therapy groups which would be meeting several days later. I told Doug that I had decided to deal with an old problem in a new way and added no details except that I was going for outside help. That he didn't push me for details was indicative of our relationship. Far from relieved, I fretted at home about having to talk to a group of strangers about my binges.

When I got to the first meeting, I presented my usual false front of confidence, because I was embarrassed to admit that I abused food in such a weird way. I didn't want to admit exactly how often I binged, how much I ate, or that I was alone so much of the time—but I did. To say out loud, "I throw up five times a day," was extremely hard. But the women in the group, all of whom were struggling with food issues, were supportive and responsive. All along I had thought that I was the only person who had such a bizarre relationship with food, but the group helped me see that I was not alone at all.

Marlene also stressed the importance of taking actions such as speaking up, honestly acknowledging feelings, and writing every day. I began a journal that I kept for several years, and just that small step made a big difference. I was learning to say in words what I had been saying with my bulimia. I was able to put off binges for a day or two and I began to gain confidence that I would get better.

I had only attended five sessions when Doug transferred back to Stanford. Although recovering from bulimia was becoming my focus now, I was still afraid to tell him anything. Also, under the strain of my secret life and his dedication to graduate studies, our marriage had turned into a distant companionship. I decided that I should live alone for a while and told Doug that I would return to California with him, but that I wanted my own place. I thought that I needed to change in order for us to be a better couple. This was *my* problem and I would return to him clean, pure, free, and independent when it was all behind me. He need never know.

When we got to California, we found separate places to live, which was painful and confusing for us both. We had never expected to be apart. We saw each other practically daily, but it was always awkward. Even though I had started to undergo changes inside, when we were together I was unable to articulate or express them.

I liked Susan, the woman from whom I rented a room, and I hoped that I could open up to her. But I missed the safety of my support group and resumed bingeing almost immediately. Being around Stanford brought back memories, and I returned to the same markets and doughnut shops that I had frequented earlier. I maintained my journal but felt disgusted with my eating and wrote only about daily life, not how I felt. Even though I had taken some daring steps towards recovery, I still clung to the magical promise of getting better "tomorrow."

I heard about an art fair in Los Angeles that was coming up in two months, and I decided to sell my "Gürze Designs" batiks and dolls there. Even though I was pretty broke, I continued overeating and vomiting, assuming that when the fair came, things would change. I would get to spend some happy time with Doug, who offered to drive me, sit in the warm Southern California sun, and make some money. But until that time, I stopped working on myself and binged and purged heavily until the fair.

At a Stanford craft fair with my dolls (age 26)

Turning Point

I'd hoped that the fair would be a turning point for me and it was, but not in any way I expected. Monetarily it was a bust, and I sold practically nothing. By the end of the third day, I was a bundle of nerves and broke down crying with Doug and his mother, with whom we were staying. I would not tell them that my greatest worries were about food, so they could not help me. I faced returning to the isolation of my single room, without a "real" job, unable to confide in anyone about the food problem that dominated my life.

It was not these aspects, though, that made the trip a turning point. It was when I met a man named Leigh Cohn, who was also a seller at the fair. I quickly felt able to relate to him, and we spent hours talking when business was slow. I had never felt so comfortable with anyone; our conversations felt intimate right from the start—so different from my other relationships. I was conscious of his presence even when we were apart, and when the fair ended, only reluctantly did we say goodbye. Soon afterward, we exchanged letters and phone calls as soon as we could and made plans to see each other.

When he finally arrived at my door, the attraction was incredibly strong. For the next three weeks we spent almost every minute together in what felt like a perfect union. Much to everyone's amazement, including our own, Leigh, who had taken a year's leave of absence from teaching, left his house—which was for sale in Los Angeles—to live with me in my room at Susan's.

Doug reacted with disbelief, and we had many confrontations. My parents had been upset by our separation, but they found it incomprehensible that I was living with a man I had known for only a month while still married. Even Susan disapproved. Everyone was against us, and I didn't blame them!

Still, I felt on a very deep level that for once I was doing the right thing, and I began to feel better in spite of the pressures. Unbelievably, the bulimia disappeared for those first few weeks that we lived together.

The sudden difference in my daily routine felt wonderfully healthy and refreshing. This seemed to be that magical, instantaneous cure I had always wanted.

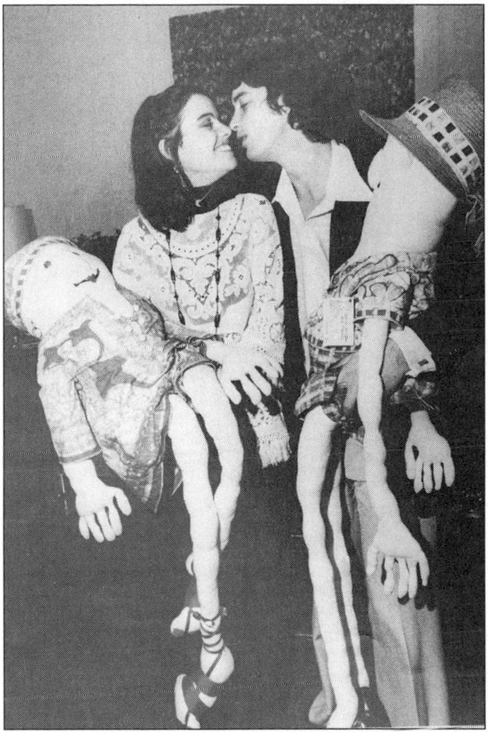

Leigh and me (age 28) with Gürze and Dash

As the days started to follow a routine, though, my newfound strength began to ebb. I worried about the hurt I was causing Doug and my parents. I felt guilty for being so selfish. I was afraid I couldn't give up the bulimia. Who would I be without it? I began to question if I really was doing the right thing and if I knew my own mind. After all, I ate and vomited for nine years knowing full well I was doing something crazy; maybe I was still crazy!

Tension increasing, I began to sneak food while Leigh slept and when I was alone sewing dolls at the studio I had rented. I could feel the desperation and loneliness building as it had in the past, and I was frustrated that being so in love hadn't completely cured me after all. I knew then that there would be no easy way out. I had a lot of work ahead of me if I was ever going to overcome bulimia, and that if I didn't take the initiative right then and there, I risked slipping permanently back into the addiction. I wanted all aspects of my life to be as wonderful, loving, and free from bulimia as those first weeks with Leigh had been.

I decided to take a chance and tell Leigh everything—otherwise there was only secrecy and hiding. Now I wanted honesty and love.

Ending the Behavior

In a tearful, emotional outburst, I described my bingeing and vomiting. At first Leigh didn't think it was a serious problem because he had never heard of such a thing. Besides, he had been a sweet-freak all his life, able to eat huge amounts of doughnuts and cookie dough without feeling guilty, gaining weight, or even getting cavities! His family loved big meals and boxes of candy. He assumed that I was just a sweet-freak, too, and threw up because I felt guilty about it. As I described the size and frequency of my binges, however, he could tell that something deeper was going on and that this was no ordinary problem. He listened to me that first day with love and compassion and said that he would try to help me.

In the past, I expected to get better "tomorrow" after one last binge. But this time I knew that I had to start taking definite steps. I made two resolutions. I would be absolutely honest by telling Leigh about all binges, and I would do anything to recover—even admit myself to a sanitarium, if necessary. At that time, there were no treatment facilities specifically for eating disorders, and this threat conjured up scary, melodramatic images I definitely wanted to avoid. Leigh promised to stick by me as long as I stayed committed to my recovery. He would help me come up with ideas about what actions I could take, listen, support, laugh, and love me; but we acknowledged that it was my responsibility to understand and overcome the behavior.

I went to see a psychiatrist primarily because of the tension and guilt I felt living with Leigh while still being married to Doug. I didn't mention my bulimia at first, but when I did, he recommended I see a woman psychiatrist who treated anorexics. I met with her once, but didn't feel comfortable. I realized the importance of confiding in someone, though, and decided to continue working on my recovery with Leigh.

Without any guidelines to help us, we brainstormed ideas. I began meditating twice a day and recommitted to journal writing. I tried to establish a better frame of mind by constantly watching what I was thinking and saying, and I consciously reframed negative "self-talk" to be more positive. I wanted to feel more relaxed, so I took walks and listened to my favorite music. I decided to drink a set amount of water each day, but I had difficulty with that, so I revised my expectations rather than feel like a failure. Also, Gürze Designs took off and required hours of concentrated sewing, during which I talked to myself about my recovery—sort of self-therapy!

I made lists: immediate goals, future goals, "Poor-Lindsey" and "Lucky-Lindsey" lists, what I liked and disliked about myself, reasons for wanting to get better, how I felt about my parents, my siblings, my life, ways to handle difficult feelings, and many others. I prepared a checklist of things I could do if I was on the verge of a binge, like exercising, sewing, gardening, soaking in a hot bath, and talking to Leigh or another friend about my feelings. Frequently I struggled, but increasingly I was able to overcome the urge to binge.

I had to approach food in a new way. In fact, it became my teacher because the way that I treated food was a lot like how I treated myself. If food were unimportant, expendable, not worth treating with kindness, then neither, I thought, was I. So, rather than labeling foods as "good" or "bad," which gave them power over me, I wanted to learn to eat anything—without fear.

One extraordinary step I took had a tremendous impact on my confidence, but I would not have attempted it alone. *No one recovering from bulimia should do something like this without support and supervision.* I went on a planned, all-day binge with the intent of not vomiting. I wanted to know, at a deep level, that I could eat anything—that I could have power over food.

On the big day, Leigh and I woke up to a bag of malted milk balls on the bedside table to start. We bought a pound of candy, a dozen doughnuts, caramel apples, caramel corn, a batch of homemade cookies, brownies, and drinks—all to take with us while delivering dolls in San Francisco. During the course of the day, we also ate hamburgers and fries, milkshakes, a greasy meal of fish and chips, and continuously snacked on white chocolate.

By bedtime, we were both exhausted and stuffed. Leigh felt sick, but I was preoccupied by how my body looked and felt—pregnant and unable to lie down comfortably in any position. Leigh would not let me out of his sight for obvious reasons. Without a support person, I would surely have vomited. In spite of stomach cramps, I was actually quite proud of myself at the end and laughed at what I had accomplished.

The next day, I had vowed not to eat until I felt hungry, and that didn't happen until nightfall. Also, I was sure I had gained weight, but I hadn't, and that made me even more confident. This was a real turning point for me—I knew I could reach a goal, and I had power over food instead of food having power over me.

For many months, I ate mostly foods that I had formerly considered "safe," like yogurt and bananas or cottage cheese and pineapple juice, but I tried to stick to three meals a day with small snacks in between. Eating that often seemed like a lot at first, but I was determined to stick to my plan even if I began to gain weight. Actually, I took a hammer to my scale after writing it a farewell note, so that I would not know what I weighed. Never again would I be ruled by a number.

I wanted out of *any* prison that existed for me. Toward that goal, I decided to allow myself one "forbidden" treat daily without guilt. This was a completely different orientation for me and was surprisingly easy. I began to treasure that one treat, which was a lot different than bingeing.

I acquired likes and dislikes of certain foods and learned to say "no" by saying it to food. I began to pay attention to how I was eating and slowed myself down. Sometimes I had soothing music in the background during meals, and silently affirmed that eating in a healthy way was an act of loving kindness towards myself. This was fundamental, because I had treated myself so poorly for so long.

I tried to change my ideas of what I thought I "should" eat to what my body actually craved by becoming aware of internal hunger cues, which I had ignored for years. I started to try new foods. This was one of the hardest things that I had to do because I was so afraid of losing control. What I discovered, though, was that the more I restricted my eating to only specified foods, the more I wanted to binge. So I focused on improving my nutrition by eating healthier foods and becoming more balanced biochemically. When I took the time to go within and discover what it was that I was really hungry for, I experienced satisfaction and fullness. Sometimes what I craved wasn't even food! Doing artwork, saying something that needed to be said, or just sitting quietly, was sometimes more appropriate and more fulfilling.

Other times, I needed to scream into a pillow until I was hoarse or cry for hours on end. I released pent-up feelings, especially anger, by wrestling with Leigh on a large foam mattress on the floor and having exhausting fights with foam bats. We put on boxing gloves and he let me hit him. He always pulled his punches, but came very close to my face several times. I took long saunas. All these things had a settling effect on both my body and mind.

I began to explore spiritual issues outside the church I had attended as a child. I read books on different religions and discovered many wonderful spiritual teachers whose lives inspired me to be more loving towards myself and others. Along these lines, I kept a picture of myself on my dresser beside a candle and some flowers to remind myself that I was a good person, worth taking care of. I learned specific exercises that showed me how my values and beliefs were influenced by my parents, my childhood, and the culture in which I lived. Taking all these things into account enabled me to discover the truth of my own heart so that I could live in accordance with who I was at the deepest level of my being. This was *real* nourishment.

My most difficult commitment was to tell the truth all the time. I started by sharing my secrets about bulimia with the people I least wanted to. Doug, who had finally accepted our separation as permanent, was astounded, but took my finally confiding in him as an act of genuine caring. He said he didn't know why he hadn't asked me about spending so much time in the bathroom, and he was saddened by what I had gone through. At that moment of truth telling, I think we were closer than we had been in years.

About a month later, I began to write letters to people, with the option to send them or not. I wrote to my parents about how I felt when I was around them. I described my recovery, but did not ask for, expect, or receive much participation. I began to confide in friends, most of whom were interested, sympathetic, and supportive, though a few dropped out of my life. I wrote the following in a letter to my childhood friend, the one who had eaten all those oranges at boarding school: *Finally, I can tell people about eating and throwing up. Do you know how ashamed I have been all these years, thinking I was abnormal and disgusting?*

Gradually, I grew more comfortable with just being myself. I had always been desperate to maintain an image of unfailing perfection and independence, but now I stopped hiding shyness, opinions, and fears. As I grew to understand who I was and why, I also understood how well the bulimia had served me. It had been my friend, my buffer, my security, and my expression when I knew no other. It had been a way to anesthetize my overwhelming feelings, a vehicle for protesting my place in my family, and somewhere to hide when I didn't want to participate in life. As an addiction, though, it allowed no other behavior but itself and had completely consumed me. I fought hard to get me back!

During the first few months of recovery, I did binge many times, but these slips became less and less frequent until, after a year, they dwindled to one every couple of months. When I occasionally binged, Leigh and I had long talking and planning sessions, and I was able to think of those slips as a way to learn. I gradually accepted that a single binge did not return me to square one. Instead, it was a red flag signaling that I needed to examine why I relapsed and what I could do the next time to intervene. This level of compassionate acceptance, coupled with a firm commitment, was just the approach I needed. The episodes stopped completely after about a year and a half, after which Leigh and I wrote our booklet, *Eat Without Fear.* It has now been over 30 years since I quit.

Family portrait 1980, the year *Eat Without Fear* was published

Lasting Recovery

Ending the binge-purge behavior was only one part of my recovery, because the bulimia had infiltrated all aspects of my being. Gradually, I underwent a transformation in the way I viewed and experienced every situation, from a simple conversation to a pressing crisis.

As I look back on what my life was like back then, the most obvious change is in my relationship to food. I no longer eat to escape, nor am I obsessed about my weight. I recognize hunger signals and eat accordingly. I no longer have food fears, and I enjoy everything from nutritious meals to decadent desserts. I stop when I am full and feel no qualms about having seconds or leaving food on my plate. I do not follow rules and have given up my compulsive rituals. I do, indeed, eat without fear!

I came to realize that my eating disorder had less to do with food than it did with feelings. Instead of being numb inside all of the time, I now experience life in a completely different way. For the most part, my waking state is one of peace and personal trust, although I do get happy, nervous, proud, frustrated, satisfied, concerned, sad, etc.! I have a full range of feelings, but mostly I try to maintain a state of love—my favorite.

Being free of bulimia has brought me in touch with an inner self I never knew existed. No one had told me that I had many of my own answers! This realization came from being honest and trusting my instincts. Once I made the commitment to practice honesty, I stopped worrying about what I thought others wanted and was able to focus on my own needs. As I learned to trust myself to make the best decisions, I discovered an inner self that would always lead me in the right direction. I came to respect and honor the wisdom of that inner self, to allow it expression in the world. It has guided everything I have done ever since.

As strange as it may sound, I'm actually grateful for my bulimia because it's partly responsible for who and where I am today, because without such a serious illness I might never have worked so hard to be happy. I had to overcome every barrier to living and loving fully, with my own set of values and ideals. From eating without fear, I learned to live without fear, and that has truly set me free.

In closing, here is a brief update. Leigh and I married shortly after my divorce from Doug, and have continued to be deeply in love. We have two great sons, Neil and Charlie, who are now adults. My "Gürze" soft sculpture dolls were a rage in the late '70s and early '80s—nearly half a million were sold—and I often tell people, "I sewed myself well," because of the long hours I spent doing that instead of the bulimia. Also, the relationship with my parents improved before they passed away, in part because I forgave them, and I forgave myself for how I reacted to them. I recognized that they both had family histories of depression, which had influenced all our lives, and I acknowledged that my own sensitive nature combined with those genetics set me up to have an eating disorder. Through the years, I've also grown closer to my siblings and numerous friends because I stopped hiding and learned how to just be myself.

Eat Without Fear was the first publication solely on bulimia, and we soon wrote two more booklets on the topic that were combined into the book *Bulimia: A Guide to Recovery* in 1986.

Family portrait 1986,
the year *Bulimia: A Guide to Recovery* was first published

It has been revised numerous times, and this 25th Anniversary Edition has also been fully updated. Leigh and I have also written and edited many more books for our publishing company, Gürze Books, which specializes in eating disorders. Our books have been translated into several languages, we have several websites (including *Bulimia.com*, *EatingDisordersBlogs.com*, and *EatingDisordersReview.com*), and our annual *Gürze Eating Disorders Resource Catalogue* is the most widely used publication in the eating disorders field—millions have been distributed.

The field of eating disorders has grown since those early days, and we have dedicated our professional lives to it. In the early '80s, I was the first person to talk about bulimia on national television, and in the intervening years Leigh and I have each been interviewed countless times by the media, have spoken at universities and professional conferences, and have been involved with all of the national organizations dedicated to eating disorders, some of which have presented us with awards for our service. More of that kind of information is in the Resources section of this book.

For years, I assumed that "Gürze" was just a name that had come to me in a dream. But one day, about ten years later, Leigh and I met a student of dialects who claimed with great certainty that "Gürze" was similar to a greeting amongst peasants in a remote region of Bavaria, the literal translation of which is, "Greet God" or "Hello, I see the God in You." This miraculous dream-name conveys exactly what I believe to be true. Every person has a source of love within. My recovery from bulimia was guided by this idea, and I hope yours is, too.

With an award from the
National Eating Disorders Association in 2008.

PART TWO

Overcoming Bulimia

Chapter Three

Getting Started

Deciding to Stop

You might think you can stop your bulimia at anytime, or that it will magically disappear on its own at some point in the future, but the truth is that many aspects of the bulimic cycle are highly addictive and will continue indefinitely—and probably worsen—unless a decision is made to finally end them. Deciding to stop does not mean promising to get better "tomorrow," which is a bulimic thought, but rather doing whatever it takes *right now* to become free.

I advocate recovery for lots of reasons: to live a longer, healthier life; have honest relationships; reach potentials of creativity; take pleasure from eating; experience peace of mind; save money—the list is endless. It almost doesn't matter what your reasons are, though—what matters is that there is something you want *more than* bulimia; and, from that decision will spring your determination, courage, and willing attitude. So ask yourself, what is important to *you*?

The path to recovery is different for every person. Some have an easier time than others, but there is no such thing as an instant cure. Recovery from a disorder as complex as bulimia is a process of successes, setbacks, realizations, and resolutions unique to each individual and without a well-defined ending. Many people think that they are "recovered" when they stop their binge-purge behaviors, and although that is an important goal, it is only a part of what I would call a "full recovery." Ultimately, you have to explore the underlying causes that drives those behaviors in order not to fall back on them in times of stress. During the process, the way you define "recovered" will probably evolve.

This is an extremely challenging task not to be taken lightly. Even life-threatening behavior is hard to quit if it helps protect you in some way. To give up that protection is daunting; with little self-confidence or experience, you might feel that you are without tools to face an uncertain future. But help is available if you take the first step. Make the decision to stop and your recovery begins.

Everyone's reason for making that decision is personal, as these actual experiences indicate:

Realizing that I am the only person who could stop my behavior helped me start my cure. It was all up to me.

Seventeen years is a long time to be in prison. I've done my time. I've earned my freedom. For me there are no concrete events or even attitudes in my recovery, rather an existential decision in favor of life, which I continually affirm.

Really, it was the decision to stop that did it. Then, I had to be quite forgiving of myself and give up my need to be perfect. Eating better was contagious—the more I did it, the more I wanted to. It took me two years to stop the cravings.

I've spent the last six months accumulating information on stopping my bulimia. But I've avoided doing anything concrete. Now hesitantly, shakily, I'm making a start.

Several bulimics in recovery mention that physical complications had caused them to question their behaviors. However, the mere knowledge of side effects did not guarantee that they would stop. Some point out that they were "experts" on nutrition, health, and psychology and understood on an intellectual level that their binge eating was unhealthy, but they still resisted making the commitment to change. A nurse described her physical problems in quite specific medical terms, yet hid this information from doctors who were also her friends. A 38-year-old woman who spent thousands of dollars on dental work from 15 years of vomiting told me that she felt fortunate that the damage to her body was not worse. Sometimes, medical emergencies led to the first steps towards recovery:

My emergency hospitalization for cardiac problems due to low potassium was not premeditated or planned. Afterwards, I quit "overnight" and never went back to vomiting, but it was very difficult psychologically.

An experience that made a big difference to me was a near-death situation from poor physical health due to numerous daily bulimic episodes. I developed malnutrition, double pneumonia, a spastic colon, and hypoglycemia. I was finally hospitalized for three weeks. Following my hospitalization, I entered a day treatment program that met six hours daily, four days a week, for eight weeks. It changed my life!

Pregnancy prompted some to stop because of a newfound respect for their bodies and love for their unborn children:

My bulimic/anorexic behavior has ceased almost entirely because I'm pregnant. I feel so much love for this baby that I want to love myself, too. A deep caring feeling toward others can sometimes set you on the road to recovery.

The experience that made the biggest difference in my cure was becoming pregnant and giving birth. The role of my body took on a new perspective. The externally motivated desire to be thin—fitting into some societal prescription for beauty and happiness—was no longer in my reach. This gave me an opportunity to find or feel my own standards and to question "theirs" from my new, noncompetitive, pregnant perspective.

I had a premature baby who lived three weeks. I'm sure that fourteen years of bulimia, in one form or another, had a great deal of impact on my body's ability to handle pregnancy. I thought this experience would be enough to "cure me forever." However, about three weeks after he died, I returned to old habits. I am again pregnant and I do not want to lose this baby, so now I am eating normally.

Things to Do Instead of Bingeing

It is rare to be able to give something up if you don't have something else to take its place. What will you do *instead* of bulimia? This is important to think about ahead of time because you will need to have some strategies in place. Plan in advance by gathering the necessary tools. Make connections with people who can love and support you. Get books to read, candles for hot baths, new sneakers if you're going to be active.

Below are some suggestions for things to do which have helped thousands of others, and they can help you, too. When you are tempted to binge, pick one idea from the "Immediate" list and do it! Use the "Short-term" list for planning how to avoid bingeing in the future. Personalize these lists in any way, at any time, by adding your own ideas. After all, it's *your* recovery.

Regardless of how you eventually address the underlying issues, you still must make a stand now. Post your list of things to do on your refrigerator or cupboard door—today.

IMMEDIATE THINGS TO DO INSTEAD OF BINGEING

- Postpone the binge for 15 minutes. Set a timer. That should give you enough time to figure out what to do next.
- Brush your teeth. Take a shower or a hot bath.
- Soak binge food in water.

- Leave the environment that's tempting you to binge. Go to a park, library, or other safe place. Take a drive.
- Call a supportive friend.
- In panic situations, relax with deep breathing. Take a deep breath for a count of ten, hold it for that long, exhale. Repeat this a few times, then think through your anxiety. *What am I feeling? Can I handle what's going on? Am I safe?*
- Get your mind on something else. Surf the web. Turn on some music or TV. Distract yourself from the cravings long enough to settle down.
- Let out your emotions in an aggressive way. Hit a punching bag or scream into a pillow. Wrestle with a safe support person. Beat your bed with a tennis racket or baseball bat.
- Cry! Sobbing can be a great release.
- Take part in physical activity. Go for a walk, jog, swim, or bike ride. Hit golf balls or play tennis.
- Write in your journal. Be intimate and honest. Look back at earlier entries for patterns or progress.
- Think about answers to these two questions, *What's the payoff to this binge?* and *Is it worth it?*
- List the foods you are fantasizing about, seal the paper in an envelope, and throw it away or burn it.
- Draw or paint a picture, play a musical instrument, or get involved in a favorite craft like sewing, knitting, needlepoint, or woodwork.
- Create and use panic cards. Each would include one idea with step-by-step instructions, such as, "Work in the Garden: a. Go to the nursery and buy seeds,

starter plants, or soil amendment. b. Return home and do planting. c. Offer gratitude and blessings to the garden. d. Show the garden to a friend or neighbor."

- Stop yourself in the middle of a binge. This may seem impossible, but those who have done it say it is a very powerful accomplishment. Take calming breaths. Do whatever it takes to stop yourself from eating more or purging. Afterward, process your feelings in your journal or with a support person.
- Keep a separate "Didn't Binge!" journal. Record the time, date, place, and what you did to distract or nurture yourself instead. Add a smiley face! Review this list when you're feeling down or on the edge.

SHORT-TERM PLANNING FOR NOT BINGEING

- Make your own list of "Immediate" things to do instead of bingeing. As you discover which activities are successful, repeat them and add options of a similar vein.
- Add relaxation techniques to your daily routine. Take a yoga class, meditate regularly, or simply take quiet time away from others and be alone with your thoughts.
- Cultivate more friends who are sensitive, compassionate, and capable of uplifting you. Someone who has overcome an eating disorder will be especially empathic.
- Call or visit a long-lost childhood friend. Track them down. Catch up on each other's lives. They are not likely to judge you and will have their own unique stories to tell.

- Plan to attend a cultural event, like a concert, art exhibit, stage play, or museum. Prior to going, learn more about the subject. For example, if you are going to hear a symphony, listen to it beforehand and read up on the composer. These kinds of personally enriching activities can take the place of bingeing.
- Make lists about your life: likes and dislikes, goals, priorities, accomplishments, things to do, people to call, etc. Lists are good for organizing your thoughts instead of letting them spin.
- For incentive, every day you don't binge or purge, mark your calendar with a big star or put money in a jar. When you reach certain goals—whether they're short or long term—give yourself rewards.
- Take a vacation. Get away from your usual routine, and decide not to binge and purge while away. Be a "new" you while you are gone, and think about ways to keep that attitude when you return home.
- Smile more often. Consider hugging! Remember that most people are a bit shy themselves. Something as small as a nod of the head or tip of a hat can make you feel good about yourself, while making someone else feel good, too..

NOTE: Many more ideas such as these are presented elsewhere in this book, especially in Chapters 5 and 8.

Setting Reasonable Goals

One effective recovery strategy is to work within a framework of success rather than failure. This means setting small, attainable goals that produce tangible results. Whether it is making a phone call to a therapist, starting a journal, or simply reframing a negative thought in a more positive way, achieving small goals results in big feelings of self-confidence and the motivation to continue. While not an excuse, even a setback binge can be an opportunity to better understand yourself and the triggers that drive your behaviors so that you don't react in the same way the next time. In the early stages of recovery, when the distance between where you are now and where you want to be can feel so vast, take baby steps. Make a list, think about what item you are capable of doing right now, in this moment, and do it.

The following quote is from a woman who had read my original booklet, *Eat Without Fear,* in the early '80s. She had been anorexic and then bulimic for 12 of her 28 years. At first, she was relieved to read that someone else who was bulimic had "gotten well," and she went several days without bingeing. But soon she realized that she needed to open up to her husband—who was supportive—and enter professional therapy. By the time she contacted me, she had considered herself recovered for several years. Here describes her early progress. Incidentally, we have stayed in touch over the years, and now, nearly three decades later, she remains completely free from eating problems:

In the beginning, I had to make very deliberate decisions to do something else—to fight off an urge that I knew would only come back to haunt me. I had to accept that each time I decided not to throw up was an experience that I could add to my repertoire. This allowed me to accept any failures because they didn't subtract from my "getting better times." A failure did not mean all was lost. I used setbacks to examine the situations that led me to throw up, and from this I learned to avoid certain circumstances. I became more self-accepting, which enabled me to feel better about myself. I began to carefully examine how I felt after I had thrown up and also how I felt when I didn't. I gained greater trust in myself and in my ability to get well.

As I have said repeatedly, recovery is an ongoing process. For every person who has shared their story with me, recovery meant experimenting with different strategies, enduring pressures, falling off the wagon of self-care, and getting back on. Practically everyone had bingeing episodes in the early stages of treatment, but even those rare individuals who went "cold turkey" had to dig beneath the bulimic behavior to uncover the emotions and triggers that previously set them off. Many shared that they worked to set reasonable goals, and some experimented with keeping simple contracts:

I used to give myself stars for every day without throwing up. I bought the shiny colored ones like I got in grade school. For some reason, this worked.

I plan my day and stick to the schedule, not allowing myself to "play it by ear" and panic at the first moment I feel alone, hungry, or unoccupied. I set small goals and achieve them. I use a checklist.

I'm trying not to be obsessed by the thought of an overnight cure. I know it takes time! Now I stop eating after less food than during previous binges—two bagels instead of six. My therapist calls it "discreet amounts." My binges have lessened greatly. They used to be my whole day, my whole life. Self-love really helps, and also not giving up. There's always tomorrow.

I put $5 in a jar for each binge-free day and saved up for something I wanted. [If I'd saved like that, I'd have over $50,000 in my jar by now!]

I stop myself from bingeing by recalling the pain I always experienced afterward. Instead, I do something positive for myself, even when feeling discouraged. Then, I really get into feeling good about what I've done. This pattern took me a long time to get used to. I took baby steps the whole way!

Getting Support

I believe that the most important step to take in recovery is to reach out to another person for support. This is because a side effect of an eating disorder is that it thrives on secrecy and is therefore isolating.

Most people with bulimia live in fear that their husbands, lovers, parents, roommates, or others will catch them bingeing or vomiting. They are adept at lying, embarrassed by the truth, and think that being face down over a toilet is an accurate representation of their self-worth: Not only is the act of bulimia disgusting, but *they* are disgusting for doing it. They are afraid of displeasing others by admitting to such an all-consuming problem and being judged as weak or less than perfect. They feel like a burden. Even though they don't know who they *are* without the bulimia, they're afraid someone might try to take it away before they are ready to give it up. Recovery is also equated with a loss of control and possible weight gain, both of which are terrifying.

If you have been isolating yourself from other people by hiding behind an eating disorder, it might be hard for you to ask for and accept support. You might not know, or have forgotten, how to actually *have* a healthy relationship. So, in recovery, this is something you will learn, one relationship at a time, as you are capable and ready. You will practice skills like communicating your needs in a constructive way, saying "no" when you disagree, and expressing feelings of all kinds. You will find out what giving and receiving love feels like, and it's pretty darn good! You will find out who you truly are and find joy in sharing that with others. Opening up to even one safe and trustworthy person—even if it is just your therapist—is a way of acknowledging that you are ready to begin this journey and find a new way of being in the world.

I cannot overstate the importance of supportive relationships; mutual respect and love between people is a powerful, healing force. Even just sitting in the presence of a compassionate support person, without exchanging a word, can touch us on a very deep level. Relationships can calm us, cheer us, expand our possibilities, make us feel both loved and loving, and validate our presence in the world. Mirrored in another person's eyes, we can see who we truly are, and that is perfectly enough.

Being honest by giving up the secrecy and pretence might seem frightening, but it's also a tremendous relief. Bingeing and purging takes a lot of energy, but so does keeping it a secret! Remember that bulimia is not a reflection of the inner person, it is a way of coping with life, and the best way you have known—until now. So start to build your support team one qualified member at a time.

Note that I said your team should consist of "qualified" members. Not everyone is cut out for the job. The best supporters should love you unconditionally, so that you are unafraid to tell them the whole truth without fear of judgment or disapproval. They should be willing to learn about eating disorders so that they, too, understand that the behaviors around food and weight are only a symptom. They should be good listeners, but also strong enough to speak up when they think your viewpoint needs to be challenged. They should help you reach your goals. And, they should be patient with the process of recovery, as should you.

Good possibilities for a support team member would be: trained health professionals, parents and other close family members, friends, clergy or spiritual advisors, or favorite teachers. Mentors who have been through recovery are also a great resource. A recovered mentor intimately understands what you are going through and can offer invaluable insight into the entire healing process. Mentoring websites exist online, although you might be able to find a "recovery buddy" through a local therapist.

I often get calls from people who admit that I am the first person they have ever told about their situation. I always encourage them to seek out a "next" person to tell—someone close to them who is safe and can be trusted to react with kindness and without judgment. Usually, support people are glad to be asked to help because it makes them feel good about themselves. One college student took my advice one step further and enlisted the support of everyone on her dormitory floor. She made a public statement about her problem and asked that they all help her to stop bingeing. They responded in full force!

Most individuals in early recovery admit that opening up was one of the most difficult obstacles to overcome, but these comments indicate the value of being totally honest and getting good support:

Telling my husband after four years of hiding has helped me the most. He is supportive, and I don't hate myself as much anymore because I'm not lying to him. Talking about it to family members and a therapist has helped a lot, too.

I had a friend call me every night and I would tell her how I did. Knowing I was going to talk to her helped me to make the decision earlier in the day not to throw up.

I felt a lot less isolated after opening up and bearing my soul to two trusted girlfriends. Their prayers and undying support meant a lot. I learned that I was not unacceptable as a person, even if I did have an eating disorder I hated.

Lying became so much a part of me, it was difficult to remember what was truth. I figured that if I was honest and admitted my imperfection, I'd be in trouble. For me, breaking free meant always telling the truth and accepting myself like that—imperfect, but fully human.

The fact that most people close to me were not repulsed when I told them about my bulimia made a big difference.

Talking to my friend, who was anorexic and bulimic for eight years, and is recovered for three, is always helpful.

Group Support

A community of people devoted to recovery can also be profoundly healing. If you're ready for this kind of support, there are several avenues to explore.

Private therapists, eating disorder treatment centers, and school counseling centers are the most likely resources for *therapy groups* specifically geared to recovery from eating disorders. These are usually conducted by a professional, sometimes require a fee, and run for a specific number of weeks or months so that the membership remains fairly constant.

Other options are *support groups* that are usually run on a no-fee or donation basis by organizations such as The National Association of Anorexia Nervosa and Associated Disorders (ANAD). An ANAD meeting is usually, but not always, run by a therapist or qualified facilitator and most states have groups ongoing. (See the ANAD listing in the Resource section of this book for referral information.)

Overeaters Anonymous (OA) and Food Addicts Anonymous (FAA) are *self-help groups* based on the principles of Alcoholics Anonymous and the belief that an eating disorder is an addiction. Both follow an abstinence model, use food plans, and draw on the experience of sponsors to help new members work the 12-Steps of Recovery. However, FAA also believes that this addiction is a biochemical disease, and that avoiding certain foods, such as sugar, fat, and wheat, is necessary for recovery. While OA and FAA might work for some people, they don't for others. An abstinence model still puts a focus on food, which you might not want. On the other hand, the structure might be good for you, especially in the early stages of recovery. Different avenues work for different people. Take advantage of whatever works best for you, knowing that you can change approaches at any time.

Finally, *chat rooms* on the Internet, preferably monitored and facilitated by a professional or recovered person, are another way of sharing ideas and successes. Other kinds of group support might be found in yoga, meditation, or self-improvement classes, where the focus is not necessarily on food problems, but on finding the best in yourself.

I encourage group support. Many heads together give different insights to problems.

The biggest key I've found is expressing myself and reaching out to others for help. In talking with other bulimics and asking people to listen to me, I gain a sense of who I am, relief from anxiety and anger, and a secure feeling that I am okay.

Today I have over seven months of no vomiting, part of which I believe is a spiritual miracle, and part is my willingness to show others who I really am.

Any support group where people share their honest feelings is really helpful. Isolation is the bulimic's greatest enemy.

The thing that has helped me the most is my group therapy. It enables me to see others with the same problem and is the only place I feel I can be honest.

Other Support

Support can also be found through unique and different kinds of relationships. Many people in recovery who write to me describe the value they place on the unconditional love of pets, ranging from horses to dogs to fish! Some mention relief from depression and anxiety by walking in nature. Others feel supported by particular books, websites, and movie characters (Cutts, 2009). Even a shell from the beach or a stone on a path might "call" to you. In all these cases, the relationship elicits heartfelt feelings of connection to the outside world, affirming your sense of worthiness.

A great decrease in my bulimic behavior occurred when I got a dog. The dog represented acceptance, companionship, something to love and care for, which was missing in my life. Gradually, I began to accept and care for myself, as well!

When I need inspiration, I go to a favorite spot in the mountains near my home. Being in nature calms me down and makes me feel like my problems are tiny in the scope of the greater universe. For some reason, that makes me feel more in touch with my Self.

Family Support

Families are at the front lines of defense in the recovery from eating disorders. Regardless of your age or the nature of your relationship, your family has had a profound influence on your life and, to some degree, your bulimia. Obviously, the level of support you get from them will differ whether or not you live at home, or if you are in a committed relationship. If you are a young person living at home with your parents, I urge you to include your family in your recovery. However, if you are out on your own, you can still get support from your parents and siblings. Finally, if you are in a committed relationship, you should have an ally there. Let's explore each of these situations.

When You Live with Your Family

If your parents don't know about your bulimia, now is the time to tell them! If they do know, then tell them you are ready for recovery and want their support. Frankly, it is virtually impossible for you to recover without their knowing about it.

Parents feel their children's pain, and no one is more likely to want to help you. Most sympathetic parents will do anything: listen to you, get involved with your recovery, respect your feelings, pay for therapy, and love you unconditionally. If you live in that kind of household, a family-based approach might work well for you. In this strategy, which is sometimes called the "Maudsley" method, parents take charge of their child's eating and everyone in the house focuses on your recovery.

However, even in "perfect" homes, an eating disorder *is usually supported by the sufferer's environment in some way.* Exploring problems within the family dynamic, such as difficulties with communication or conflict resolution, can create a new, positive foundation for your relationships. Parents and siblings might need to examine their own attitudes surrounding the same issues that you are facing—weight prejudice, women's roles, intimacy, spirituality, low self-esteem, getting needs met, etc.! While family members might not be bingeing and purging, they may share some of the same unhealthy attitudes that you do, which will not help you get well.

Family therapy, whether it includes everyone in your family or just those most able to participate, is a perfect opportunity for exploring these kinds of issues. It a safe place where everyone can express thoughts and feelings, using a trained, objective professional as a middleman. You can talk about things you might be afraid to say at home on your own. Your family will learn that no one is to blame for the eating disorder, but that everyone is responsible for taking productive steps towards healing. And, together with the therapist, you and your family will become a team for solving any problems, so you do not have to shoulder the entire burden of recovery on your own.

Studies have shown that family therapy, coupled with assertiveness training, is an extremely effective tool for recovery. In some cases, therapists treating adolescents *require* that the family be treated as a whole. Ideally, all family members would share the goal of improving their relationships, so that not only would the individual with bulimia feel supported, but the entire family dynamic would also improve, affecting every member in a positive way.

Sometimes *multi-family therapy groups*, where several families get together in a facilitated meeting, can be beneficial. This type of setting encourages families to share their experiences and get the support that they need, as well. A child with an eating disorder is a scary thing and parents need a place to voice their concerns, ask questions of other families, and find reassurance. *You* might also benefit by seeing the way other families interact and apply the best ideas to your circumstances.

Family support comes up regularly when people tell me their stories:

My bulimia has decreased almost 90% and I have my parents to thank for that. They have been very supportive and are always there when I need help.

The biggest help in my cure was the Sunday night reports I would give my mom. After an entire week without bingeing or purging, I told my mom about my accomplishment. I could see the relieved expression on her face, and that was enough to get me through any rough spots I encountered through the week. As each week went by, it became increasingly easier to not throw up. Whole days went by without even a thought of vomiting.

When I reached adolescence, my father seemed to avoid me, and I thought it was because of my weight. When I told my parents about my vomiting, he showed genuine love and concern. Having him involved in my life again helped me most of all.

If you are a family member, do not coerce the bulimic into therapy with the belief that you are immune to counseling. You might play an active part in her history and recovery. Be ready to take a deep look at yourself and your own coping patterns.

There has been a vast improvement in how I regard my parents. Hatred is replaced by love and understanding on my part. They now show more genuine affection, and all of us are more honest.

When You Live on Your Own

If you are living on your own, your parents may be less involved in your recovery, or not all. It's up to you. Obviously, they can't monitor your eating as if you were a kid, but they can provide emotional support, care, and love. They, and your siblings, can potentially be your greatest sources of support, because they know you so well. I hear all the time from parents with grown children, and they mainly want to know what they can do to help.

Regardless of how involved they get in your recovery, you will *still* want to personally explore any familial beliefs and habits that you may have brought along with you to your new environment. For instance, you may still be bound by some ground rules that were established long ago, like no dessert unless you eat everything on your plate, or girls should be seen and not heard. Or you might think that anger is an unacceptable emotion, or that misbehavior is best disciplined authoritatively rather than with rational discussion. These kinds of myths and rules may have served a purpose when they were created, but they do not necessarily apply to your present life, or to the process of finding out who you are, independent of your family. Explore your beliefs about food and weight, judgments, perfectionism, and self-esteem and the ways these were influenced by your family. By discussing these issues within the context of recovery from an eating disorder, you may discover new levels of honesty and insight. Want to know more about your childhood? Talk to your family!

Most people can turn to their families for support, but some cannot. In situations where parents and siblings are too toxic, abusive, or unwilling, you may be better off on your own. Whether you decide to involve your family in your recovery or not, it is still helpful to acknowledge and explore their influence. Here are some reflections:

I have difficulty getting support from my family, especially admitting to them that I need the help, and asking for it, since I have always been the one to help and support others.

I have confided in my sister whom I have never been very close with, and we now have a bond and are beginning a relationship.

Now that my parents understand, they are very supportive. The best support I received was from my mother, who calls everyday and sends cards.

I told my parents after my first therapy session and they were pretty surprised, but they have been wonderful. They are even paying for my therapy since my insurance won't cover it.

I've been bulimic for 22 years and my family does not know. I am still afraid to tell them.

When You Are in a Committed Relationship

Although many individuals describe how hard it is to open up to their husbands, wives, or partners, the response they receive is usually extremely compassionate and helpful. Most spouses do an excellent job!

I recently spoke with a man a couple of times about his fiancé, whose bingeing and purging had been increasing as their wedding date neared. They'd already gone through about a year of her recovery together. We discussed his concerns, and then he went to her with a list of questions: Was she secretly vomiting again? How often? What pressures were most stressful? How did she feel about her body? Which wedding guests' opinions did she fear? Does she feel sexually desirable? He came up with almost 50 of them! They spent three hours talking and crying until both felt spent. They then meditated together and let the emotions subside. Eventually that night they had another conversation—about their future—and came up with some ways for her to better cope with stress. When he told me about that cathartic night sometime later, her binges were in check, and she was even enjoying some of the wedding planning.

On the other hand, too often I've seen marriages ripped apart when an anorexic or bulimic gets engulfed by the disease. It becomes the primary relationship, and no life partner wants to play second fiddle to an eating disorder. My own first marriage didn't stand a chance against my secrecy, and my second one has thrived for over 30 years with honesty. Take my word for it, if you're in a committed relationship, enlist your partner's support.

The most important factor in my recovery has been the support of someone who loves me unconditionally, in spite of the ugliness of my problem. My husband now, boyfriend during many of the years of my bulimia, did not reject or leave me when he found out about my vomiting. He also never lectured me about giving it up. The way he put it, though, made it clear that whether or not I chose to quit vomiting, I would be doing it mostly for my own benefit—although clearly he would benefit, too.

My lover helped me greatly by not being critical. Her feelings of love and acceptance took the pressure off. Telling her when I failed allowed me to deeply experience my sadness, yet know I was still loved. She had faith in my ability to recover.

I am learning to ask for help, something I have never ever done before. My boyfriend came up with "Super Sunday," a day of fun and no throwing up. We rented our favorite movie, got a reasonable portion of our favorite foods (I had a low fat hot fudge sundae, my first in five years), and kissed and cuddled.

Encouragement: Why Get Better?

The most important thing I can say about the struggle to end bulimia is that it is worth it. Even though it is more of a journey than a goal, and it begins in what feels like total darkness, there is a light that exists within your own self, which will guide you on your path to health and wholeness.

It might surprise you to hear that many women who have recovered from an eating disorder believe that they are better off in the long run for having had one. They consider their problems with food and weight to have been their greatest teachers, without which they might never have seriously questioned their beliefs and values, or faced their inner fears. Recovery made them strong enough to resist cultural pressures to be thin, and they stopped judging other people based on size or shape. They learned to respond to old patterns in new ways, enabling them to tackle other problems with confidence and compassion. Although they are not focused on food, they eat well and enjoy the benefits of good nutrition. They are usually healthy, happy people.

All these changes might be difficult to fathom now, when you feel caught in the cycle of bingeing and purging, but remember that "eating" disorders are not really about eating. They are evidence of other issues which, when healed, will transform the rest of your life. In time, you will find other things that will fill you up—physically, emotionally, and spiritually. As one person said to me, "Self-love can be delicious."

Inside of you is a creative, worthwhile, loving person. In your heart, you know this is true. Stick to your commitment; continue to participate in life instead of bingeing. Practice love and believe in yourself. Make lists, get support, enter therapy, follow our two-week program. It takes time for such a big change. Don't worry! Be willing to try anything to get better. In the words of one woman, "My life has not changed with recovery, it has begun!"

Since I have been completely free of bulimia, I sleep better, have more energy, and am happier and less nervous. I laugh more, and I'm told I'm more outgoing and fun to be with. I also have more money and more time to do the things I really enjoy.

Every aspect of my life has changed. I now like myself. I am productive, positive, and enjoy beautiful relationships with my family, friends, and children. I am going through a divorce, and I'm happy about that, too!

Most of the time I'm fairly serene and better able to cope now that I'm no longer escaping through food. In some ways, life is also more painful though, because I must deal with the emotions instead of covering them up.

I feel much more grown up, and that is wonderful. I am more confident. I don't avoid walking into a room of people. I approach each task with more strength. I enjoy little things. I am not so self-centered.

Physically I feel great. My hair is healthier. I just look and feel more attractive. I take better care of myself. I love my husband more. I am going back to college and I feel a lot happier and much more relaxed.

Although my eating disorder had many negative aspects, I feel that without it, I would not be the person I am today. It gave me a reason to really discover my own truth.

I have ups and downs, like everyone else, but mostly my life is great! I experience happiness on a daily basis and share love, humor, and vulnerability with others. I never knew life could be this way, or that I could be this way. With recovery, I gained the self-confidence I never had.

Chapter Four

Professional Treatment

Most bulimics agree that talking about their food problems is extremely difficult, especially when they have maintained an appearance of competence and well-being for so long. While they may be embarrassed to "tell all" to a friend or family member, especially at the beginning of recovery, confiding in a professional therapist can feel safer and easier. Also, one misconception shared by individuals with bulimia is that they can get well on their own, but this is rarely true and possibly the result of a fear of relationships in general. Thus, therapy is a way to face what feels like shameful behaviors and difficult feelings, as well as an opportunity to learn how to trust and interact with another person.

You might worry that no one other than a bulimic could truly understand your pain. Actually, many therapists specialize in this field because of their own experiences with food issues. But even if they haven't had an eating disorder, therapists are trained to listen, accept, challenge, and provide coping skills. They are trained to fully "be there" for their clients, which is crucial for overcoming feelings of loneliness and disgust. A healthy, therapeutic relationship will positively influence nearly every aspect of a person's life, and I strongly recommend that all bulimics seek out some form of professional therapy. But no matter whom you choose for professional guidance, keep in mind that their role is not to "cure" you but rather to empower you to help yourself.

As previously mentioned, eating disorders have a wide variety of causes and relevant issues, so the best treatment is multidimensional. For this reason, professionals from many different types of disciplines specialize in this area, including psychologists, psychiatrists, marriage and family therapists, social workers, dietitians, and others. However, not all mental health professionals treat eating disorders. For example, only a small percentage of psychiatrists have full-time experience with these complex problems. Therefore, when you are seeking professional treatment, it is essential to find someone who has been trained specifically in this field. (See "How do I choose a therapist?" on pages 65–67.)

Just as there are different kinds of professionals treating eating disorders, there are also different therapy approaches (psychotherapy, family based, etc.) and levels of care (outpatient, inpatient, etc.), which will be explained further in this chapter. In many instances, someone in recovery works with a *treatment team* composed of a primary physician, therapist, nutritionist, and perhaps other members, including parents and loved ones. So, your treatment will likely include an eclectic mix of techniques based on your individual needs and the unique skills of your team members.

When combined with other forms of treatment, support groups are a great way to enhance relationship skills, increase motivation, and provide feelings of connection in a semi-structured environment. Look for groups that are led by qualified professionals who are knowledgeable about eating disorders or individuals who are fully recovered. Group meetings should not be turned into gripe sessions or ways to share disordered behaviors.

Individual Therapy

Individual therapy with a local therapist is the usual place to begin. During your first sessions, many professionals will administer an assessment test with questions about your eating attitudes and behaviors in order to give you an initial diagnosis. They will try to determine the nature of your disorder (bulimia, anorexia nervosa, EDNOS), its severity, your nutritional status, how much you exercise, and readily apparent underlying issues. Together, you will make a plan with concrete goals, time frames, barometers for monitoring the benefits of treatment, and contingencies to increase the level of care if measurable progress isn't being made. A treatment team should be formed, and you should have medical and dental exams.

In subsequent sessions, you and your therapist will work together to modify your behaviors, understand and gain insight from your experiences, and explore the skills you need to create a recovery that is deep and everlasting. Nevertheless, talk therapy alone can sometimes be limiting, which is an advantage of the team approach.

Most traditional psychotherapy has three basic stages of treatment. In the initial stage, you and your therapist talk and form what is called a *therapeutic alliance*. He or she listens carefully to your story and tries to uncover the causes of your bulimia. During this phase, you also learn about the medical and psychological effects of eating disorders and begin to take small steps. The middle stage is when deeper inner work is done. You develop ways to "talk back" to your inner critical voice, become more autonomous, increase intimacy in outside relationships, and focus on body image issues. In the last stage, you prepare for the termination of therapy. By this time, your therapist may feel like one of the most important people in your life. Together, you work through the emotions connected to ending this partnership, and by the time therapy ends, you are both ready (Zerbe, 2008). Of course, you can always return for further sessions, if needed.

Depending on your particular situation, access to treatment is a primary consideration. For many people, individual therapy may be sufficient, but more severe cases might require a higher level of care. Most large cities offer many options, but in smaller communities, local choices will be limited, requiring you to travel or find someone who will do therapy via phone and email. Additionally, finances are often an issue. Staying at a treatment facility is expensive, and even individual therapy has its costs. Insurance policies vary in their coverage, and you might have out-of-pocket expenses. However, recovery is the best investment you can make!

Finally, in building a trusting relationship with a therapist, you may feel sexual or other needs for physical intimacy. A solid therapist will *never* take advantage of that—they will talk about those feelings but not act on them. If a therapist does, it is time to get out, seek other consultation, and report him or her to the appropriate authorities.

Locating the right therapist for me was the most important element. Involvement in a self-help group was also valuable.

My therapist has helped me look at many aspects of myself of which I was either unconscious or that I had pushed aside because they were too painful for me to deal with.

Seeing my psychiatrist by myself, and at times with my mom, has been the best help to me.

I give my therapist a lot of credit. She never pushed me or put me down. She kept the attitude that I'd do it when I was ready.

I've been at it for two months, and I'm working with a team of a psychologist and a dietician. We began with a goal-driven plan, adding a new goal each week. Using this plan, I progressed from purging every time I ate to keeping down up to sixteen meals in a row!

One of my teachers recommended I go to the counseling center at school. This was the best move I could have made. My counselor has been very helpful in getting me to talk about my feelings and anxieties, which were being ignored or substituted for by my eating.

I saw many different therapists, from psychiatrists to non-credentialed counselors, but the last therapist I saw was the only one that helped me!

Types of Therapy

Psychology has many approaches to the study of human behavior, some of which have been adapted to the treatment of eating disorders. A few of these approaches have been meticulously studied and their effectiveness has been well documented; others have been less studied, but are still widely used. *Most therapists and programs use a combination of techniques.* Here is a brief overview of the eating disorders field's most common therapies and others that are often used as adjuncts to treatment.

Cognitive Behavioral Therapy

More studies have been published on Cognitive Behavioral Therapy (CBT) than any other form of treatment for bulimia, and it has been shown to be highly effective using a manualized approach. Some therapists have training in CBT and others also use it to some degree, although it is being continually revised and defined for treating eating disorders patients. The state-of-the-art version is called CBT-E (for enhanced), and encompasses about 20 sessions of one-on-one, individualized therapy. After an initial assessment and introduction to the treatment plan, the focus is on stopping the bingeing and purging, which involves keeping a self-monitoring record of all food consumed as well as the context and associated feelings. Simultaneously, patients are educated about "regular eating," and significant others are involved for support. As the treatment progresses, it addresses the over-evaluation of shape and weight, including issues of body checking, "feeling fat," and the eating-disordered mindset. Finally, problem-solving skills are systematically developed for relapse prevention (Fairburn, 2008). The CBT-E manual is not intended to be combined with other methods of treatment, but practically speaking, most therapists and programs use their own hybrid of CBT rather than CBT-E exclusively.

Interpersonal Psychotherapy

The primary aim of Interpersonal Psychotherapy (IPT) is to help patients identify and address current relationship issues and is particularly appropriate for individuals who are either socially isolated or in unfulfilling relationships. In studies, it has comparable long-term outcomes to CBT, though the behaviors might not stop as quickly, because the early phases of IPT are not as concerned with eating. Instead, the patient is assisted in understanding how their eating disorder is fueled by such influences as: grief (death, the loss of a relationship, etc.), role transitions (going away to school, changing jobs, divorce, etc.), disputes with family, friends, or coworkers, and interpersonal deficits. The therapy focuses on goals, questioning beliefs, making connections, improving internal and external communication, and redirecting attention from food and weight to the underlying issues (Tanofsky-Kraft, 2010).

Dialectical Behavior Therapy

Dialectical Behavior Therapy (DBT) is an expanded form of CBT. It is based on developing skills for effective behaviors, and includes modules for mindfulness, avoiding self harm, emotion regulation, and distress tolerance. Originally developed to treat borderline personality disorder, it is proven to be effective for a subset of patients with bulimia. It is especially useful for those bulimics who have difficulty with emotion dysregulation, which means being so upset that they can't think clearly or make good judgements. DBT would also be an especially suitable treatment for bulimics with other self-harming behaviors, such as substance abuse, cutting, suicidal thoughts or attempts, or trouble with anger management. DBT treatment typically involves group sessions designed for learning skills, and individual sessions to work on applying them to personal goals (Safer, 2009).

Family Therapy

Traditional family therapy is a well-established approach in which the individual with the problem and the family members meet with a therapist. Together, they explore how the family dynamic contributes to the eating disorder and ways to help the recovery process. Oftentimes, communication skills are emphasized, like honesty, assertiveness, independence, speaking directly, and listening. Some therapists make use of Attachment Theory, which concerns the emotional bond between two individuals—most specifically a child and parent. Regardless of their approach, most therapists have family sessions, especially when the recovering bulimic lives at home. Likewise, couples therapy is standard when the person is married or in a committed relationship.

Family-Based Treatment

Family-Based Treatment (FBT) is an approach originally developed for treating anorexics at Maudsley Hospital in London. Used primarily for adolescents living at home, FBT for bulimia relies on parents to take charge of their child's eating. Through love, understanding, and collaboration, parents help their child control the symptoms of bulimia and resolve the issues that led to it. The goals are to: first, reestablish healthy eating; second, help the adolescent eat on his or her own; and third, to have a positive relationship that is no longer focused on resolution of the eating disorder. Usually parents work with a therapist, who follows a manual that includes forms, worksheets, and a schedule (Le Grange, 2007).

Psychodynamic Therapy

Only a few controlled trials of the psychodynamic treatment of eating disorders have been done, but it is a widely practiced approach that has evolved from the work of Sigmund Freud, incorporating an ever-expanding blend of modalities. Central to this approach is the relationship that forms between therapist and client. It emphasizes self-discovery and understanding feelings, and because the individual's recovery unfolds gradually, psychodynamic therapy typically takes longer—usually at least one year and frequently a few years or more (Zerbe, 2010). In psychodynamic therapy, issues are explored on many levels, for example: food might be seen as a transitional object, a binge might represent a daughter's inability to feel her mother's love, and purging may be a form of punishment for being "bad." Practically all therapists will have had training in psychodynamic principles and will assimilate aspects of it into their treatment.

Other Therapies

In addition to the predominant approaches used by your therapist, he or she and other members of the treatment team might provide adjunct forms of treatment, including, but not limited to, any of the following:

ADJUNCT TREATMENTS

- Nutritional therapy – meal plans, nutritional supplements, facts about food and weight, etc.
- Feminist-oriented therapy – empowerment to fight gender-related issues
- Experiential therapies – art, music, psychodrama, dance, etc.
- Acceptance and Commitment Therapy (ACT) – a branch of CBT stressing acceptance and mindfulness
- Mindfulness – meditation, yoga, journal writing, guided imagery, etc.
- Psychoeducation – media literacy, facts about eating disorders, advocacy, etc.

- Pharmacotherapy – use of medications (see pages 60–62)
- Body image therapy – addressing issues with weight and shape
- Eye Movement Desensitization and Reprocessing (EMDR) – uses elements of other therapies (CBT, psychodynamic, etc.) and bilateral stimulation (moving the eyes back and forth as directed by the therapist) in a series of sessions
- Biofeedback –monitors and helps to modify the body's reaction to stress
- Internal Family Systems (IFS) therapy – methods for accessing the "higher" Self
- Equine therapy – working with horses to restore notions of self-care and confidence
- Ropes courses – for personal empowerment, achievement, getting over fears, etc.
- Therapeutic touch – balancing and promoting the flow of human energy
- Body work – massage, Reiki, acupuncture, exercise, strength training, etc.

Inpatient and Outpatient Care

Sometimes, sufferers need a higher level of care than an individual therapist can provide. There might be medical issues, comorbid behaviors such as cutting, acute depression, or a degree of severity that need to be monitored more closely than at a weekly or bi-weekly appointment. Other recovery efforts may have failed, and a more concentrated treatment might seem like the next logical step. In such cases, the options are staying at a hospital in an eating disorder unit or at a center devoted exclusively to treatment of these problems, which is called *inpatient* or *residential treatment.* Going to this type of center a specified number of hours a day, several days a week, is called *intensive outpatient treatment (IOP)* or *day treatment.* In the latter case, patients usually stay in their homes (or other local housing for out-of-towners) and commute to the facility.

These facilities come in a variety of forms. Some are distinct units in hospital settings, some are residential programs in houses or on ranches. Each one is different, even when they are satellites of the same program. They also have separate philosophies that might stress, for example, spiritual or religious viewpoints, a feminist orientation, challenges like ropes courses and equine therapy, a medical model, holistic approaches, or the personal convictions of its owner or clinical director. Some specialize by age or gender. Some treat only eating disorders, others include treatment for comorbid conditions, such as substance abuse.

Many centers treating eating disorders offer both inpatient and outpatient services, and most employ a multidimensional approach using a team of skilled professionals, including: a medical director who is often certified in psychiatry; a program director; a psychologist who specializes in eating disorders; licensed clinical social workers or marriage and family counselors; a registered dietitian; plus a well-rounded medical and nursing staff. Treatment usually includes: individual and group therapy sessions; nutrition counseling; structured meals; relaxation and exercise programs; experiential therapies; medical monitoring; and sometimes the use of medications.

Typically, the day will include therapy sessions, meetings with nutritionists and physicians, support groups, educational classes, and structured meals. Groups and classes may cover such areas as: body image; stress management; coping skills; nutrition education; relapse prevention; assertiveness training; art or music therapy; and expressive writing.

Although cost may be a limiting factor depending on your insurance coverage, inpatient treatment can be beneficial for a number of reasons. You will be removing yourself from the familiar temptations and triggers that kept your compulsive bingeing and purging alive. You will be devoting yourself to around-the-clock recovery, and such a dramatic change can lead to accelerated progress. And, by going to a facility that specializes in eating disorders, you will be getting constant expert care at the hands of skilled, dedicated professionals.

If you are going to make the commitment to spend time, money, and energy to go away to a treatment center, pick one wisely. No program is right for everyone. Ask local therapists for recommendations and do homework on your own. Websites of national eating disorders organizations, as well as the Gürze Books website (*bulimia.com*), link to many of the most prominent facilities in the United States. Find a facility that reflects your values and goals. Visit their websites, call their intake coordinators with a list of questions, and, if possible, visit the facility before making your decision. Consider more than one option, and be diligent in your research. This is one of the most important decisions of your life!

Picking a center and having your insurance company pay for it are two different things. Currently, managed care companies dictate terms of treatment, and oftentimes families and doctors must fight for adequate coverage. You cannot stand on the sidelines and let third-party payers make restrictive decisions about your health, for instance, who will treat you or for how long. Be an advocate for yourself! Organizations such as the National Eating Disorders Association and Academy for Eating Disorders can provide you with more information on this topic.

Medical and Dental Exams

If you have had an eating disorder, your body has been through a terrible ordeal. For this reason, you should have a complete physical examination from a physician who is familiar with bulimia and who will encourage you to begin caring for yourself.

The secretive nature of this illness kept the medical profession in the dark for a long time, but even in this day and age doctors and nurses sometimes make inappropriate comments. However, most doctors are now familiar with the symptoms and side effects. Be sure yours is. If not, ask for a referral from a local treatment facility or therapist who specializes in eating disorders.

Do not make excuses to avoid a physical examination. Even though a basic exam, blood tests, and EKG are often normal in patients with bulimia, they are necessary to be sure that nothing worrisome is missed. Find someone with whom you feel comfortable and confident. Be sure to tell the doctor your complete bulimic history. It is important to be honest. Sometimes doctors are intimidating because of their time constraints and implied stature, so be assertive and get all of your questions answered. Prepare for the appointment by reviewing the medical dangers that are summarized on pages 50–53.

It is also important to have a dental checkup, especially if you vomit. Stomach acid removes tooth enamel, and constant exposure to food, especially simple carbohydrates, causes serious tooth decay and gum disease.

I was afraid to go in for a checkup, but my therapist insisted. Finally, I went for an examination, terrified that I had every problem that I had read bulimics get. To my relief, I was okay, and that made me feel better about myself and my recovery.

I was a rock bottom bulimic and was hospitalized with low potassium. The doctors couldn't believe I wasn't in a coma!

My gynecologist found a benign tumor the size of a lemon attached to the base of my spine. She said that it wasn't caused by the bulimia, but I believe that it was.

I had polycystic ovary syndrome and learned that it may have been associated with my binge eating.

My teeth were an absolute mess for years and have cost me thousands of dollars worth of dental work, but I have not had a single cavity since I stopped bingeing.

Chapter Five

Tools for Recovery:
What Has Worked for Many

While I highly recommend professional help as part of your recovery, I know from experience that there is a lot you can do on your own. This chapter is full of ideas, many of which I used while I was actively stopping my bulimia and have continued to use throughout my life. In addition to my own experiences, the suggestions provided here came from hundreds of people who have sent me letters and answered recovery surveys, as well as from therapists who specialize in this field.

This chapter has been greatly expanded and revised for the 25th Anniversary Edition. I recommend that you first skim through it one time completely, and then go back and begin implementing its action-oriented tools, exercises, and things to do in whatever way suits your needs.

You might construct a *recovery plan* by doing daily, regularly scheduled activities from this chapter. I always recommend starting with the basics: meditation, journal writing, and affirmations. Then, begin to explore some of the other tools that are offered here. An example of a structured plan is the "Two-Week Program to Stop Bingeing" in Chapter 8. Otherwise, depending on where you are in your recovery process, you might select just the topics that are most pertinent to your situation.

Recovering from bulimia requires hard work. When you choose to embark on this journey, you will most likely be exploring unfamiliar and sometimes scary territory. Not only will you be investigating the origins of your problem, but you will also be radically transforming your current behaviors. This will probably feel uncomfortable at first; take baby steps if you need to.

I urge you to make recovering from bulimia your highest priority. Even if you think you are being selfish or irresponsible for placing your recovery ahead of other commitments, remember that *understanding and healing your relationship with food will enhance all other aspects of your life.*

1. Looking beyond the symptoms

Bulimia is not just about food and weight. Bingeing and purging, repeatedly weighing yourself, counting calories, and similar habits are actually ways of coping with *other* problems in your life. The symptoms are just the tip of the iceberg; underneath are all the reasons why you turn to bulimia. It is serving a purpose in your life, and although stopping the behaviors is essential, the underlying reasons must eventually be explored before you can be completely free.

Why do you have an eating disorder? There are lots of possibilities, such as: avoiding memories of a trauma that once occurred; beliefs that result in low self-esteem; painful emotions; or something about your present circumstances. Every person who has bulimia has a different constellation of hidden motivations. Whatever the causes, they manifest in some aspect of your bulimia.

Your eating disorder is trying to tell you something in a language all its own. So listen. Go into the thoughts, feelings, and behaviors and ask questions. Your approach here is key. It's much more productive and downright kind to come from a stance of curiosity and acceptance rather than judgment and blame. You are exploring solutions now, so instead of trying to control your bulimia, you are going to learn from it.

Understanding the role that bulimia plays in your life is a way of getting to know and care for yourself. Now, you are ready for something different, something more meaningful that nourishes you on a deeper level. Start by answering questions that will reveal some of the ways that bulimia functions in your life.

QUESTIONS FOR REFLECTION

- What were the circumstances that led to my earliest bulimic episodes?
- Why did the bulimic behaviors increase and begin to dominate my life?
- What triggers my binges?
- How has bulimia been taking care of me?

An eating disorder is just a symptom that something is seriously wrong in our lives. In fact, it is an invitation to grow, emotionally, and spiritually. Every crisis is an opportunity.

I just had my first consultation with a therapist and feel much calmer. My life has a new glow. Maybe it's because I realize that there's more to my bulimia than just bingeing and purging.

I told my boyfriend I was going to prove to myself that I could be bulimia-free for two weeks. Guess what, I did it! Instead of focusing on food, I focused on my thoughts and feelings and kept a journal every day. I learned so much and he supported me the whole way.

2. *Trusting the process*

Recovery is a gradual process. It's a journey that starts with your intention to heal; and, once you embark, you will experience a whole new way of being in the world. When I left my bulimia behind, I developed a wonderful relationship with my inner self. That didn't happen overnight, I had miracles and I also had setbacks. I didn't know what my life would become, but I believed wholeheartedly that it would be better than having bulimia. I became willing to do anything to recover and committed myself fully to that goal. As a result, I've had more than 30 years of happiness, meaningful service, and fulfillment on many levels. Not only was my recovery enlightening, but I even came to appreciate having had bulimia because it compelled me to go through the steps of self-discovery and emerge transformed.

The process begins with a leap of faith, because you are giving up the familiar for the unknown. Bulimia has been taking care of you, and you'll need to find different ways to cope before it is gone completely. But what will take its place? You might be frightened about who you will be without it. Let me reassure you: I've read hundreds of testimonies and have heard countless firsthand stories, and—without exception—every single person said their life improved by giving up their eating disorder.

Recovery means looking at things in a new way. Try to view the whole process in a positive light. Accept that you are doing the right thing at the right time. Follow your intuition, not the critical voice that has become all too familiar. When you have successes, celebrate them and pat yourself on the back. Reflect upon your setbacks and learn from them. Incidentally, there's a difference between a setback and a full-blown relapse. One binge can be a teacher if you stop to take the time to explore why it happened. That's how you learn to avoid bingeing a next time. On the other hand, a significant increase in bingeing would signal a problem that requires extra support.

You might want a quick fix, or think that there is such a thing as a "perfect" recovery. But that's not how recovery works. It's a process of steps forward and steps back, hits and misses, milestones and everyday steps. Gradually you discover what works specifically for you and what doesn't. Furthermore, there is no final destination in this journey. Whether you consider yourself "recovered" or "in recovery," your life will continue to unfold in new and surprising ways.

I resolved to trust my body's inner wisdom, particularly when it came to hunger and weight. I followed my instincts, stopped counting calories, quit weighing myself, and have felt better ever since.

I used to think that I needed to be healed to work in the world, but I discovered that by doing service I became healed.

My recovery became less about getting rid of a problem than journeying through it.

3. Journal writing

You can literally write yourself well.

In recovery, one of the most effective ways to sort out your thoughts is by writing. I always recommend keeping a journal, because it's a great way to get to know who you are. While I was ending my bulimia, I wrote in mine every morning. I also made lists, did values clarification exercises, composed letters, and jotted down insights from time to time. I cannot overemphasize how much this helped me, but that might be expected from someone who has spent the last 30 years writing, editing, and publishing.

The benefits to journaling are many. When you write, you are having an honest, caring relationship with your inner self. Giving your innermost thoughts and feelings tangible form makes them more real. If you sometimes have trouble expressing yourself, a journal is a safe place to explore this inner life. If you have difficulty slowing down, writing is an excellent way to take quiet time and explore the issues that come up when that time is taken. A journal can reveal patterns that you might need to challenge, be used to chart long-term progress, or help you problem-solve. It's like having a best friend who is always there, valuing what you have to say. When you have the urge to binge, turn to your journal instead.

You can buy a nice notebook or create a personal and confidential place on your computer. If you are more comfortable speaking than writing, try a recording device. Regardless, treat your journal with love and respect, because it is a representation of your own inner experience. Be spontaneous and let the words flow. No one else will read what you write, you won't be graded on content or grammar, and you don't have to explain yourself. You can be honest without being afraid.

Schedule a block of time every day for writing, and use your journal for times of stress as well as contemplation. Consider keeping a dream journal. If you don't know where to begin or get "writer's block," some topics are provided here to get you started. More are woven throughout this chapter and Chapter 8. Remember, there are no rules—write about whatever is on your mind. Actually, by documenting your thoughts, you literally take them *off* your mind!

WRITE YOUR STORY

Write the story of your life, especially the parts that are related to your bulimia. Include childhood influences, events that shaped your beliefs, the emergence of thoughts about weight and body image, and the history of your eating disordered behaviors. Try to get to the heart of your bulimia: Why it started, what sustains it, and why you are pursuing recovery.

Note: This exercise can take days, months, or years as you get to know yourself better during the course of your recovery.

Writing Letters

Writing a letter is a great way to express your most intimate thoughts and feelings, and you don't even have to send it! Whether you write to a person, situation, institution, or even an inanimate object, just getting the words out can have a powerful healing and calming effect. For example, you could write a letter of appreciation to your body for all it does for you on a daily basis, or a letter of goodbye to your bathroom scale. You could write letters of forgiveness, sympathy, anger, or other emotions that you've held back. You could write to friends explaining what you have gone through and asking for support, or to your family to rehearse for actual conversations. Write to your culture, advertisers, your bulimia, your therapist, yourself, God—anyone or anything to whom you want to communicate something straight from your heart.

Letters are particularly effective at resolving pent-up feelings about people. In my case, I wrote letters to my parents, most of which I did not send. This was a perfect way for me to say things to them that I could not express in person, because they were not interested or involved in my recovery. I needed to explain that they made me feel invisible, why I was compelled to move 3,000 miles away from them to go to college, that I didn't like the way my father treated my mother, how I was affected by their judgmental opinions about other people, and every other injustice I could think of! These were cathartic for me, and healing on many levels.

These kinds of letters can be written to anyone, whether they are currently in your life or not. Tell them how you have been mistreated. This is your chance to be critical and even blaming. Refer to specific incidents. Tell them what they did or said that hurt you, and convey how that made you feel. This is a much healthier way to purge than you are used to! Once you've gotten out all of the negativity, try composing a letter of forgiveness, affirming that you are ready to move forward and leave the past behind. These kinds of letters should not be sent without consultation with a professional, because they can have strong repercussions.

TOPICS FOR WRITTEN EXPLORATION

- Make a list of things you want in your life, such as: nurturing relationships, self-respect, a new skill, etc.
- Make a list of at least 25 goals (immediate, short-term, long-term).
- Explore your family's contribution to your eating disorder. How were you parented? Whose body shape do you have? What relatives have struggled with depression, alcohol, substance abuse, anxiety, or social avoidance?

- Pick a family member or friend and write your impressions of them. Describe your relationship. How has this person influenced you? What would you like to say to them that you haven't?
- Draw a timeline marking important events in the life of your bulimia.
- Describe a particularly happy moment. What gives you happiness?
- Write a non-judgmental description of your body. Next, write a non-judgmental description of your character. How do these differ from your usual views about yourself?
- Make a list of at least ten personal strengths. How can you best use these in your recovery?
- List ten people you admire (half from your personal life and half from contemporary society or history). What attributes of theirs do you admire? How do these compare to yours?
- Make a list of myths and rules that you want to change. A myth is a belief such as, "Skinny people are happier," and a rule has consequences, such as, "If I eat dessert, I have to throw up."
- What can you do to become more self loving?

When I began my recovery, I tried to make the journal my friend instead of the bulimia. In it I said whatever I wanted to say, knowing that it wouldn't judge or reject me.

I could always tell when there was something bothering me because I felt a twinge of anxiety right in the pit of my stomach. I always wondered if my bingeing wasn't directly connected to that physical sensation. Journaling helped me identify what I was anxious about before I began to binge.

Putting my thoughts and feelings down on paper made them seem more real. It helped me to feel less isolated, and I knew I'd eventually be able to communicate with people better.

I have kept detailed journals over the past 15 years. When I want to remember how distraught and obsessed I was, I read these. I am reminded of how far I have come, and how my desire for life, love, and happiness keeps me strong and clear.

4. Taking time for relaxation and meditation

People with eating disorders are obviously under tremendous stress. Their thoughts constantly jump from idea to idea, moving from past to present to future without rest. Much of this chatter revolves around eating, weight, and general negativity, along with the ordinary complications of everyday life. Although bulimia can be somewhat calming in its mindless repetition and emotional distance, these effects do not last. In the long run, the constant pressure and hyperactivity only adds stress to what already exists. Recovery requires slowing down and quieting the mind, which is achieved through relaxation.

Hyperactivity tricks you into thinking that you are only as good as what you can accomplish, including a smaller size and lower weight. You then become a "human doing" who has to stay busy to be worthwhile, instead of a "human being" who is valuable solely because you are alive. Taking time to relax and empty the mind will connect you to the quiet wisdom of your heart. At the same time, it will allow your body to return to its natural, balanced state.

This is the magic of relaxation. Although you feel like you are doing nothing, a great deal is actually occurring. Instead of being in the "fight or flight" mode, your blood pressure, heart rate, breathing, and circulation return to normal. Instead of churning and spinning, your mind turns inward and rests. You feel calmer, more connected to your inner self. And, when you return to your life, you are more centered, better able to handle not only the stresses of everyday life, but the challenges of recovery, as well.

In her book, *Desperately Seeking Self,* Viola Fodor says that "quiet time" helps us get in touch with the deeper realm of self and its healing capacity:

> Your inner self is wise and strong. You have an abundance of inner resources on which to draw. Your healing potential is boundless. Deep down, you already know what you need and how you are meant to be living. Your inner self is always there to help you. Your inner self is forever present. It can help you through any life situation. If you are prepared to listen to your inner voice, you will receive guidance and support whenever you need it.

Meditation

Meditation is one of the best ways to get in touch with your inner self. In fact, I think *everyone* should meditate regularly and those in recovery should do it twice a day! Meditation, in its many forms, has been practiced for thousands of years. It is a way to bring silence to the mind and has many practical benefits—from the obvious, such as relieving anxiety, to the sublime, such as getting in touch with both the inner self and the infinite universe.

Instructions for various meditation practices can be found on the Internet, in books, and from teachers. Some originate in Eastern philosophies and religions and others have been developed in more recent years by "gurus" of the self-help movement. I do some form of meditation every day, either sitting and repeating a mantra or the word "om," or doing a moving meditation based on the Chinese practice of Qigong. I've chanted for several hours at a time and have done one-minute meditations, but 20 minutes is an average session, and that's what I recommend to you.

Find a quiet place, sit comfortably, and close your eyes. Play soothing music if you wish (I like a recording of ocean waves). As thoughts arise, notice their existence, and then let them pass. Purposefully avoid being attached to a sequence of thoughts. Try to *not* think! Here are some simple ways to meditate:

3 SIMPLE WAYS TO MEDITATE

- Count your breaths from one to ten and repeat. Breathe in, silently say "one" and hold that word through the out breath. Breathe in, "two," etc. When thoughts arise, gently return to your counting.
- Repeat the word "om" over and over with each breath. Om is a sacred syllable in several languages and is used in many religions and meditation practices. Some think of it as the name of "God," which might be another good term for you to use.
- Think of a slowly flowing river. As thoughts enter your mind, drop them like leaves into the water and allow them to float away.

MORE WAYS TO RELAX

- Observe silence.
- Listen to soothing music.
- Take a bath.
- Be in nature.
- Stare at a body of water or a fire.
- Get a massage.
- Sit in a beautiful or holy place.

- Watch a bowl of fish, pet your cat, brush your dog.
- Chant or sing.
- Walk a labyrinth.
- Recite prayers.
- Practice yoga or T'ai Chi.

(See Chapter 8 for more ideas.)

When I felt sad, troubled, panicked, angry, or lonely, this disease jumped out on me like a Jack-in-a-Box. I just wanted to get numb! Taking quiet time made it easier for me to choose not to binge. I felt more connected with the part of me that wanted to get well.

I am thinking about taking some time off from school to find out what I really want to do with my life. I am so busy that I honestly don't know.

We have a hot tub in a cedar room with plants. I went in there last night, after feeling very stressed, lit some candles and climbed in.

My mind goes a million miles a minute and I have a hard time with the relaxation stuff. My husband and I are going out to get some CD's, such as whales, the ocean, and rain, to help.

Sometimes during a relaxation session, I see a small ray of light and get a feeling of hope that inspires me to go on.

5. Practicing mindfulness

Mindfulness is the practice of becoming aware of the present moment—without judgment. Rather than emptying the mind, like in meditation, mindfulness focuses the mind. Instead of being caught up in the chaos of an eating disorder, it changes your stance from being actively involved in the drama to being an impartial observer. It encourages you to become a witness to the unfolding of your thoughts and emotions—less critical, more accepting—and thereby increasingly present to the richness of everyday life.

Mindfulness practices separate you from your disorder. Although the voice of your bulimia might be loud in the beginning, you are purposefully creating a more powerful relationship with the voice of your own heart. You are touching that place within that has answers, ideas, and empathy when you most need them. By consciously bringing yourself into the present moment to experience all that "is," instead of distracting yourself through your bulimia, you are committing yourself to the highest goals—loving yourself and finding new meaning in your life.

Even a mindful experience lasting only a few minutes can have tremendous lasting value. Virtually all eating disorders treatment facilities and most therapists use mindfulness approaches in their treatment protocol. Here are two examples:

2 SIMPLE MINDFULNESS ACTIVITIES

- ***Notice sounds*** – Carefully listen to the world around you, either while sitting still with eyes closed or while walking outside. Form no opinions about what you hear, neither the birds singing or the drone of cars on a boulevard. The sounds are not better or worse than one another, they just are.

- ***Do a mental body scan*** – Sit or lie down in a quiet, safe place. Slowly and progressively concentrate on parts of your body, starting with your toes, then feet, ankles, calves, knees, and thighs, continuing upward until you finally arrive at the top of your head. Notice physical sensations like tingling or pulsing. Bring your consciousness to the inner experience rather than the outside world. If you get focused on your body in a way that isn't helpful to you, stop and concentrate on your breath instead.

MORE MINDFULNESS ACTIVITIES

- Practice being the observer.
- Engage fully in a particular activity.
- Practice acceptance of "what is."
- Write non-judgmental statements about your experience.
- Set and hold an intention.
- Bring yourself back to the present, gently and persistently.
- Use your senses to return to the present (sight, sound, smell, sensation).
- Notice how media images make you feel, why, and some ways to resist.
- Focus on a quality like kindness, generosity, gratitude.

6. Being authentic

Who are you, really?

Most people with bulimia spend years trying to conform to external standards, constantly questioning whether they are doing a "good enough" job. They tend to identify themselves in terms of their shameful behaviors and personal shortcomings. The voice of the eating disorder has become their voice—criticizing, judging, comparing, and offering bingeing as the solution to every situation. It all but silences the voice of their heart, so they are left feeling unsure, fearful, and empty inside. Bulimia is a relentless, symbolic quest to "fill up" this empty place—over and over again—which obviously does not work.

Recovery requires discovering who you are apart from the eating disorder, which means getting to know and express your authentic self.

Deep down, you are an important, worthwhile human being, a source of compassion, creativity, wisdom, contentment, and happiness. For some reason, which you will surely discover in the process of getting well, you have become cut off from this knowledge and don't even believe that it could be true. Without a foundation of self-awareness, however, nothing you do, buy, think, or eat will fill you up enough.

Start by acknowledging a separation between you and your bulimia. In her book, *Life Without Ed*, Jenni Schaefer defined her eating disorder as "Ed" and wrote, "He was abusive, controlling, and never hesitated to tell me what he thought, how I was doing it wrong, and what I should be doing instead." She gained her independence from Ed by distinguishing his voice from her own.

In the early stages, Jenni simply recognized when he was speaking and agreed with him. If he said she was fat, she believed she was fat. At this point, she was only ready to notice and acknowledge his existence. Over time, however, she began disagreeing with and eventually disobeying Ed. For example, if he told her she'd feel better snacking, she'd counter, "No. I think I'll pick up the phone instead and call someone for support who understands what I am going through. I don't need you anymore." She learned that life with Ed was no life at all, and that by divorcing him she was free to be her authentic self.

You are *not* your eating disorder. Inside, you are a person who dreams of a better life. Your self-worth is not dependent on the number on a scale or whether you can fit into a pair of old jeans. Underneath your "bulimia coat," you have wonderful qualities, such as honesty, trust, thoughtfulness, humor, sensitivity, understanding, forgiveness, and unconditional love.

Get to know yourself. Accept that you have strengths and weaknesses. We all do, that's part of being human. Learn how to listen to your inner voice, the one that wants you to be happy and healthy. Follow your intuition, often experienced as a "gut" reaction! Don't worry about what others might think. Appreciate who you are instead of trying to be somehow "perfect." You are always a perfect *you*.

The truth is that people come in all shapes, sizes, colors, aptitudes, interests, faiths, etc. There are infinite combinations, and no one else is exactly like you. However, we all share one divine similarity: self-love is available to all of us. No matter what challenges or hardships you have endured, it's okay to just be you.

QUESTIONS FOR REFLECTION

- Who am I, separate from the eating disorder?
- What gives my life meaning?
- Realistically, what are my strengths and what are my weaknesses?
- What are the layers that hide my most authentic self?
- Can I hear the difference between the voice of bulimia and a conscience that is trying to guide me in the right direction?
- Who do I dream to be?
- What issues are important to me?
- How can I be of service to others?

My value as a human being is not about my size.

I have discovered at last how important I am as a person—a human that God created and loves. I realize that I am worthy of love and friendship; I deserve a good life, like everyone does.

As I became more comfortable with myself, I saw my life change in many ways. I found myself surrounded by friends who really liked me. And they were happy people, not miserable and depressed like my old friends. I have learned how to say "no" to people, and earned a lot of respect for doing so.

My self-concept has changed with recovery! I no longer have a secret life that

I am utterly ashamed of! I no longer hate myself for continuing destructive behavior that does nothing but temporarily alleviate pain. I now love myself. I am a good person. Sometimes life is scary, but I can face it head-on now, instead of hiding in food.

I have found happiness. Once I stopped using food to cope with life, I started getting to know myself. To my delight, I like the person I discovered, and I now enjoy life.

I never dreamed I could like myself this much!

7. Expressing yourself

Once you begin to recognize that the "voice" of your eating disorder is different from your own, you will want to start speaking for yourself, rather than letting it speak for you. This means learning how to express your most authentic self in the world, whether in your relationships with other people, the work you choose to do, the causes you support, the kinds of art you create, and the like.

Expressing yourself can feel awkward at first, especially when you haven't had much practice. You may be used to holding back your feelings and opinions rather than making waves or standing out. You may be a "people pleaser" and put everyone else's needs before your own, or not feel comfortable saying "no." You may think that no one would like you if they knew who you really were. But *you* don't even know who you are!

The beauty of recovery lies in the fact that as you weaken the connection to your disorder, you strengthen the connection to your inner self. And as that relationship gets stronger, you will discover that expressing your truth is satisfying, meaningful, fun, productive, creative, and financially rewarding, among many other great things. People might disagree with you sometimes, or not like what you have to offer, but that's okay. When you come home to yourself, you have the confidence to be in the world in a whole new way.

In my recovery, I was driven to express myself through creativity. I had never considered myself creative before, but the process turned out to be exciting to my soul, and an incredibly motivating force. As I wrote in Chapter 2, when I was "sewing myself well," the joy of creating my goofy soft-sculpture dolls was much more fulfilling than sneaking away to eat. And when I needed to put my artwork out there for the world to see, I felt compelled even though I was afraid of the unknown. It was scary to go to a craft fair with a carload of life-sized dolls, price them (almost like measuring my self-worth), and not know how anyone would react, but I did it anyway. I put my sense of humor out there, and the response was tremendous. People loved my dolls and over the next few years proved it by buying hundreds of thousands of them. I know without question that I would not have achieved so much, both personally and professionally, had I stayed stuck in my bulimia.

Don't let your eating disorder make any more decisions. You are a person with likes and dislikes and an interest in things that don't have to do with food and weight. You have passions and talents and a unique personality. Learn to appreciate your qualities and quirks instead of worrying about how people view you. Stop trying to please others when it means devaluing your own needs. "No" is an acceptable answer if it reflects your real feelings. Be honest and be yourself. You are different from other people—everyone is—and that's the way it is meant to be!

Everyone has a song to sing. Write. Draw. Dance. Have a heartfelt conversation with a friend. Play an instrument. Give money to a cause. Get to know who you are, and offer the gifts you discover to other people. Have confidence in what you think and say, anchored in the knowledge that you are worthwhile and that your thoughts and feelings matter. You have a place in the world, there is meaning in your life; shout it loud and clear, "I am here and this is who I am!"

WAYS TO EXPRESS YOURSELF

- Think about what you say and how you say it, to yourself and others. Increase your use of the pronoun "I," and follow it up with active verbs, such as: feel, think, want, wish, and am.

- Instead of swallowing your emotions, let them out and express those feelings with words.
- Pursue your creativity.
- Seek out uplifting friends and support each other.
- Take the risk of letting family and friends get to know the real you.
- If you have a problem being authentic with someone, rehearse a conversation with a sympathetic friend or in front of a mirror. Maybe write out what you'd like to say. Consider role-playing the conversation from both points of view.
- If you are angry, hit or kick a punching bag or pillow. Scream out loud.
- Use your journal!

I have gone from a person who went along with whatever anyone else said or did, to someone who expresses opinions of her own.

From the moment I first told my parents that I was "recovering" from bulimia, my whole perception of myself changed. I started to feel more in control of my own decisions.

I had always been told that I had no imagination. But in recovery, I started to paint portraits from photographs and discovered something that I love and am good at. My life has taken on an entirely new direction because more and more of the time I would rather paint than binge.

A big piece of my recovery meant letting my family know who I was. In the safety of family therapy, I told them that I needed it to be okay for me to be a quiet person even though they were all outgoing. It sounds so silly now, but at the time I needed to tell them that.

8. Thinking positively

If you tend to think of the cup as "half empty" instead of "half full," fill it up! Although positive thinking doesn't change the circumstances, it does change how you approach them. Your mind is a filter for every thought, word, and action. Approach the present moment from a positive perspective, and you are likely to react with compassion, expect good things to happen, look for solutions, even see lessons in misfortune. Since the way you view the world is reflected back to you, and you can consciously choose your approach to life, make yours more positive.

In the process of "cleaning up" my mind, I spent (and continue to spend) time practicing mindful awareness of my thinking. My goal was to separate what was going on in my head, which was often fearful and negative, from what I truly believed in my heart or what I *wanted* to believe. What I discovered was that most of the time, my mind was on automatic pilot. (My mind had a mind of its own!) I was a worrier who needed to be on the alert because bad things were right around the corner.

Until I started my recovery, I took it for granted that there was nothing I could do about these thoughts. Not only was I unaware that my mind was filled with negativity, but I also avoided the reasons why, such as: my upbringing, cultural pressures to look a certain way, guilt from bingeing and purging, as well as the important fact that my brain was malnourished from years of bulimia. But once I began to eat more normally and take an objective look at my attitude, I discovered that my mind could be a friend if I put it to good use, but it would remain an enemy if I left it to react on its own. So, trying not to judge what I uncovered, I explored my negative thinking patterns and worked to change them. Here are a few examples that may resonate with you:

NEGATIVE THINKING PATTERNS

- **General negativity**

  Expecting the worst. You instinctively have a pessimistic outlook about situations, relationships, the future, and the world at large.

- **Seeing everything as black or white**

  Judging based on extremes. Food becomes good or bad; weight gain equals obesity. You repeatedly look in the full-length mirror but never like what you see.

- **Magnifying the negatives**

  Filtering out the positives, and letting only the negatives through. Minor problems are seen as catastrophes and offhand comments get blown out of proportion. If you see an increase on the scale, the day is ruined. If someone disagrees with an opinion, you think they hate you.

- **Taking everything personally**

  Thinking that the world revolves around you. You feel guilty over matters that often have nothing to do with you, or feel that people are judging you, or that the world is against you.

- **The "shoulds"**

  Having rigid rules about how you and others should act. This would manifest in thoughts such as as, "Anger should not be expressed," or "I should not eat salad dressing."

- **Justifying**

  Using excuses to justify being stuck. If you eat "one bite too many," you give in to the urge to binge. You think that bingeing is an okay way to find comfort when faced with something difficult.

- **Critical self-judgment**

  Thinking you are not good enough. You are your own worst critic, thinking about yourself in harsh terms no outside observer would ever use. Thoughts about yourself are so dark and insulting that you would never voice them for someone else to hear.

Changing Your Mind

If you make a conscious effort to fight these habitual patterns, you can change how you experience everything. Begin by focusing on recovery and make that your highest priority. When you have "bulimic thoughts," recognize, examine, and rephrase them in terms of recovery. For example, if you think, "I want to binge," notice that thought and change it to, "It's more important to me to not binge," or "I don't need to binge in this moment—I can take care of myself another way." Then, imagine what steps you could take next that are not part of the old chain of events.

Transforming your thoughts from negative to positive has powerful consequences. If you instinctively think, "I'm not worthy," and change that thought to "I am worthy," the result is pretty dramatic—you feel more worthy! Even if you have to "fake it till you make it," repeating positive statements that you might not even believe will help them manifest in your life. Filling your mind with thoughts of gratitude is far more uplifting than feeling resentful or dissatisfied. Expressing compassion for the pain that surely drove you to bulimia will ease the guilt and shame. Believing that you are learning the right lesson at the right time can free you from doubt. Plus, this "mental housecleaning" has the added benefit of silencing your inner critic and making it possible for you to hear the voice of your inner self more clearly.

How you think has the power to change your life. Here are some activities to help you in this pursuit of positive thinking:

ACTIVITIES FOR CHANGING YOUR MIND

- Stop thinking of yourself as "bulimic." You're "*recovering* from bulimia."
- Set the intention to think more positively, and continuously remind yourself of that goal.
- Make lists of short, medium, and long-term goals.
- Observe negative thoughts with non-attachment. Take note of the ideas, but let them pass without having a mental conversation.
- Choose your words carefully so that you consciously speak positively and with optimism.
- Counter negative thoughts by reframing them with positives.
- Say "do" instead of "don't," "will" instead of "won't," and "can" instead of "can't."
- Pat yourself on the back for large and small accomplishments.

Positive Affirmations

Repeating positive affirmations is a great way to reprogram the mind. Make the conscious effort to articulate at least one positive statement over and over throughout each day. Say it aloud, if possible, as many times as you can: in front of a mirror first thing in the morning, while you get dressed, as you open and close doors, while you drive in a car, sit at a desk, hug a friend, make dinner. When you catch yourself in negative self-talk, stop it with a positive affirmation.

While it might be hard at first, and even feel dishonest to verbalize phrases that you don't yet believe, repeating them does have a transforming effect on your mind and mood. Eventually, you will turn a corner and begin to believe them, and in yourself. Here are a few ideas to get you started.

EXAMPLES OF POSITIVE AFFIRMATIONS

- I love myself.
- I am great!
- I deserve good things.
- My weight has nothing to do with my worth.
- I have a good heart.
- Every day, in every way, I'm getting better and better.
- The universe supports me.
- My body is a temple.
- I am enthusiastic and confident.
- People like me just the way I am.
- I am thankful for the lessons of recovery.
- I honor my individuality.

I know that I should try a new way of thinking because the old hasn't worked.

My bulimia was a symptom of very poor self-esteem, feelings of guilt, and helplessness. Through therapy I learned how to treat myself with respect, control my own emotions, and use frequent affirmations, which have turned my world around.

I used to feel like I was on automatic pilot. I let my thoughts dictate my life. Now, I dictate what I think!
I like to imagine a paper shredder in my mind where I destroy all the negative thoughts.

Although recovery was the most difficult challenge of my life, I can now experience the beautiful things that I couldn't from the inside of a toilet bowl, like the smell of leaves, butterflies, wild flowers, and how it feels to love myself and others.

9. Visualization

One particularly powerful use for the mind is visualization. When you visualize something, you are creating a mental image with the express purpose of influencing your experience. You are healing the past or pulling your dreams into the present. You can visualize a safe place to go when you need it, evoke feelings like safety or courage, realize goals, or just relax. It can complement or augment healing practices, for example, to boost the effects of chemotherapy in cancer treatment. Athletes regularly use it before competing. And, it can be a powerful ally in stopping eating disordered behaviors.

In recovery, which is a process of getting to know who you are at ever-deepening levels, visualization can set the stage for self-reflection. For example, imagine a favorite place, perhaps alongside a stream or in a forest. Relax and feel the breeze, hear the sounds of the rushing water or the wind rustling the leaves in the trees. Then bring to mind a question or troubling situation, or allow one to come up on its own. You might ask, "Why am I so shy?" The reply might be, "Because I fear my father's anger." Answers may come in the form of words, images, colors, feelings, memories, songs, or prayers. In this way, visualization gives you access to your inner self. You are inviting your subconscious to speak, and learning how to be present for whatever realizations occur.

There are many kinds of visualization techniques, and detailed descriptions of these are easily found in books and on the Web. Most involve entering a state of relaxation and then either creating a mental image, allowing one to emerge, or following outside prompts (to stop smoking, sleep better, etc.). Sound recordings—sometimes combined with visual effects—may include music, electronic sounds, or "white noise," along with guided imagery or subliminal messages.

Imagine your life without bulimia right now. Really give it some thought. Come up with the most positive ideas you can so that you have an image of an almost "perfect" life. Some aspects of your dream will be attainable, like eliminating your bingeing and purging. Others will not, like changing someone's personality. But the simple act of imagining your heart's desire increases the chances of it coming true.

GUIDED IMAGERY FOR APPRECIATING YOUR BODY

Get settled and close your eyes in a quiet, comfortable place. After a few cleansing breaths, imagine yourself as a toddler. See how round you are as you roll on the floor or pull yourself up to stand. Hear the adults saying, "What a darling child." Feel happiness in knowing that they are talking about you. The fat on the child is okay, because it is natural for all children to have baby fat. Then, picture yourself as a young teenager, just starting to mature. Your body needs to grow at this time; it needs some extra fat, too. Now, see yourself moving into adulthood, getting some wrinkles and letting gravity take over a bit. Can you accept these changes? Finally, imagine yourself at 90 years old. How far your body has taken you! What do you look like? How do you feel towards your body now? Bodies change. Relax. Get comfortable with this idea and appreciate what nature gave you.

IMAGINE...

- a day at the beach. Synchronize your breath with the waves.
- a conversation with a wise and respected teacher.
- feeling good while you eat a forbidden food.
- being licked by a puppy.
- how you'd feel after a year without bulimia.
- the next step you need to take in your recovery.

10. Feeling your feelings

Emotions are a part of being human. Everyone has them—good and bad. They connect us to our inner experiences, much like the senses connect us to the outside world. People with bulimia, though, usually keep their feelings at bay. Obsessing about food and weight, fearing the next meal, keeping secrets, and other hallmarks of an eating disorder take time and focus away from what is really going on inside. Like a dam holding back water, it's a lot easier and quicker to get numb by bingeing and purging than drown in anger, loneliness, shame, or even happiness that you feel you don't deserve.

Think about approaching your feelings in a new way. Consider the possibility that they exist for a reason: to help you navigate your life by reflecting your inner truth. Feelings are not something to avoid, but something to *value*—messages from an internal guidance system that fights for who you are and what you need as a person. They help you make decisions, give you a reason to stand up for yourself, and articulate what you want out of life, all of which you are learning to do as you let go of your bulimia.

So, in your recovery, you will be getting in touch with your feelings, not just the bad ones, but the good ones, too, since bulimia affects both.

Begin by simply naming them. Use specific words, such as "invalidated" or "lonely" instead of more general terms, such as "bad." See if the feeling has a physical sensation, a color, a shape, a past, or a "voice."

Then get curious. Since feelings serve a purpose, try to mindfully observe them as they occur and interpret what they mean. If you feel overwhelmed, do you need to slow down? If you feel frustrated or vulnerable after a conversation, did you assert yourself? Discover when, why, and how the emotion took root. Notice the ways in which bulimia helps you cope with that feeling. Is there another way you can handle it? Become like a private eye, whose job it is to investigate your inner life and, in particular, how bulimia has robbed you of your feelings.

Getting in touch with emotions you are not used to, or don't know what to do with, can be frightening. You may have memories, physical responses, or particularly strong reactions at first. You're processing not only the feelings of the present moment, but also those underneath the bulimic behavior. You probably have feelings about being bulimic, too. Take it slowly. Get support from someone you can trust, for instance a close family member, friend, or recovery buddy. Open up to your therapist or counselor, with the understanding that they won't judge or dismiss what you have to say. Write a letter about a feeling. Paint a picture. And with each feeling that you honor, you get a little more comfortable with yourself, a little more honest, confident, and real. As Karen Koenig, author of *The Food and Feelings Workbook* writes, "With practice and patience, both feelings and food will begin to serve you the way they were intended: feelings as a way to nourish your emotional needs, and food as a way to nourish your body."

FEELING EXERCISES

- List 25 positive and 25 negative emotions. Match them in columns side-by-side (e.g. happy and sad) as much as possible.
- Music can intensify feelings. Do you listen to the blues or rock anthems? Try playing upbeat music

when you're feeling down. Listen to different types of music and see how they make you feel.

- Smells can evoke powerful emotions. Keep a "smell" log for a day or two. Write down whatever scents you notice and if they evoke a particular feeling. For example, does the aroma of cookies in the oven give you feelings of comfort or anxiety?
- Feelings are often based on underlying, sometimes faulty, beliefs. List some of your beliefs and how they make you feel. For example, if you believe people who are outgoing are more popular, and you are shy, then you'll feel inadequate.
- Feelings are also triggered by passing thoughts, so watch what you're thinking! List some thoughts you might have, like "I look fat," or "I ate too much," and how they make you feel.
- Laugh more! Read jokes aloud (you can find tons of jokes on the Web). Watch funny movies, TV shows, and video clips. Try pretending to laugh out loud with other people, and before you know it, you'll all be in stitches!

11. Improving body image

People commonly think of body image as the way we "see" our body—a mental picture of our physical attributes. While this is true, body image also includes how we think and feel about our body, how it feels to be *in* a physical form, and all the messages we receive about appearance—especially misinformation about the relationship between weight, health, and beauty. It is influenced by how we take care of our body, how other people respond to us, and any medical issues we might have. So, body image is a very important and complex issue for everyone.

As children, we adopt beliefs about how we look based on feedback from family, friends, classmates, and culture. The opinions we develop become ingrained as we age, and unfortunately, those messages are often negative. More than 80% of women *and* men are dissatisfied with their bodies, although for the majority, this does not dominate their lives. But it does for people with eating disorders. In fact, disliking the body is such a crucial symptom of anorexia nervosa and bulimia that both *DSM* diagnoses include the criteria that a person's self-evaluation is "unduly influenced by body shape and weight."

For someone with bulimia, whose body is the battleground where daily wars are fought, improving body image is essential. Your recovery is not complete by simply stopping the bingeing and purging; you must also make peace with your physical self. It's a package deal. This is because body image and self-image are so closely tied. The approach you take with your body is a reflection of the approach you take with yourself.

So, the best way to improve your body image is to get to know and appreciate who you are as a unique, multidimensional person. Being mindful of your many facets will lessen the emphasis you place on your appearance, while helping you to be grateful for the mystery and miracle of even having a physical form in the first place.

Instead of obsessing about your body, recognize the many ways in which it serves you. Obviously, without it you wouldn't be alive! It is the house for your mind and spirit, a means to experience pleasure and joy, the vehicle in which you drive through life. It will pass through stages from childhood to old age, and there is nothing you can do to control that process. However, even as your body transforms, who you are at the core of your being remains the same. When you place a higher value on your inner self, you become more accepting of your exterior. You can then appreciate it for taking you on the journey of life itself—a tall order, but entirely possible.

A lot of the tools for recovery we've mentioned in this chapter also apply to improving your body image. Changing your internal self-talk will change how you think and feel about your body. Knowing that phrases like, "I hate the way I look" or, "I feel fat" have a deeper meaning will make you more curious than critical. Being mindful of the body without judgment can feel like coming home. So, many of the tools we recommend in this chapter for self-discovery will help you approach your body in a new way, as well.

This section on body image is a little longer than the others in this chapter, because we feel it deserves extra attention. It is organized to help you attack negative body image on several different fronts by: negating toxic cultural influences, understanding the role of heredity, taking back the power you give to the mirror, and taking advantage of other practical approaches.

Be a Cultural Revolutionary

Start improving your body image by becoming media literate. You can do this immediately by being critical of what you read, see, and hear that deliver subtle (and not so subtle) messages about issues, such as weight loss, health, joy, and success. We, as a culture, have been duped into thinking that image is everything and that thinness has value. Multi-billion dollar corporations depend on our feeling insecure about our bodies and spending our money on a particular look. Open your eyes and ears to what you are "consuming"!

While playing with fashion and style can be fun, being a slave to it is not. Too many people believe there is something about their physical bodies that should be changed or fixed before they can feel good "enough." Women are expected not to have rounded bellies, wrinkles, or allow their hair to grow gray, although these are all perfectly natural and predictable consequences of aging. They're supposed to have well-developed breasts, but not too big or too small. Men face similar pressures, for instance being muscular and thin, and having hair on their heads but not necessarily on their bodies. We're told that anyone can have a "perfect" body if they go to the "right" gym, eat "good" foods, or buy the "best" products for trimming thighs, hardening abs, and losing weight.

To love your body, you will have to be a cultural revolutionary! Stop buying into the mentality that you need to look somehow "better" or different, or that thinness has value. Begin noticing how often you receive these kinds of messages. Do you really think diets are about health? Think again. They're about corporations getting rich. Be aware of the economics of body image and spend your money and time wisely.

Media Images

Research has consistently shown that exposure to media images makes people feel worse about their own appearance. Even the models themselves are affected. Many, who are paid fortunes for their "beauty," are actually insecure about how they look (especially body details), and as a group have a higher frequency of anorexia nervosa and bulimia than the general public. Ironically, most images are digitally altered anyway, so what is presented as a "gorgeous" body is really just an artist's creation designed to get you to buy a product. So be mindful of images, both how they affect you and how you can become resistant to their influence.

Here is an exercise to help you fight back:

MEDIA MINDFULNESS EXERCISE

> Buy a popular magazine, like the glossy ones at a supermarket checkout stand. As you page through, tear out every image, idea, or bit of advice that hints at changing or improving yourself. This means things such as dieting, having a better love life, coloring hair, firming abs, and looking younger. How much of the magazine is left when you're done? Go to their website and see the same useless information. Then, write a letter to the editor explaining why this is offensive, and what you would rather see instead!

Find Your Body on Your Family Tree

Bodies come in all shapes and sizes, that's a biological fact, and yours can be found somewhere on your family tree. You can change your weight to some degree by the food you eat and the amount of exercise you get, but you cannot radically change your inherited body type without harming yourself through obsessive exercise, surgery, or an eating disorder.

Your recovery from bulimia in part depends on your ability to accept the body you were born with, even while you think it's imperfect. Face it: there is no such thing as perfection. It is an unattainable goal, and precarious at best. Self worth is not a size. Your body is neither good nor bad, it is just the one you inherited. Also, those "imperfections" that you focus on are probably genetic, as well. You might have your mother's hips or your father's gut. Recognize their attributes in you, and treasure these physical traits as if they were family heirlooms.

Observe groups of people in a busy public setting and see that they do, indeed, come in a wide variety of shapes, sizes, and colors. Do the thin ones look happier than those who are of average size or larger? You can't miss the ones who are related, because parents and children, regardless of age, often have such obvious similarities. They look alike because they share genes! And there's absolutely nothing they, or you, can do about that.

WHO DO YOU LOOK LIKE?

> Look through family photos to find pictures of yourself and family members to determine whose body you inherited. You may resemble a parent, grandparent, aunt, or uncle. If your figure is like your mom's, for example, match up her pictures with yours as children, teens, and at your present age. You will be amazed at the similarity of your shapes, and if you shared the same body type as kids and young adults, you can expect to continue to look like her as you get older. Accept it, and honor this special connection.

Be aware that this exercise won't work if either one of you is pictured with an eating disorder, while on a severe diet, after years of binge eating, or during an extended illness.

Mirror Work

You probably check yourself in the mirror several times throughout the day and have anxiety about it every time. Perhaps you even try to catch your glance in windows, silverware, and on the chrome of cars. Every time you see yourself, though, you only notice the "defects" and believe that everyone else sees them, too.

You are not alone in this behavior. I doubt that anyone feels great *every* time they look in a mirror, but people with eating disorders rarely see anything they like. Every time you see yourself, you mentally distort the image as if you were looking in a fun-house mirror. You see your thighs and think they look lumpy. You see your face and it seems to be sagging or stretched. You become preoccupied with every bump and blemish, and you focus on those areas continuously throughout the day—for weeks, months, and even years. Challenging negative mirror talk that has persisted for so long means training your mind to think differently and changing your rituals.

You have to stop the body checking! You would probably be better off covering over all of the mirrors in your home so that they don't distract you so often. Otherwise, shorten the time you spend in front of the mirror, and when you find yourself overdoing it, tell yourself something like, "I look really good today," or "Stop looking!"

Take a Mindful Look

A basic step in improving your body image is to get to know your body! This may be scary, but cathartic. Being afraid of what you see only gets in the way of reality, though, and we are aiming for truth here.

Go into a private room with a large mirror, such as a bathroom, and take off all or some of your clothes. You are going to stand in front of the mirror for several minutes and observe mindfully. Stay as present as you can. Start by giving yourself a quick once-over. Tell yourself, "This is my body. It is beautiful. It is the house for my heart and soul." Try not to judge it, and instead feel appreciative of everything it does for you. Next, study the details, slowly from head to toe, again without opinions. As you do this, stay aware of your breathing. If you have a negative thought or feeling as you stand there, notice it, but don't pursue it. Let the thought pass, focusing again on your breath. Finally, look at your body as a whole and, with conviction, repeat five times, "I accept and love this body just as it is."

After you get dressed, write about the experience in your journal. Here are some questions to get you started:

BODY IMAGE QUESTIONS

- How did it feel to look at myself that way?
- What do I like and dislike about my body?
- What do I believe about the importance of looks?
- What influenced my body image?
- How does my poor body image interfere with my relationships?
- What would I like to change about my body image (as opposed to my body appearance)?
- What concrete things can I do to improve how I feel about my body?

Suggestions for Improving Body Image

Over the past 30 years of having a company that specializes in eating disorders resources, I've had the opportunity to read virtually every book ever written in English on body image. Obviously, I cannot share all of that knowledge in one section of this book. However, here are ten of the most important lessons and practices gleaned from numerous sources:

WAYS TO IMPROVE BODY IMAGE

- **Have compassion for yourself.**

  Be honest and kind to yourself as you examine your beliefs, thought patterns, and assumptions about your body and the bodies of other people. This is fruitful but demanding work.

- **Expand your idea of beauty.**

  Expand your concept of what is beautiful. View art. Observe different cultures. Spend time in nature. Constantly remind yourself that everyone is beautiful in his or her own way. Think about people you admire. In what ways are they beautiful?

- **Let go of perfectionism.**

  In the same way that you are learning to accept yourself—flaws and all—you will also be learning to accept your unique body. Striving to reach an arbitrary idea of physical perfection is a form of self-sabotage, and is not possible anyway.

- **Fully experience your senses.**

  Get more in touch with your body by noticing all of your senses. Concentrate on smells, sounds, colors, and touch. Best of all, connect with taste! Eat something you love (that's not triggering). Try something you hate! Your body enables you to have physical experiences, so get brave and enjoy them.

- **Reconnect your mind and body.**

  Certain activities—yoga, stretching, dancing, Pilates, Tai Chi—bring the mind and body together by focusing on the physical experience of the moment. These are wonderful practices for both quieting the mind and building a friendship with the body.

- **Tolerate negative body talk without acting on it.**

  You don't go from bulimia to loving your body in one day. Acknowledge that it's a process, and that negative body talk is inevitable. But don't act on the thoughts by turning to old habits. Instead, learn to talk back, or decide that you just aren't going to listen right now.

- **Understand the deeper meanings of negative body talk.**

  Negative body talk is a symptom of an eating disorder, just like bingeing and purging. There can be deeper meaning behind the phrases "I feel fat" (I feel worthless), "I have to lose weight" (My life lacks meaning), and "I hate the way I look" (I hate my life). When you have these thoughts, recognize that they are code for bigger issues, and investigate.

- **Talk back to harmful body thoughts.**

  When you hear yourself being self-disparaging, talk back. Use positive affirmations and use rational, rather than emotional, language.

- **Process body trauma with support.**

  Sometimes, body image issues are symptoms of past trauma, such as teasing, abuse, rejection, or abandonment. Healing the pain of trauma is a challenging and intimate process. I recommend working with a qualified therapist.

- **Write a love letter to your body.**

  Thank your body for all the good things it does for you. Appreciate it for giving you a life. Tell it the kinds of things you would say to a soul mate, because, after all, your body is your soul's companion!

MORE THINGS TO DO TO IMPROVE BODY IMAGE

- Smile more. It can't hurt.
- Be aware of how you carry your body. Walk and speak with dignity.
- Get rid of your scale. I took a hammer to mine. Write it a good-bye letter!
- Pamper your body with massages and long, luxurious baths.
- Embrace your sexuality and have an orgasm!
- Buy clothes that fit and get rid of those that don't.
- Accept and offer compliments graciously.
- Get moving! Participate in physical activities that you enjoy.
- Develop a new skill that involves dexterity, like sculpture, knitting, or playing an instrument.
- Don't compare your body to others.
- Do something that you've been putting off because you are unsure about your body, such as taking a dance class or wearing a bathing suit in public.

I didn't see my body the way others did. The difference now is that I acknowledge my perceptions to be distorted by my low self-esteem, and let it sit at that. I recognize that I didn't "feel thin" at 85 pounds, so losing weight is not my answer anymore.

I like my body! And, it is ten pounds heavier than I thought I could live with. My physical body is a map, a reflection of the totality of every experience I have had since conception, and the genetic disposition of my family of origin. It is unique, like I am.

My body image is based on my feelings about myself at that moment. In other words, how I see myself is based on my emotions. More and more now, I have times when I am at peace with my body image because I feel more at peace internally. I am glad I am healthy and not emaciated, as I used to be.

Most of my life I have used my body size to evaluate my self-worth. It wasn't until my mid-forties that I finally began to recognize that others valued me for who I was, not how I looked.

12. Cultivating relationships

Secrecy and isolation are part of an eating disordered lifestyle, because the primary relationship is with food rather than other people. It's a lot easier to take refuge and comfort in familiar rituals and patterns than open up to someone and risk rejection, anger, or dismissal. Your bulimia is always there, keeping you at a distance from yourself and other people. It may even have talked you into an exclusive relationship, because you are afraid of what others would think of you if they knew the truth.

So, in the course of recovery, as you get to know yourself apart from your disorder, you'll also be opening up to other people and learning how to be in healthy, caring relationships. The rewards are many: trusting another person calls up courage, telling your story and asking for support means being honest and accepting honest feedback, expressing your needs and preferences is affirming that you are worth fighting for, and sharing a hug feels like heart-to-heart resuscitation. Remember, you are *not* your bulimia, you are someone who has *used* bulimia as way of coping with life. Put down your embarrassment and your feelings of disconnection and separation. Get to know yourself, get to know other people, and you'll discover the richness to be found in close relationships.

Finding the right people to confide in is crucial, especially if your boundaries are unclear or you have been hurt in the past. Therapists are good choices because they are trained to listen, guide, teach, challenge, and be there for you when needed. (I recommend finding one that specializes in treating eating disorders.) In the safety of that fundamental connection, you can explore your true thoughts and feelings and begin to express them. You can practice communication skills and thinking patterns. You can safely take risks and be more open. You have a collaborator who believes in you—without judging or shaming. Also, in a good therapeutic alliance you will learn to maintain a connection with yourself even when you're in relationship with another person.

In addition to professionals, there is an eating disorders recovery community which is available for support. Groups can be found through local therapists or by searching the Web. In addition to regular meetings, organizations like Eating Disorders Anonymous also match "sponsors" with attendees who are new to the process. Some eating disorders treatment centers have referrals to alumni who are on hand for support, and an online program, MentorCONNECT, matches mentors who have had sustained recovery for at least one year with those who are just getting started. Mentoring relationships can be conducted by phone and email. Finally, discussion groups for support can be found online, but they are obviously less intimate.

Spending time with a willing friend or relative can "fill you up" in ways bingeing and purging never has. Start by reaching out to someone who you are, or have been, close to, even if you haven't talked recently. The important thing is to interact with people who will mirror your earnest effort to love and be loved. Gradually and gently, allow others to know who you really are. You might be amazed at how supportive some can be. Eventually, as you make new connections, you will become more comfortable and confident being yourself with others.

IDEAS FOR CULTIVATING HEALTHY RELATIONSHIPS

- Be honest at all times.
- Assert yourself; say what's on your mind.
- Reach out to long-distance friends with letters, calls, and e-mail.

- Make eye contact when you talk in person.
- Ask questions, listen, and be supportive.
- Seek out a long-lost friend, who knew and liked you before you had bulimia.
- Volunteer at a retirement home and "adopt" someone who is lonely.
- Spend time with small children or animals—they will accept you unconditionally.
- If you anticipate a conversation to be difficult or confrontational, try role playing it first with a friend or therapist.
- See the best in everyone, especially yourself.
- Keep good company!

Because most of us who have bulimia are ashamed of our behavior, we tend to hide and keep our addiction a secret. We isolate from the ones who care and want to help us. There were many times I wanted to go to someone for help, but fear of rejection kept me isolated. I can't tell you what a relief it was when my secret was finally out in the open—everyone who knows has been very supportive and understanding.

My saving grace has been your book and my sister, who is a recovered anorexic. I've debated telling my best friend who will be at college with me next year but I know unless I do, the relationship won't be honest and we will grow apart.

Not everyone I told about my bulimia had the same caring response, but I was able to accept that. I have no regrets about telling anyone. In fact, one of my closest, lifelong friends shared that she was suffering from the same disease. We were able to be there for one another in a way we had never been before.

In my recovery process, I started to socialize again, and this time I chose a couple of friends I thought I could trust with my secret. Their reactions were the very opposite of what I had feared—they were understanding and supportive, offering to help me in any way they could. I was so relieved. Their acceptance gave me more confidence and made it easier for me to tell other people.

When I was honest, our relationship deepened, and I discovered that I was a good person. That gave me confidence. Now I have a close girlfriend and generally feel more comfortable around other people.

Difficult Relationships

With increased confidence, you will be also able to tackle relationships with some of the more difficult people in your life. Be aware of old, restrictive roles, and especially do not allow yourself to be abused. Separation and independence are preferable to being misunderstood or mistreated. Also, if you have low self-esteem, you may tend to have superficial "friendships" with others who also have low self-esteem. You don't need people who bring you down when you are sincerely working on your recovery. Develop positive relationships with those who want to be uplifting and self-accepting. Keep good company! This is so important, I will repeat it: Keep good company!

If there is someone you blame for actual or perceived misdeeds, your recovery will gain by examining that specific relationship. Depending on the situation, you can either discuss it with the person directly, or process your thoughts on your own or with a therapist. If you'd like the relationship to continue, work on repairing it. If not, you can still gain a sense of closure by writing the person an honest and assertive letter, just to get your feelings out. Later, you can decide about sending it or not, and whether you want to offer them the gift of forgiveness.

Just as forgiveness can help heal relationships with others, I especially encourage you to forgive yourself. You can acknowledge and be accountable for your actions, but you don't have to punish yourself anymore. Don't regret past decisions that led to and sustained your eating disorder. In whatever ways the bulimia took care of you, it is becoming a thing of the past. The time you have spent on this unsatisfying obsession cannot be relived. Move forward.

When I look back at over three decades of recovery, I certainly don't begrudge those long ago days when I was so sick and unhappy. Not only do I forgive myself for having had an eating disorder, but I am actually grateful to my bulimia for the lessons I was forced to learn through recovery. I know how good it feels to be well and know who I am, to trust my choices and believe in myself. When I think back to who I was with bulimia, I feel only compassion for the young woman who felt it necessary to binge and purge to make it through a day.

Sexuality

Finally, with regards to relationships, you may want to address issues concerning your sexuality. Bulimia has probably interfered with your ability to be comfortable in sexual relationships. You may have inhibitions related to poor body image, anxiety about sexual responsiveness, lack of maturity, and a fear of passion that seems wild, crazy, or out of control. An eating disorder is often used to avoid physical intimacy, for example, as a response to previous sexual victimization or because of a belief that you might lose yourself in an intimate relationship. Bulimia can also be a substitute for sexual stimulation—a way to have a predictable physical release by yourself. Bingeing and purging is similar to the act and feelings of sexual intercourse—the buildup of intensity, emotional craving for intimacy, stroking of the body, explosion of physical sensation, and for some, a conditioned guilt.

However, recovery creates the opportunity for having all kinds of love in your life. As you improve your self-esteem, body image, and your capacity for intimacy, you will be more ready and capable of having satisfying sexual relationships, as well.

Having a fulfilling love life requires accepting your partner's basic humanness—and your own. You will have to embrace someone else's body without being concerned about their imperfections; and, perhaps even more challenging, allow your partner to caress and savor your body, as well. You have to be playful and be willing to enjoy each other. Mutuality, balance, and trust are fundamentals for having a happy sex life, all of which are developed by working on relationship skills (Zerbe, 1996).

SUGGESTIONS FOR IMPROVING YOUR SEXUAL RELATIONSHIPS

- Educate yourself about sex and sexuality.
- Enjoy your sexuality alone.
- Build a solid friendship before becoming sexual with someone else.
- Accept that your partner is attracted by how you look.
- Try to turn off negative body talk during lovemaking.
- Assert yourself and your needs; tell your partner how to please you.
- Be willing to try safe, new sexual activities.

Eating can be very sexual. I'm sure it's not a coincidence, but I never had an orgasm until I stopped purging. Bulimia was almost a type of oral masturbation.

I think maybe initially I was getting better for my husband and hoped that eventually I would want to get better for me. This is exactly what has happened, and our sex life improved.

13. Finding your purpose

Finding a purpose in your life is difficult to do when you have bulimia and symptoms get in your way. For example, *anxiety* limits your authenticity because you worry about what others think, *fear* hinders your ability to express opinions or take chances, and *perfectionism* keeps you concentrated on unimportant details instead of seeing the bigger picture or trying new things. You may be an expert at it, but bulimia saps your time, energy, and resources.

As you progress in recovery, though, and leave the bulimia behind, you will want to find something to take its place—healthier passions and an alternate sense of mastery. Who are you and what issues are important to you? What are your talents and passions? How will you fill your bulimia-free time?

In his classic 1946 book about survival in a Nazi concentration camp, *Man's Search for Meaning,* Victor Frankl wrote that we can find meaning in life three ways: "(1) by creating a work or doing a deed; (2) by experiencing something or encountering someone; and (3) by the attitude we take toward unavoidable suffering." His observations also hold true for people who have been oppressed by eating disorders.

Your primary "deed" at this point is to create your own recovery! Letting go of an obsession with food and weight and replacing it with a meaningful connection to your heart, mind, and soul is a powerful goal. Taking that inner wisdom—your recovery—into the wider world is even more so. Eventually, you won't be thinking about the next binge, because the last one will be a distant memory. Without bulimia, your calendar is wide-open. You can do anything! People get satisfaction from creating and doing all kinds of things: art, music, literature, architecture, manufacturing, technology, science, business, etc. Parents create children, people develop friendships, teachers inspire wisdom.

Whatever you decide to do, be fearless and passionate. Choose something that you believe in; after all, you can't believe in bulimia. Look for value in the process—the doing—rather than the outcome, and try not to be a perfectionist. No one is a perfect artist, musician, inventor, parent, teacher, or friend.

Frankl's second way of finding meaning, by "experiencing something or encountering someone," can be achieved in a variety of ways, but the one I particularly like is selfless service. Giving your time, energy, and presence is a way of contributing to the greater good, while at the same time taking the focus off your personal drama. The act of serving others can be done in large or small ways. When you smile at a stranger or listen to your friend describe their troubles, you are being a positive influence. You are giving to others when you contribute to a charity or cause, volunteer at a senior center or animal shelter, coach youth sports, tutor students after school, or pick up trash at a local park. Ironically, these kinds of deeds enrich you at the deepest level of your being, because they are focused outside of yourself. You lose yourself in giving.

Frankl's third point is about attitude, which was discussed in the section on "Thinking positively." To summarize: While there are many things in life we cannot control, we can control our approach. So listen to what you think and be more positive.

Even so, life is not as simple as *one, two, three*. Figuring out who you are and what issues are important to you is a nonlinear process. With every opinion, revelation, and choice, you get to know yourself a little better. You learn another lesson and go a little deeper. Also, the path to self-discovery is not a straight one. There are twists and turns, setbacks and dead ends, and a few express lanes. Nor is there an end to the journey. Your purpose will continue to unfold for the rest of your life, and presumably, somehow, even after your death.

Bulimia has distanced you from finding meaning in your life. It hasn't contributed to your wellbeing, other people, or the world. Imagine if you were recovered, had a bright outlook, worked in a fulfilling job, and somehow served mankind—you'd definitely be having an improved experience of purpose then! Living a good life depends on having a positive approach, participating fully, and feeling like your life has meaning—all of which you will develop through recovery.

Still, how will you know what to do with your life? Follow your heart! Act in ways that make you feel good inside. Nurture your strengths, talents, and creative interests. Take risks and believe in yourself, even if you have fears or anxiety. Don't be afraid to live an unconventional life! Above all, trust the process—the universe will support your efforts.

QUESTIONS FOR REFLECTION: FINDING MEANING

- What issues are important to me?
- What do I want to do with my life?
- How can I use my talents and interests to serve others?
- How do I want to live? Contemplative? Activist?
- What would I like to accomplish?
- What would I like to leave as a legacy?

14. Pursuing spirituality

Throughout this chapter, I have encouraged you to go inside and get to know yourself. I have done this because I believe that tending to the health and calling of our spirit is one of the most transformative things we can do in recovery. No matter what your definition, creating a place for the sacred in your life connects you to it. And in that relationship to the "divine," you will learn lessons of immeasurable worth that will touch the deepest core of your being.

Most people respond well to this kind of inner exploration. In a survey of recovered and recovering bulimics we conducted over 30 years ago, 60% found spirituality helpful in their recoveries, and a recent study (Richards, 2007) showed similar results, with prayer mentioned as the most helpful spiritual intervention. Many programs and therapists follow a 12-step model, adapted from Alcoholics Anonymous, which acknowledges and relies on a close relationship with God or a Higher Power. Some Christian-based 12-step programs look to biblical scripture for guidance. Regardless of the orientation, spiritual practices are commonly recommended by medical and psychological professionals and have been a foundation of the recoveries of many, many people.

You do not need to believe in God or be a worshipper of any religion to pursue spirituality. Simply learning to approach life with love in your heart, which anyone can do, is a spiritual practice. Being compassionate, truthful, and grateful are also ways to connect with your deepest values. When you commit an act of kindness and feel good inside, that's your spirit glowing. So, when I advise you to "pursue spirituality," I mean for you to think, feel, and behave in ways that make you feel good about yourself and your place in the world. Recovery is fueled by love; it is the inner self, wanting to be known. Viewed this way, living with an eating disorder is the opposite of living a spiritual life.

In the highly praised professional text, *Spiritual Approaches in the Treatment of Eating Disorders*, the authors describe many practical activities. One I particularly like uses the heart as a metaphor. In the early stages of treatment, patients' artwork often has the image of a broken heart representing the loss of their "sense of spiritual identity, with all its worth, dignity, and capability." But, as they progress, their self portraits show a healed heart, often glowing with vibrant colors and with powerful words written on them. What's the state of your heart?

Being on a spiritual path has given my life meaning. Ironically, I have my bulimia to thank for it, because recovery taught me how to love myself—and that has made all the difference. As we wrote in our book, *Self-Esteem Tools for Recovery*:

> When we practice love, we are making a connection with our real selves. This love cuts through the layers of false selves that we wear for protection, and makes clear that we are at our core, not flawed, but divine. We come in contact with our capacity for compassion, creativity, humor, goodness, and love. We realize that we are truly worthy of self-esteem.

A SHRINE TO YOURSELF

Choose a small area on a table or other surface to put a picture of yourself, just as you would a picture of a loved-one or a religious icon. Add candles, flowers, special items like seashells, gems, or stones, and anything else that holds significance for you. Write yourself a note or an affirmation and add that as well. Take some time every day to look at your picture with great love and respect, and perhaps offer a prayer for whatever comes to mind.

MORE SPIRITUAL ACTIVITIES

- Embrace spiritual concepts, such as grace, honesty, and service.
- Read religious or spiritual books, such as the scriptures of your chosen religion or New Age selections.
- Pray, meditate, or take quiet time.
- Imagine a wise, inner teacher. Ask him or her questions and listen for answers.
- Listen to sacred or uplifting music.
- Maintain a list of inspirational quotes.
- Get involved in a religious, spiritual, or self-improvement community.
- Seek spiritual guidance from teachers who are positive and uplifting.
- Participate in activities that are "soulful" to you, such as being in nature, playing music, doing artwork, gardening, etc.

The main thing that has helped me is my faith and trust in God. We all need someone to trust, whom we know loves us unconditionally, not for how we look or what we do, just for us as we are.

Today, I am reclaiming my feelings and working very hard to see that I am lovable and valuable. I deserve to live a joyous, fulfilled, serene life. Many times I've gone walking instead of bingeing, and I've never come home still wanting to binge.

Usually I pray while I walk, pouring out all of my burdens, fears, joys, and hopes, knowing that God is hearing me and is delighted in me. I really enjoy this time alone with Him.

15. Handling setbacks and preventing relapse

I've talked about the fact that there is no such thing as a "perfect" body, and that striving for one is an exercise in futility. Same goes for recovery. There is no perfect or right way to do it. Practically everyone has setbacks, because they are part of the process of growing and learning. There will most likely come a day when your emotions get the best of you, or the cravings for a binge are just too much. Even though your recovery might be going reasonably well, you let down your guard. What will you do?

Your response is crucial because you can learn a lot from a setback and feelings of guilt and shame will just get in the way. Try to be curious, but not judgmental. Write about what led you to binge or purge and the feelings surrounding it. Talk to a support person, because keeping secrets is counterproductive. Forgive yourself and move forward. Even if you have moments when you are feeling hopeless, your recovery is not hopeless. When you have a setback, you are not back to square one. Plus, you have valuable information for next time. A setback is a bump in the road, a temporary detour, not the end of the road.

Also, it *is* possible to stop yourself on the verge, or in the middle, of a binge. This can be a tremendously empowering experience, because you are proving to yourself that recovery is more important to you than bulimia. You also gain confidence that, in the moment, you *can* make the healthy, self-nurturing choice.

However, if you don't take steps to intervene, setbacks can turn into full-blown relapse. Be aware of the warning signs, for instance an increase in: bingeing (with or without purging), concerns about weight and shape, negative self-talk, or isolation. About one-third of eating disorders patients are faced with a relapse in the first 6-18 months of treatment. Common causes are ambivalence about recovery, lack of treatment follow up, overwhelming emotional states, problems with relationships, and stressful circumstances (Pearle, 2007; Wasson, 2003).

Preventing relapse is a vital step in the recovery process. Therapists commonly employ post-treatment techniques to limit relapse for their patients. They may schedule follow-up sessions, recommend a support group, or have ongoing contact through email. Some encourage former patients to send text messages regularly as a way of checking in and staying connected.

If you are using a purely self-help approach, you must be diligent about your recovery. Keep using the techniques that have been working for you. Maintain your journal writing and relaxation techniques even after you've have recovered from the bingeing and purging behaviors. Continue building relationships, especially with the people you've turned to for support. And, if you find yourself slipping back to the bulimia and nothing is helping, find professional help as soon as possible. The sooner you reverse a relapse, the better!

Be an Activist

I have found that one of the best ways to prevent relapse is to be an activist. When you work for a cause, you are caring about something bigger than yourself. Not only do you become involved with other like-minded individuals, but you also become connected to the greater good, feel generous, and promote the welfare of future generations.

Many people who have recovered from an eating disorder feel a desire to give back, and they become therapists, authors, mentors, and advocates for the field. You can serve the eating disorders community in countless ways. Browse the Internet to find organizations devoted to eating disorders education, treatment, and prevention. They can all use volunteers! Local high schools often welcome recovered speakers to meet with peer advocates or support groups. Throughout North America, events are staged during National Eating Disorders Awareness Week, and the local planners always welcome additional help. The Eating Disorders Coalition invites individuals to participate in National Lobby Day, when legislators in Washington, D. C. are lobbied about health care initiatives.

Ultimately, you must advocate for yourself. Be willing to do or say anything that will help your recovery, and don't back away from that goal. Every exercise you do, choice you make, decision you come to, conversation you have is *you being an activist on your own behalf.* So I encourage you to continue to be active in your recovery. Do whatever it takes for you to get to know who you are and live from your deepest values.

Chapter Six

Healthy Weight, Eating & Exercise

Although much of recovery focuses on inner work that has nothing to do with food, you still have to face decisions about eating every day. This is obviously a challenge for someone who has been bingeing and purging on a regular basis. You are probably unsure about how much to eat because you've been out of touch with your body's hunger and fullness signals. Having relied on fad diet information, you may not know what constitutes good nutrition or normal eating. You may be afraid of particular "forbidden" foods or of losing control if you allow yourself to eat one bite more than you are "allowed." But learning how to eat and the inner work of recovery go hand in hand. Every healthy bite you take is an act of self-care. And as you grow to love and respect yourself more, the choice to nurture yourself with good nutrition and healthy exercise gets easier. Win-win!

Eating normally and attaining a weight that is both natural and healthy for you *is* possible. First, let's lay some groundwork.

Healthy Weight

Most people mistakenly think that when it comes to weight, "healthy" means thin. This idea has been so ingrained in our culture that it is practically inconceivable to think that a large body could be fit, vital, and functioning at a high level. Yet, weight is actually a poor indicator of health and longevity. What's more, the false premise that thinness is possible for *every* body fuels a multibillion dollar diet industry, and, in part, an epidemic of eating disorders.

Your goal, as someone in recovery from bulimia, is to make peace with food so your body can return to balance at a healthy, "natural" weight that is right for you, in spite of cultural, familial, or peer pressures to diet. If you eat generally well and get moderate, regular exercise, you will attain that weight. It might be higher than you'd like, lower than you'd expect, or even the same as you are right now, but you won't know for sure until you have ended your bulimic behaviors for (at least) several months. If you have been bulimic for an extended period of time, readjusting your metabolism may take longer. Reaching your natural weight is a process not to be controlled or rushed, but rather gently and patiently encouraged over time.

Eating in a new way requires thinking in a new way. You have to stop believing conventional wisdom about weight. Instead, I'm going to ask you to accept three basic concepts: dieting does not work; your weight is primarily determined by family genetics; and thinness has no inherent value.

1. Dieting does not work.

I bring up the subject of dieting here because the majority of people with bulimia either have been on diets, or they are using bulimia as a way to "control" their weight. However the idea of weight loss or weight control through caloric restriction, purging, or laxative or diuretic abuse is fundamentally flawed. This is because the human body has a variety of survival mechanisms designed to maintain the weight at which it operates best. Inadequate supplies of food or water are perceived as emergencies and adjustments are made so that the body holds on to precious pounds instead of letting them go. That's why 95% of people on diets gain back lost weight, *if not more.*

Everyone's body has a particular weight range of between about five to ten pounds at which it works most efficiently. This *set point*, or settling point, can be somewhat influenced by diet, age, health, and activity levels; but, generally speaking, each of us has a natural weight that our bodies want to be. And our biology fights to maintain this optimal weight. Too little food is interpreted as starvation, causing your metabolism to slow down to preserve calories; too much food is a signal to speed up metabolism to compensate for calories that are not needed.

In this way, our bodies are fighting our efforts to be thinner by working to keep us at our set point. Again, this natural weight might be higher or lower than you think it should be, but it is the weight at which your body is most healthy. As long as you are not starving or stuffing, you can eat a variety of foods—more on some days and less on others—and stay balanced. Your best weight size is not yours to determine, it is only yours to accept and ultimately love.

One point that you may not be aware of is that a significant percentage of the calories consumed during a binge are retained after purging. Even though you think you are getting rid of every last bite you have eaten, your body clings to whatever it can to do its job of keeping you alive. So, your bulimia is not "helping" you the way you think it is.

In the early stages of recovery, you might gain weight—though not everyone does—because your metabolism is slower than normal, still in survival mode trying to retain calories. This is similar to the weight rebound experienced by people who go off fad diets. Be aware that your body will have to go through a period of adjustment to life without bulimia.

2. Your weight is primarily determined by family genes.

As I've said before, you can pretty much find your body on your family tree. Extensive studies have been conducted—including some with identical twins reared apart—and although the research is not absolute, it does indicate that body weight is predominantly established by inherited genes. For example, when a naturally thin person is adopted by obese parents, he or she is likely to remain thin. Likewise, someone with a predisposition for obesity, who is brought up by thinner adoptive parents, will usually grow up to be obese.

Although weight can be somewhat influenced by food choices, activity levels, and biological factors—such as metabolism or illness—you are essentially born with a specific body type. Just as you cannot become shorter or taller than what nature gave you, changing your inherited size and shape is a waste of time, energy, and often money. Improving fitness levels, metabolic function, and muscle tone are far more worthwhile and achievable goals.

3. Thinness has no inherent value.

We live in a culture that worships thinness. This is not news to anyone, least of all people who suffer from eating disorders. The media are filled with images of skeletal models who look healthy, happy, successful, smart, and sexy—implying that the key to such a wonderful life is to be thin. Billions of dollars every year are spent by the diet, fashion, beauty, and anti-aging industries to convince us that we need to be different from the way we naturally are. This relentless barrage of advertising makes us think that our hair should be lighter or bouncier, our teeth should be whiter or straighter, and, most important of all, we should be thinner.

The flip side to the drive for thinness is a phobia about fat. While our society has become more accepting of differences in race, religion, and gender, weight prejudice is still rampant. People with large bodies are often contemptuously stereotyped as stupid, lacking in willpower, undesirable, and failures. Bombarded with messages of "thin equals good" and "fat equals bad," it is no wonder that we are terrified of gaining weight and wish to be thinner.

But thinness actually has no inherent value—it is an arbitrary yardstick, promoted by the media, by which we measure others and ourselves. Do you honestly believe that thin people are more valuable human beings than fat people? Do they have greater integrity or love more deeply? And while losing weight might seem to be a way to feel better about yourself, that's based on how well you conform to society's expectations, not on who you are as a person. Bodies change, styles change, your health and age will change. Better to anchor your self-esteem in qualities and abilities you know in your heart have enduring meaning, like how compassionate or generous you are, or how good a friend—*not* how thin.

What's more, despite what you have repeatedly heard, *research has proven that thinner is not healthier*. In fact, among individuals who are generally fit, those who weigh above the "ideal" standards on weight charts have significantly lower mortality rates than those who weigh below the "ideal." In contrast, large weight gains or losses, or yo-yo dieting, are associated with early mortality (Gaesser, 1996).

The idea that a large body can be healthy may be a difficult truth to swallow given how brainwashed we have been by money-grubbing industries, nonsensical insurance company standards, and our misguided prejudice against fat. The real health culprits in today's obesity epidemic are not weight and body fat; they are sedentary living and the excess consumption of food.

Good health is determined by factors such as blood pressure, heart rate, fat in the bloodstream (cholesterol, low-density lipoproteins, and high-density lipoproteins), endurance, strength, and psychological outlook—not by weight. A fat person who exercises and eats well is likely to be healthier than a thin person who doesn't. Having an eating disorder, overexercising, or drastically cutting fats might result in a temporarily lower weight, but will not make you feel better or cause you to be physically healthier. Instead, they create hunger, depression, anger, feelings of deprivation, weakness, loss of focus, and a preoccupation with food—*and* probable weight gain.

I understand that these three ideas are diametrically opposed to popular beliefs. You may even think they are crazy, but they certainly make more sense than trying to control your weight by bingeing and purging! Nonetheless, they are true and can support your desire to eat in a new way. You deserve to take up space in the world so that you can live a full life—

of love, laughter, creativity, service and a host of other wonderful things. Whether you do so in a naturally small or large body does not matter.

GET RID OF YOUR SCALE, TODAY!

> Weighing yourself is a bad habit and can be especially distressing if you've recently stopped bingeing and purging, and your metabolism is still in starvation mode and conserving calories. I've already suggested getting rid of your bathroom scale earlier in this book, and if you haven't, you should do so today.
>
> I took a sledgehammer to mine when I started my recovery, and I haven't weighed myself since (although I have been weighed at my doctor's office). You cannot imagine how freeing this is until you do it! Your scale is cursed and fills you with anxiety and fear every time you step on it. Do not donate it to a thrift store—no one else should be cursed by it either. Drive over it with your car, throw it in the recycling bin, or destroy it in some other (safe) way. Just let it go!

I had to accept myself and not feel the compelling urge to be "perfect" as reflected by my old need to be "perfectly" slender. I had to acknowledge that with my genes I'd never look like a model, and that was okay.

Nobody told me that when girls hit puberty, they put on weight in preparation for childbirth. I thought that I was the only one! When dieting didn't work, I turned to bulimia and was caught for thirteen years. I am now fighting to get my "natural" body back and love it, no matter what its size or shape!

Last year, I made a resolution that I would say something whenever one of my friends mentioned that they felt too fat or wanted to lose weight. It has been hard to be so honest, but when they hear what I have been through, they are a little more accepting of themselves. Even I can be a teacher!

Healthy Eating

Everybody has an opinion about how to eat. That's why there are tens of thousands of books and millions of websites on eating, cooking, and dieting. Even experts in the eating disorders field don't agree. Many advocate "legalizing" food and becoming an intuitive eater, others encourage abstinence from certain foods, like sugar or carbohydrates, and still others have their patients follow detailed food plans. I think different approaches work for different people—and there's a path for everyone. In this section, I am going to recommend what has worked for me in my 30 years of being recovered from bulimia.

During that time, I have eaten nutritiously, without food restrictions, and with great enjoyment. Though I have read up on nutrition, I have not dieted or followed any outside plans. Mostly, I've relied on internal cues: eating what I want when I'm hungry and stopping when I'm full. I eat a generally well-balanced selection of foods with a combination of regular meals and snacks. I stay in touch with my feelings of hunger and fullness by eating slowly and savoring tastes and textures. I enjoy a big meal now and then, and am happy to top it off with a small dessert. Essentially, in recovery, I learned to *eat without fear*, and by following the guidance in this chapter, perhaps you can, too.

Physical and Emotional Hungers

People have various kinds of hungers—physical, emotional, social, spiritual, and sexual, among others. If you have an eating disorder, you may have difficulty recognizing these different hungers because you are separated from your inner experience. So, in recovery, as you start to connect with yourself, you'll also be learning to differentiate between your hungers and "feed" them appropriately.

Emotional hunger is the longing to be loved, have self-worth, be understood, and find meaning in life. It is the desire to find peace, be whole and happy, connect to other people, and do meaningful work.

Bulimics are often oblivious to these hungers of the heart, and are instead preoccupied with their weight and feelings like self-loathing, loneliness, and shame. Emotional eating is a way to numb those painful feelings, and, for bulimics, all eating becomes emotional.

Emotional eaters are also oblivious to *physical hunger*, the body's physiological craving for nourishment. Instead of recognizing what their body naturally needs, they try to control their appetite and waiver between a diet mentality and binge eating.

Bulimia is an addictive cycle on both physical and emotional levels. As you can see from the figure that follows, this sequence involves a self-sustaining series of events and predictable responses:

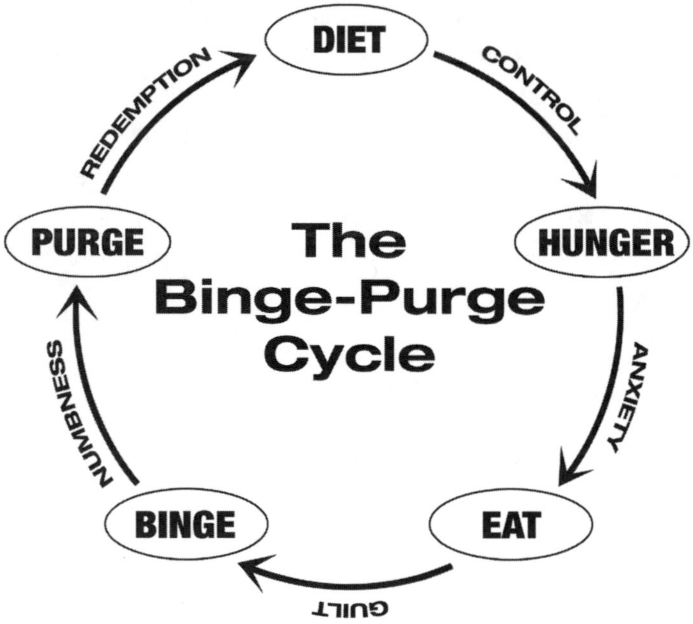

The Binge-Purge Cycle has no beginning or end, but for the purpose of this brief explanation, let's start with **DIET**. If you believe losing weight will make you feel better about yourself, you control what you eat. Before long, you obviously experience physical **HUNGER**, which brings up anxiety (as in the tension between "I want to eat" and "I shouldn't eat"). At some point, you finally **EAT**, but feel overwhelmed by guilt, shame, a sense of failure and insecurity, and other negative emotions. For bulimics, this translates into a **BINGE** that takes the focus off all these feelings, leaving a sense of numbness. But pressures build, and redemption is only a **PURGE** away. A "high" follows, along with the resolutions "never to do it again" and be a better dieter in the future. Then, the process repeats itself. In this way, the binge-purge cycle is not only about food and eating, it is also about painful emotions and using and abusing food to handle them.

You can break this cycle at any point by intervening on an emotional or physical level. Intervention can take many forms, for instance, you could refuse to purge after a binge, eat a dessert without guilt, or challenge the value of dieting. At the very least, begin to question. If you *are* hungry for food, acknowledge that your body usually knows what it wants because it is responding to biological needs, and ask, *What is my body craving? What will give me feelings of satisfaction and fullness? What can I eat right now to nourish my body—without guilt?* Before the binge begins, ask, "What would *truly* ease my hunger? What feelings need to be expressed? Is there a way of satisfying my emotional hungers directly instead of using food?" In the middle of a binge, ask, "Can I take back my power and stop right now?" These kinds of questions can help you begin to take steps towards distinguishing and feeding *all* your hungers—one of the biggest challenges of recovery.

A healthy pattern of eating excludes bingeing, purging, and dieting along with the negative emotions that accompany them. Here's what the Healthy Eating Cycle looks like:

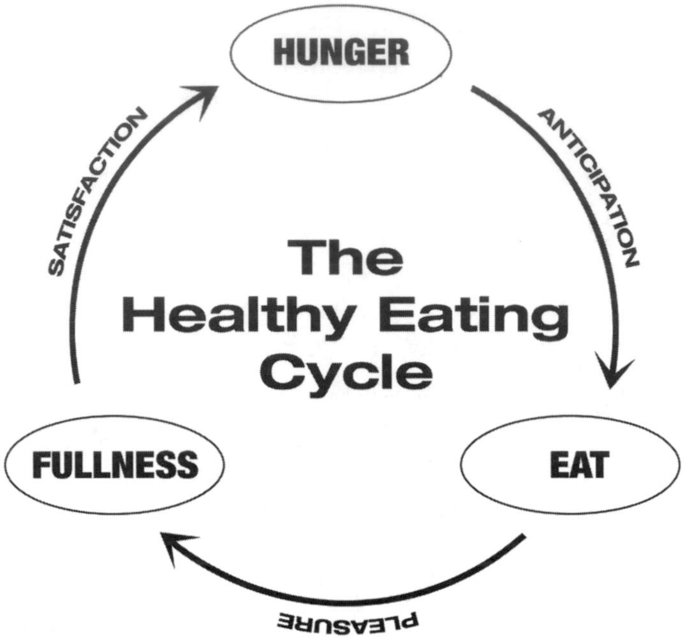

In this second scenario, natural **HUNGER** is followed by the anticipation of the next meal. For "normal" eaters, this is a period of excitement when they think about what foods they crave. When they **EAT**, it is with pleasure and enjoyment, leading to **FULLNESS** and feelings of satisfaction and nourishment. Instead of the turmoil of the bulimic, their physical and emotional hungers are fulfilled, and they feel energized and ready to get on with their lives until they feel hungry again.

Keep in mind that your body needs a combination of carbohydrates, proteins, fats, water, and minerals. If you have been purging or restricting for any period of time, both your body and your brain are probably starving for nutrients. You might not be able to think as clearly, respond as positively, or make as good decisions as you would if you were eating healthy food and keeping it down. This is why you must satisfy physical hungers by eating regular meals and snacks so you will be better able to incorporate the insights of recovery into everyday life.

I feel best about myself when I eat in response to physical hunger. This feels like I am honoring my inner self. To eat in response to emotional hunger, without the presence of the physical, is my definition of compulsive eating.

Being terribly abused by the man I loved was the precursor to my bulimia. I binged to stuff the hurt and fill the void. Now, I am filled with love, but it comes from within me, not from someone else.

Without realizing it, I substituted food for many emotions. In my recovery, I'm learning to recognize that my sudden hunger or cravings are actually emotions or signs of something bothering me.

Mindful Eating

Mindfulness, as introduced in Chapter 5, is the practice of experiencing the present moment without judgment. It involves slowing down and taking a closer look, not at whatever external circumstances are going on, but at your internal reactions. You become curious about your thoughts, feelings, and bodily sensations—not critical. You begin to connect with an ever-present, unchangeable "observer self," which is separate from the unpredictable, unstable cycle of your bulimia. And in the space of mindfulness, there dawns the awareness of choice. You are not your bulimia. It is something you have used to cope with life, and now, in recovery, you can choose another way.

Mindful eating is a powerful way to break the Binge-Purge Cycle. When you eat mindfully, you purposefully connect with the body by observing physical sensations without attaching meaning or value to them. This is a much different approach than controlling, shaming, or distancing from your body. You slow down the pace of each meal and become aware of taste and texture, savoring every mouthful. You might notice your chewing or breathing to counter anxiety or distress. Instead of being caught in a mindless cycle, you learn to discern levels of hunger and fullness and are more attuned to choices about what and how much to eat. Eating becomes an act of self-nurturing—putting fuel in the tank—instead of a threat. This is intuitive eating: learning to trust and honor the wisdom of the body.

In addition to observing your bodily sensations, mindful eating also involves non-judgmental awareness of any thoughts and feelings that arise. By keeping your mind on the present moment, its focus is shifted away from your problems, giving them the chance to fall into the background. If thoughts do surface such as, "I can't eat this, I'll get fat," be aware of them, but let them pass. If you experience feelings like guilt, shame, or anger, acknowledge that these feelings are important teachers, but return to your observer self. In this way, you still honor your experience and what it has to teach you on the path to recovery, but learn that you do not have to act on impulses and cravings. In the calm space of observing, you can learn to tolerate a variety of difficult internal states—a fundamental lesson of recovery.

Like learning any new skill, mindful eating gets easier with practice. In a way, you are exercising a mental muscle when you turn inward and observe; and the more you do it, the more normal it becomes. Here are a few things to try:

WAYS TO PRACTICE MINDFUL EATING

- Eat slowly and pay attention to each bite.
- Gauge your hunger and fullness levels on a scale of 1–10.
- Notice the colors, smells, tastes, and textures of food.
- Avoid mindless eating situations that are distracting, like watching TV or multitasking while you eat.
- Keep your focus on eating without forming opinions or thinking about anything other than the moment.
- Feed yourself as if you were providing a meal for someone you genuinely admire.

A Healthy, Well-Balanced Diet

Everyone has food preferences, and yours have been based on principles of dieting, rather than taste, physical cravings, or balanced nutrition. You may not even know what flavors or textures you like, except for your favorite binge foods.

My recommendation is that you follow a lifelong approach to eating. Discover what you like in each of the food groups, and eat a well-balanced diet that includes carbohydrates, proteins, fats, vitamins, and minerals. Don't count calories. Don't calculate fat grams or carbs. Don't follow any weight-loss diet. *That's the entire food plan!*

Although this may seem simple, it works very well for me. Here are a few basic guidelines:

HEALTHY EATING GUIDELINES

- Eat plenty of complex *carbohydrates*. Foods like whole grain breads, granola, brown rice, vegetables, and beans are good sources. Simple carbohydrates such as refined wheat products (white breads or rice, bakery goods, etc.) and sugars (fruit, honey, sweetened sodas, etc.) are burned faster by your metabolism and have less nutritional value.

- Most meals should include *protein*, for instance found in dairy products, meat, fish, poultry, tofu, and legumes. People who have problems digesting dairy products may prefer soy. Proteins are digested slower and provide energy for longer periods of time.

- *Fats* are stored for energy, used in the blood, and important for proper brain function. Those that are considered most healthy are monounsaturated (avocados, almonds, and olive, peanut, and canola oils), which help in the development of healthy HDLs that counter cholesterol and dangerous

LDLs. Polyunsaturated fats (corn and safflower oils, walnuts, sesame seeds, tuna) are fairly neutral. Saturated fats (butter, hard cheeses, coconut oil, animal fat) should be used sparingly. Most foods are made up of a balance of different kinds of fats. Some vitamins can only be gotten from eating fat.

- Most of your *vitamins* and *minerals* can be found in a well-balanced diet, however I do advocate taking a daily multivitamin. Consider nutritional supplements, but only with expert counseling.
- Eat a small dessert whenever you want. In addition to being enjoyable, a sweet signals the body's appetite regulators that a meal has ended. Avoid artificial sweeteners.
- Drink lots of water!
- Limit or avoid junk food and sodas; do not drink diet beverages.
- Primarily eat fresh, home-cooked meals.
- Eat a variety of foods.

Getting Past Food Fears

People with bulimia usually follow countless rules about eating. In most cases, these are based on someone else's (usually outdated) ideas about food, weight, and health. For instance, believing that eating anything that contains sugar will cause you to gain weight is not true. Equally false are the beliefs that you should eliminate fat or that eating only fruits and vegetables is a healthy, vegetarian diet. While labeling foods either "good" or "bad" might make you feel safe or give you goals to achieve, it can also create a prison of control. Eating "bad" food is breaking the rules, bringing up feelings of failure, which often trigger binge eating and the expectation that purging will make everything "okay" again. Obviously, it doesn't.

In fact, foods are intrinsically neither "good" nor "bad." Some are more nutritious than others, but eating dessert doesn't make you a bad person, and eating health food doesn't make you a saint. This insight is often a crucial milestone in recovery. When eating a certain way no longer defines you as "good," what does? What *is* a life well-lived? And how can you learn to eat like a "normal" person?-

As simple as it sounds, getting past your food fears is yet another step towards facing the fears you have about life—which is why it feels so profoundly difficult. Do not belittle this challenge! Making peace with food is a way of saying "yes" to the experience of being human, of affirming the importance of your contributions and your right to take up space in the world. This approach is fundamentally different from your drive to be smaller and take up *less* space! What's more, getting to know yourself through recovery, and embracing your many positive qualities, makes way for a new reality: self-worth cannot be measured by what you eat (or don't eat) or the size of your body. The challenge of every bite, every meal, and every food decision is to enrich your spirit as well as your body.

The negative associations that you attach to foods *can* be recognized and eliminated, especially if they are tackled head on in a systematic and determined manner. First, identify some "safe" foods. Make a list so you know what you will permit yourself right now. This gives you a starting point and establishes a positive "can have" (rather than a "can't have") mentality. Gradually, when you are ready, take some risks. Knowing that new foods will likely make you uncomfortable, implement some of the skills you've learned in this book, such as mindfulness and relaxation. Be kind to yourself. Use your journal, your support people, and repeat affirmations. Be patient. It takes time to change long-term behaviors, beliefs, and reactions, but it is possible. Over time, you will be able to increase the variety and amount of food you eat with growing confidence, and this sense of mastery and accomplishment will spill over into other areas of your life, as well.

A discussion of food fears would not be complete without mentioning that some individuals find specific foods to be particularly addictive and act as triggers. They use an "abstinence" approach to those foods, which is both effective and appropriate for them. However, this vulnerability must not be used as an excuse to avoid facing food fears, but instead as a guide for choices that are both selective and diverse.

INTRODUCING NEW FOODS

> A way to introduce new foods is to choose one that was previously forbidden, and try a bite. Concentrate on the texture, flavor, and smell. Be persistent about pushing away troublesome thoughts by focusing on the sensation of chewing. When you swallow, savor the aftertaste for a minute or two. Then, time yourself for ten minutes and do something else, like writing in your journal, calling a friend, or going to a park. Don't dwell on habitual thoughts like, "I won't be able to keep this food in; I want to vomit." Affirm that you are a strong person, with new skills, who is creating a positive relationship with food. When the time is up, firmly say out loud, whether you believe it or not, "That felt great. I can eat without fear!"

I allow myself anything I want, but in moderation. I have cake and ice cream, bread and butter, even cream in my coffee. The serving size is appropriate to my needs at the time. Being able to allow myself anything to eat has taken away the guilt, where before one bite of a "forbidden food" would lead to a binge; I eat it, enjoy it, and keep it down.

There are no forbidden foods for me. Certain foods don't have the power that I once gave them.

Structured Meals

Many individuals in recovery find it helpful to have a structured approach to meals, because their eating patterns have been so chaotic and impulsive. Some respond well to food and meal plans, the point of which is to remove the responsibility and fear of choosing what, when, and how much to eat. These plans can be particularly helpful in the early stages of recovery, when emotions are surfacing, hunger and fullness signals are difficult to recognize, and the temptation to resort to old habits is strong.

Most eating disorders inpatient and outpatient treatment programs, as well as many individual therapists, use meal plans with their patients. If you are working on your recovery on your own, I recommend that you at least consult with a nutritionist or dietitian who is familiar with bulimia. But if professional help is not available or not your choice, you can also create your own structured eating plan.

The goal of a good meal plan is to provide proper nutrition and restore a balanced metabolism so the body will reach its healthiest, natural weight. Experts generally recommend eating three balanced meals and two or three between-meal snacks daily. Some people do better with six small meals, or eating every couple of hours. If possible, include a combination of carbohydrates, proteins, and fats. Snacks are obviously smaller in quantity, but you can plan for them, too. Arrange for a preset amount of food, like a few crackers and slice of cheese, rather than eating crackers directly out of the box. Also, allow no more than three to four hours between meals so you don't feel deprived or so hungry that you set a binge in motion.

Write out which foods you are going to eat, in what proportion, and at what time. Shop in advance so that you are not caught without food from your plan at mealtime. Although nutritionists will commonly prescribe serving sizes or calories, I won't do that here. Instead, I advise you to educate yourself about nutrition, and be as sensible as you can, given that this is new to you. Start with foods that feel safe, and then slowly introduce new ones as you gain confidence. Scheduling in small helpings of "fun" foods or desserts—even items that you might typically choose for a binge—might give you a sense of satisfaction that will actually prevent you from bingeing (Herrin, 2007). Make an effort to stick to your plan, returning to it even if you stray; and, if necessary, make adjustments in order to be successful.

Meal plans aren't for everyone. Some people think they put too much of a focus on food, and the rules and limits feel similar to a diet. And, like a diet, if they were to "go off" it, by skipping a meal or snacking at a time that wasn't predetermined, they might feel like they'd failed at recovery. Also, while meal plans can be helpful in the early stages of recovery, a more intuitive, spontaneous way of eating might be preferable later. You'll be ready for less structure when you have learned to recognize and respond to internal cues for both hunger and fullness. Do what works for you. If sticking to a schedule frees your mind from worries about food and weight gain, great! If you want more freedom, be flexible.

NEW WAYS TO APPROACH FOOD & EATING

- Eat food you enjoy.
- Introduce a new food at least once a week.
- Include fun foods or desserts.
- Experiment with (even a taste of) different cuisines. A little risk-taking can result in big feelings of competence and mastery.
- Allow someone else to cook and serve a meal for you.
- Grocery shop with friends to see what foods they like. Talk about your concerns.
- Rely on your support team for reassurance, such as using an "eating buddy" to sit with you during meals.
- Don't try to eat "perfectly."

- Make eating a sacred event—say a blessing.
- Cook with reverence and serve with style! Does this sound like an advertisement? That's because I'm trying to sell you on eating and enjoying it!

I try to eat several times a day in small portions. The foods that I eat now leave me feeling satisfied, and I have no desire to binge.

Allowing myself all foods (in small quantities) has helped me, although I must remind myself I "deserve" cakes, cookies, etc. Cutting out all sugars set me up to binge, which reinforced that I was "bad" and couldn't control myself. I pretended not to eat sugar and carbohydrates, only to binge on them in private. I now eat sweets in small amounts in front of everyone, not trying to be "perfect" in my diet.

Special Situations

Just as particular foods pose a challenge for someone in recovery from bulimia, eating situations that involve other people can also prove problematic. Eating in public, whether it is in a familiar setting or one that is completely new, can be hard. Holiday meals, parties, and restaurants are all stressful situations, but having strategies in place can transform even these kinds of difficult events into pleasurable occasions.

Many bulimics live in fear from Halloween through New Year's Eve, but Thanksgiving and Christmas dinners are understandably the most worrisome. Planning ahead is an effective way to survive and thrive. If you'll be eating at someone's home, eat as you normally would on the day of the holiday rather than restrict yourself in anticipation of a big meal. Since anxiety comes from the unknown, call ahead and find out what is being served. Perhaps mention your situation to the host or hostess and enlist their support. If you are worried about the menu, bring some safe foods you feel good about. When you serve yourself, take normal portions of only the foods you think you'll enjoy. Be sure to eat adequate protein instead of just rich carbohydrates. You don't need to be overly polite and try everything, nor do you have to clean your plate. It's okay to leave food that doesn't appeal to you or decline more helpings if you are full. If the meal is at your house and you're afraid of bingeing on what's leftover, give everyone food to take home. (Keddy, 2007).

Many of the strategies for getting through holiday meals also apply to eating at restaurants. If possible, go online beforehand and look at the menu, even deciding what you want ahead of time. Practice what to say in different situations, for instance, if you are served more food than you want, don't like the food, or want to take home leftovers. Restaurants often serve large portions, so be assertive about how much you want to eat. You can always separate what seems to be an appropriate amount on your plate and finish only that much. You also could order from the appetizer menu or share a meal with a friend. Remember, if you are uncomfortable about something that is served, you are under no obligation to eat it. Above all, try to maintain a connection with that calm inner self and your resolve to be able to eat in all kinds of situations.

Sometimes, stress over holidays, parties, and restaurant meals has more to do with the social aspects of these situations than the task of eating. You might be worried that you are being judged or that people are watching how you eat. You might be a loner or uncomfortable in groups. This is where all of your practice in techniques such as mindfulness, self-appreciation, trust, and seeing God in everyone will pay off. Before going to the event, take some time to slow down. Perhaps write down some affirmations you can use at the event, a few easy discussion topics, and your feelings about some of the people who will be there. If you start to get anxious once you are there, use a relaxation technique or talk about your fears with supportive companions.

Eating in social situations is a double whammy. Not only are you faced with issues around food and eating, but you are also doing it in a social setting! You can't expect to feel comfortable at first, but practice will make it easier. Challenge yourself by making and accepting invitations. Eventually, you'll feel nourished in more ways than one.

I remember being terrified about going to restaurants when I had bulimia, but I've asked my partner to go with me to the bathroom so I could not purge, which really helps.

Now that I've been open about my bulimia and recovery, I actually look forward to seeing my family at holiday meals. They no longer insist I eat everything that is served, and I focus on enjoying my time with them instead of on the food.

Healthy Exercise

Exercise is a wonderful way to enhance feelings of well-being and general health, but there is a difference between beneficial, moderate exercise and working out obsessively. Extreme training can masquerade as a fitness regime and trick you into thinking you are being "good" when you most certainly are not. While it may be healthy to jog 10–15 miles per week, running that many miles every day is extreme.

People with eating disorders often abuse exercise for a variety of reasons, the most obvious being to purge unwanted calories and regain the control that was lost during a binge. It can also be an escape from responsibilities, difficult issues, and overwhelming emotions. So, knowing how and why you are using exercise and creating a balanced program are all important goals in recovery from bulimia.

Disordered Exercise

There's a fine line between exercising for health and overdoing it, and you can tell the difference by looking at your motivation and degree of obsession. If you exercise primarily as a way to control your weight or to compensate for food you've eaten—especially binges—then you are approaching it in a harmful way. That's also true if you feel compelled to work out when you are injured or sick, and if your routine interferes with relationships or other important activities, or puts you in dangerous situations. It is also unhealthy to always exercise to the point of near exhaustion, not take days off, or devote hours a day—on average—unless you are in supervised training.

Studies have shown that between 33% and 80% of anorexics and bulimics engage in excessive exercise—the wide range probably due to inconsistencies in defining the term "excessive." However, regardless of the statistics, a strong connection between eating disorders and overexercise exists, resulting in serious psychological, emotional, and physical consequences (in addition to those previously described for food-related behaviors). Exercise also has an addictive component because of neurochemical changes in the brain, which make recovery more difficult.

People who overexercise, and isolate themselves by escaping into their routines, can suffer from fatigue, sleep disturbances, and depression. Common medical problems include decreased sex hormones, reduced immune function, potentially fatal cardiovascular complications, strained or torn muscles and ligaments, and bone loss (osteopenia or osteoporosis) that can lead to fractures. Many women athletes suffer from the "Female Athlete Triad" (amenorrhea, osteoporosis, and an eating disorder), and men can suffer from the "Male Athlete Triad" (with lowered testosterone as the hormonal component). Furthermore, eating disorder sufferers who excessively exercise usually have more severe levels of body dissatisfaction, preoccupation with weight, and hyperactivity; and, they often have poorer outcomes in treatment (Powers, 2008).

It's not surprising that elite athletes are at high-risk for eating disorders. In one study among females, 46% who participated in *lean* sports (requiring a lean body: gymnastics, diving, long-distance running, etc.) and 20% in *non-lean* sports (requiring a more muscular body: ball games, speed skating, sprints, etc.) met the clinical criteria for an eating disorder. Other studies with men have shown that *weight-class* sports (wrestling, martial arts, and jockeys) have particularly high rates of bulimia. The reasons are fairly obvious. Athletes commonly, but mistakenly, think that less weight is an advantage both physically and aesthetically. But the truth is that an eating disorder is actually a hindrance to competition: an athlete can lose his or her edge when they are focused on food and how they look rather than performance; player confidence can be eroded by insecurities and low self-esteem; and eating disorders cause a decrease in strength, power, and endurance (Thompson, 2010).

Changing the goal from thin to healthy means creating balance both in eating and exercise. While you uncover the mental, emotional, and spiritual issues that drive your eating disorder, also look at how they influence your choices about exercise.

Healthy Exercise

Some people love to exercise—getting all hot and sweaty, feeling their heart beating faster, and breathing hard. Others do it begrudgingly or not at all. However, everyone can benefit from moving his or her body, regardless of age, size, gender, or fitness level. As with eating, I recommend taking a lifelong approach to exercise. Find a variety of activities that you enjoy and will look forward to day after day.

There are four main types of exercise, each of which has its merits. *Aerobic* (also called cardiovascular or endurance) makes the heart and lungs work harder and increases oxygen to body tissue. *Anaerobic* (strength or resistance training) makes the muscles and bones stronger. *Flexibility* tones muscles and is important in preventing injuries, which is also true of *balance,* which becomes increasingly essential in later life. Ideally, try to include all four of these in your exercise program (Powers, 2008).

Exercise regularly. Barring any medical limitations, try to average a minimum of 20–30 minutes (and no more than 60–90 minutes) of fairly vigorous intensity about five days per week. Include anaerobic activities, like lifting weights, a couple of times weekly. Varying your routine will result in fewer injuries and the use of more muscle groups. Plus, change helps to keep things interesting! Don't do high-intensity workouts every time, so if you run a few miles one day, you might walk the next. Don't continuously push your body too hard—even elite athletes take days off to recuperate. Don't give yourself the option to avoid exercise, but use good judgment in determining how much is right for you. Moderation is key.

Make exercise fun. Whether you are a team player or like to be alone, opportunities for getting a good aerobic workout abound. Sports like tennis, soccer, basketball, and volleyball are great avenues for socializing, competing, and playing. On the other hand, going for a hike, bike ride, jog, or swim allow you to get away and be with your own thoughts. Walking the dog, pulling weeds in the garden, choosing the stairs instead of the elevator, and other everyday tasks are also great ways to keep moving. And don't forget to stretch!

I've found exercise to be very helpful. Afterwards, I'll tend to eat normally instead of my usual cram session. I jog, but I suppose any type of exercise that works up a good, honest sweat will do!

To help ease anxiety and frustration, I swim or bike ride. After exercising I feel so much better about myself. I'm proud because I chose to do something good for me instead of destructively bingeing.

I used to compulsively jog five miles a day and work out at the gym. Sometimes I hadn't eaten in a long time and felt dizzy and weak. When I started to recover, it was hard to normalize both patterns at the same time, so first I quit exercising altogether and just concentrated on my fear of food. After I was able to tolerate feeding myself fairly well, I added walking, and now swim or jog a few times a week. I'm really doing well.

Daily exercise is essential for my mental, emotional, physical, and spiritual health. I try to do some aerobics every day—walk, swim, bike, etc. But if I miss a day, that's okay too.

Chapter Seven

Advice for Loved Ones

A few words from Leigh:

Lindsey and I fell in love at first sight. A few weeks later, she told me she had a horrible secret. I was a bit relieved when it turned out to be "only" an eating disorder. Of course, at that time the general public had virtually no awareness of eating disorders, and I certainly knew nothing about them. Actually, she didn't even use the words "eating disorder" or "bulimia," which was not an established term yet. Instead, she fully described the scope of her bingeing and vomiting, and I realized that I had underestimated the seriousness of her problem.

I quickly discovered that there was no instantaneous cure for Lindsey's bulimia. For nine years, it had monopolized her time and attention, and I was astonished that no one knew—not even her estranged husband. She acknowledged that her food issues had affected their marriage, and we both feared that unless she gave it up, our relationship was in jeopardy, as well. So we both became willing to do *anything* to help her recover. That became the top priority in our lives.

Although I was ignorant about eating disorders, I responded with compassion and creativity. I had been a high school teacher and used skills in lesson planning and values clarification to help structure her recovery. We brainstormed things for her to do to avoid bingeing and to get to know herself better—the kinds of things that are in this book.

Although she felt terrible about having such "bizarre" behavior, I kept reminding her to appreciate the goodness that I saw—a loving, funny, talented, brilliant, beautiful woman. Eventually, she started to see herself that way, as well.

For many months, Lindsey's battle with bulimia was our primary focus as she took steps to put it behind her. During that time, I had to continually remind myself that she was the only one who could do the work. I could make suggestions, be a sounding board, or even take punches with boxing gloves, but I could not "fix" her. Of course, I was not an unaffected bystander—our staying together was predicated on her recovery. But even though her struggles forced me to examine my own values on such subjects as family dynamics, weightism, media, feminism, and healthy eating, I never lost sight of the fact that *she* was the one in recovery.

Sometimes people who have heard her story give me more credit than is due. I merely provided love, support, and ideas. I didn't have difficulties with food or self-esteem, so I never experienced firsthand the pain that Lindsey endured or the courage it took to get better. Instead, I reaped the benefits of her recovery: Our love has flourished for more than 30 years, and I stumbled onto my life's work.

I never expected to become an expert on eating disorders, but that's what happened. I've spent a long career writing, editing, and publishing books and peer-review journals in this field. I've lectured throughout the United States and Canada at universities and professional conferences and have interacted with many thousands of people concerned with food problems. I have counseled both sufferers and their loved ones, and am confident that the advice that Lindsey and I offer in this chapter can be helpful to you.

General suggestions

If you are supporting someone in recovery, I encourage you to learn about eating disorders. Start by using the information in this book! It will give you knowledge and insight about bulimia as well as suggestions and guidance for recovery. Also, discuss with the person you are assisting *their* expectations for your involvement. At the same time, set boundaries that make it clear that he or she* is responsible for their own recovery, yet affirm that you will do whatever possible to help. Here are more general suggestions:

- Remember that your loved one has the food problem, and it is up to her to do the work.
- Make a pact of complete honesty.
- Be patient, sympathetic, non-judgmental, and a good listener. Let her know that you care and have her best interests at heart.
- Accept that recovery is a process and does not happen quickly. Help her to be patient, as well.
- When her behavior affects you, express yourself without placing guilt or blame upon her. Try not to take her actions personally. Use "I" messages, explaining your feelings and concerns. You may need to disengage from her to take care of yourself.
- Have compassion. Your loved one may be overwhelmed as she gets in touch with the painful issues underlying the behavior. She will need your love and support at these times more than ever.
- Continually remind yourself that your loved one uses bulimia as a way of coping with life. Encourage her to find healthier ways.
- Do not try to guess what she wants, but urge her to express her needs and boundaries. Assure her that she can say "No" sometimes! If you have questions, ask.

*Although bulimia affects many males and everything in this chapter is applicable to both genders, we use female pronouns for simplicity.

- Learn about issues related to eating disorders, such as: societal pressures on women, the glorification of thinness, weight prejudice, set point, family dynamics, and self-esteem.
- Campaign for professional therapy, keeping in mind that no single approach to recovery works for everyone. Be available for joint counseling. Be flexible and open in supporting whatever method she chooses.
- Don't comment on her appearance. You may think you are offering compliments, but they can sometimes be misinterpreted.
- Recognize that she needs to learn to make her own decisions, and that the direction of her recovery is her responsibility. Don't constantly check up on her unless she asks that of you.
- Consider options for intervention if the bulimia is severely out-of-control.

Food and Eating

Although bulimia is not just about food, developing healthy eating behaviors is an essential part of recovery. In some cases, especially when the person with the eating disorder is a minor, parents are encouraged to provide *parent-assisted meal support*. This means that in the early stages of recovery from bulimia, they would typically be responsible for providing all meals and snacks, monitoring intake, and staying with their child after meals to prevent additional eating (bingeing) or purging. As the young person becomes more mature and trustworthy, she would be given more freedom—the goal being to learn to make healthy decisions about food and to cope with life stressors without returning to bulimic symptoms.

Whether you are a parent, partner, or another type of support person, the following guidelines are relevant:

- Remember that food is not the problem, and bulimia is a symptom. Look past the immediate situation to the deeper issues.
- Allow her to establish reasonable rules and goals about food and eating, but assert your rights as well. Only make rules that can be enforced; work within a framework that will result in successes rather than failures.
- Make it clear that she is responsible for the consequences of her bulimic behavior. For example, if she binges on the family's food, she should replace it using her own money. If she vomits, she should clean the bathroom.
- If she binges, she should face it afterwards by talking about why it happened, writing in a journal, or exploring options with you for how to avoid bingeing the next time she is in a similar situation.
- Do not allow meals to be a battleground. Avoid turning her eating into a power struggle. Don't be confrontational, but instead be calm, firm, nonjudgmental, and try to maintain a degree of levity.
- Mealtime conversations should not revolve around her bulimia.
- Encourage your loved one to develop a safe, healthy, and achievable meal plan on her own or with a nutritionist or dietitian.
- Plan activities that do not revolve around food. Take walks together, visit museums, go to the movies, play sports. If she is uncomfortable about eating in public, then do something besides going to restaurants for entertainment.

Care for the Caregiver

Caregivers usually experience numerous emotions about their loved one's situation. They may blame themselves for not recognizing the warning signs and intervening earlier, or feel guilty for somehow contributing to the problem. They often "walk around on eggshells" for fear of upsetting the person or making matters worse. Exasperation over lack of communication is common, as is frustration over lack of progress and feelings of isolation and helplessness. Some parents fear that their child will never live up to her potential because of the eating disorder. Certainly everyone worries about health and whether or not recovery is really possible.

With so much stress on you, the caregiver, it is mandatory that you take care of yourself even as you support your loved one's recovery process. Here are some suggestions:

- Consider getting professional counseling for yourself.
- Take quiet time everyday to be alone with your thoughts. Just as activities like meditation and journal writing are important for her, they can also benefit you.
- Be open to the possibility—without blame—that, despite your best intentions, you might be somehow contributing to her problem. You might need to challenge some of your own behaviors and beliefs.
- Recognize your strengths and limitations. Don't try to do more than you are willing or able.
- Be a good role model by eating healthfully (but don't diet!), exercising regularly, and expressing positive self-esteem.
- Don't allow the eating disorder to be the only focus of your life. Try to maintain regular routines around meals, housekeeping, responsibilities, friendships, etc.

- Indulge yourself from time to time with hot baths, massages, and doing activities just for you.
- Don't deny yourself the pleasure of dessert or foods that she fears, but instead model healthy enjoyment for her to see as normal.

Specifically for Parents

Nothing hurts worse than seeing your child suffer, regardless of his or her age. Most parents would do or give anything to help their child recover from an eating disorder. We've known of parents who have had to sell their homes and go into debt to finance treatment, and we've spoken to countless mothers and fathers who have been scared, confused, and desperate about what to do to help their children.

Your pain is very real and the task at hand is enormous. Here are some suggestions:

- Share the burden with other family members, and also let friends know what you are going through so that they can support you.
- Be willing to re-evaluate your family dynamic and make changes to accommodate the recovery process.
- Feel compassion not only for her, but also for the entire family and especially yourself.
- Read some of the numerous books for and by parents of children with eating disorders (a few are included in the bibliography and many others are easily found at *bulimia.com*.
- Consider joining a family support group through local therapists, or investigate online resources for support.

- Determine whether family-based treatment or parent-assisted meal support techniques would be appropriate for your family's situation.
- Become an advocate by seeking out groups such as the National Eating Disorders Association, which have programs specifically for families.
- If possible, pay for treatment for your child.

Specifically for Spouses and Life Partners

Compared to parents, little has been written about the roles of spouses and life partners or the topic of marriage and eating disorders. However, these are vitally important subjects for the many couples involved with recovery. Bulimics are often secretive and self-shaming, and these characteristics—and others like poor body image, low self-esteem, and guilt—get in the way loving relationships. Also, bulimia and its treatment can be expensive and the process of recovery can take a long time, putting stress on even the best of marriages. Faced with such burdens, most spouses and partners are eager to actively participate in their loved one's recovery.

As discussed at the beginning of this chapter, couples can work together to overcome an eating disorder—or see their relationship deteriorate if they don't. They share a common cause, and by supporting each other through the healing process, recovery rewards them both. In addition to the suggestions previously listed in this chapter, the following recommendations are for spouses, lovers, boyfriends, and girlfriends of individuals with bulimia:

- Make your partner's recovery your top priority.
- Love her unconditionally.
- Ask how she wants you to help.

- Listen without judging or trying to get in the last word.
- Share the shopping and cooking.
- Eat meals together when possible.
- Attend couples therapy.
- Tell her that you love her.
- Be affectionate and let her know that you find her beautiful and sexually desirable.
- Be honest about your needs and, if necessary, improve your sex lives together.
- Be accessible and compassionate during setbacks, help her process them, and remind her why you think she's so wonderful.
- Be a supportive coach, cheering her on and offering constructive input.
- Let her know when you are overwhelmed and need her to support you.
- Deal with disappointments and distrust without blame or placing guilt on her.
- Communicate directly, honestly, and punctually without holding on to problems for days without speaking up.
- Acknowledge any ways in which you enable or contribute to her bulimic behaviors, and be willing to change.
- Do not hide the basic facts from your children about Mom having an illness and needing treatment.

Chapter Eight

A Two-Week Program to Stop Bingeing

The purpose of this program is to give you—the person with bulimia—specific goals and tasks to help put you on the road to recovery. It is not an instant cure, but it will give you an experience of what it might take to recover, and some tools to get you there. It can also offer insights into the healing process for loved ones, be a resource for therapists, and is equally appropriate for men or women.

The course requires spending time and effort. Even if you're not ready to do the full two weeks or even one complete day, you can benefit from doing any of the numerous suggestions. This two-week program is simply a structure for the things that Leigh and I recommend in this book, such as having things to do instead of bingeing, writing in a journal, getting to know yourself better, learning to relax, taking advantage of professional therapy, and talking to people.

This is *not* a test. There are no right or wrong ways to do it. *But if you* follow the daily schedule faithfully, you will develop a variety of skills as well as a degree of self-awareness and confidence that you can apply to your healing process as it continues forward. At the very least, your bingeing will probably decrease.

Obviously, you have a life apart from bulimia, but you can do this program even if you go to school, or have a job, a family, or other important responsibilities. Time for the assignments can come from time *not* spent planning and executing binges. Feel free to rearrange the order of days to accommodate your usual, busy routine.

Let us remind you again that your bulimia has taken care of you in many ways, most notably to protect you from a complex array of feelings. Experiencing past hurts, present shame, or other unfamiliar, unexpressed emotions can be frightening as well as overwhelming. Moreover, if you are not used to having feelings or even differentiating one from another, you may be tempted to turn to your fond friend, bulimia, for safety. This is a natural reaction, and we urge you to fight it!

Our advice is to be aware and prepared. On pages 106–108 is a list of things to do instead of bingeing. Keep a list such as this handy at all times, and be sure to include some of *your* ideas. Evaluate how well they work. Have a variety of support available, such as a therapist, friend, relative, eating disorders support group (either online or in person), recordings of your own soothing voice, special music, hotline or local treatment phone number in case of emergency, as well as your journal and other books. And if you do binge, forgive yourself, use it as a learning experience, and get back to the program. Would you quit school if you received a poor grade on one assignment? No, you would study a little harder next time. So, here's some extra-credit homework for exploring slips. Write your answers to any or all of these questions (and more of your choosing) in your journal:

QUESTIONS FOR REFLECTION: IF YOU BINGE

- What do I think led me to do the binge?
- What were my thoughts before, during, and after?
- What was I feeling before, during, and after?
- What did I eat?
- Did I purge?
- How did you purge?

- Did I try to do something instead of bingeing?
- Why didn't that work?
- What else could I have done?
- What will I try to do instead of bingeing next time the cravings are so strong?

Incidentally, *Bulimia: A Guide to Recovery* has gone through extensive changes since it was first published in 1986. Early versions included a "Two-Week Program to Stop Bingeing" which was, at one time, expanded to three weeks. However, in this edition, we have taken the "best of" all prior programs and distilled them into what we feel is the most manageable, least-intimidating length.

Over the years, we've received thousands of letters from people who have used our advice. Some have followed the program exactly and others have simply used various ideas from the book. Hearing from readers is gratifying and humbling, as you can appreciate from the following quotes:

I am seventeen years old and am on Day 13 of your two-week program. How can I begin to thank you? It's weird, at first I didn't want to do the program or even read the book. I felt like I didn't have a problem. Now I can recognize negative thoughts and say NO! I will not give in to this excuse of a disease! Bulimia is something I have control over and I will not let it win!" Thank you for caring, you are true angels.

I have been in and out of treatment and am trying to recover. Whenever I find myself relapsing, I use your program to get myself back on the right track.

Just a note to say thank you. You were both a great inspiration to me when I made the decision to begin recovery from bulimia. Your book has been a blessing. I have just completed the program and I can honestly say things are looking a lot brighter. I feel more in touch with myself and who I truly am. I have learned how to ask for support when I need it.

I have just completed the two-week program and am going through it for the second time starting today.

I found your book to be very useful, especially the two-week recovery program. It helped me to set aside time for myself each day. I have worked through it slowly, actually taking three months.

Your book has helped me so much. I carry it with me just about all the time. I feel more secure with it and know some day I can leave it on a shelf and refer to it from time to time. For now, though, I keep it with me and do homework assignments I hadn't gotten to yet. Appreciate how it has given me a structured way to focus on my needs. Thank you so much.

Introduction

Before you begin, either buy a journal or create one in a folder on your computer specifically for the two-week course. This is not only to give you a sacred, safe place to write your innermost thoughts and feelings, but you will also use it to complete various homework assignments we ask you to do. A journal will support you by being a good "listener" and by being a record of the patterns and progress of your journey.

Also, be prepared to spend a little money for materials and field trips. These costs are generally low, and by the end of the course you will have saved money that you probably would have spent on food. Also, Day 9 may require some planning in advance or rescheduling of other activities, so look it over and prepare.

As you will see, each of the 14 days in the program has a similar schedule that includes:

THEME: A general subject to focus on throughout the day, which is relevant to eating disorders recovery, such as attitude, assertiveness, eating, body image, having fun, and living in the moment.

THOUGHT FOR THE DAY: An affirmation that represents the theme. Copy it into your journal first thing in the morning and repeat it over and over all day long. Say it when you sit down, stand up, open doors, start the car, wash your hands, and especially when you eat. Say it with conviction and, most of all, repeat it!

MORNING WARM-UP: A short, physical exercise connecting you to your body in some way first thing in the morning. If you have roommates, a spouse, kids, or others that require your attention, make them wait. Afford yourself this bit of time.

MORNING JOURNAL ENTRY: A written assignment to get you to think more deeply about your life by focusing on recovery before beginning your daily routine or eating breakfast.

TODAY'S THINGS TO DO INSTEAD OF BINGEING: More ideas to add to the ones on your own list. Record how successful the various options are for you in your journal. Some of these can also be used for self-improvement purposes as well as to avoid bingeing.

HOMEWORK: More written assignments and tasks to complete. These can be done any time during the day. We strongly suggest that you do all of the homework, but there may be days when you simply cannot. Do each day's work that day and, if necessary, catch up later.

MEDITATION & GOOD NIGHT: A regular 10 to 20-minute period devoted to some form of meditation every night (see pages 145–148 for ideas), followed by a message from us to you. We hope you will then sleep well, feeling both centered and supported.

DAY 1

Recovery, the journey begins...

As the saying goes, every journey begins with a first step. You are ready! Let's start with baby steps. Today, do the recovery work that's in front of you. (Incidentally, read through the entire day's description every morning when you awake.)

THOUGHT FOR THE DAY

My life is better without bulimia!

Repeat this affirmation over and over with conviction, because it is absolutely true. As you will discover, everything improves when you stop focusing on food and weight.

MORNING WARM-UP

Today, let's begin with a good stretch for about ten minutes. Put on some music, if you wish. Here are some hints for getting the most from stretching:

1. Instead of copying someone else's routine, make up your own as you go along.
2. Relax and enjoy the feel of your muscles. Touch them with your fingers.
3. Groan, sigh, laugh, and make noise—it's fun and releases tension.
4. If you feel tension in your face, there is tension in your body—relax your face!
5. Don't overstretch or push yourself to go further than feels good.
6. Slowly stretch your whole body. Include your eyes, neck, back, shoulders, chest, arms, fingers, thighs, calves, and feet. For balance, alternate bending and arching your back, twisting one direction and then the other.

7. Remember to keep repeating the Thought for the Day: "My life is better without bulimia!"

MORNING JOURNAL ENTRY

Describe one of the happiest moments of your life. Try to remember why you felt so good about yourself at that time. We want you to remember that good feeling throughout the day.

TODAY'S THINGS TO DO INSTEAD OF BINGEING

1. If you have not already made a list of your own as suggested earlier in this chapter and in Chapter 3, do so now!

2. Vent your frustrations and tensions, and loudly express those feelings that you've been swallowing. Punch, kick, yell, and go wild! Use inanimate objects, such as beds and pillows, punching bags, or a hammer and wood. Look at a clock and go three rounds of two minutes each. Make that pillow feel your anger, beat the #$&!! out of it!

3. Buy colored, sticky stars to put on your calendar for every day that you do not binge.

4. Go for a long walk in your neighborhood. Weather is no obstacle; even a brisk walk in the rain or snow can be invigorating. Bring your journal or computer to record any ideas that you have during the walk. Literally stop to smell the roses! Smile or talk to people you see; look them in the eye. Observe everything, even the sky. Do not eat or go into any stores during this walk.

Important note: We often recommend that you "get away" in order to avoid a binge, but it is crucial to maintain your positive feelings and commitment to recovery when you get back to your usual environment. So upon your return, sit quietly for five minutes and relax. After that, write in your journal again. This is actually a great combination of two great recovery tools because the relaxing connects you to your heart, and you can explore any insights through writing afterwards. Other choices are to call someone, drink a cup of hot tea, check your email, or do whatever else works for you.

HOMEWORK: DAY 1

1. Write about your bulimic habits of the last weeks, months, or years. Include frequency of binges and purges, and describe in detail your last episode. Also answer the following questions: How much time do you spend each day on bulimic behaviors? How much of the time are you *thinking* about bingeing? What do you think are the drawbacks of having bulimia?

2. List the various ways in which your life would be better without bulimia. Be both general and detailed. For instance, you would have more time and money, but time and money for what? Your health would improve, but in what way?

3. Read your answers for #1 and #2 and write a brief reflection about how they differ.

4. Make a final journal entry: How do you feel about what you did today and what is your intention for this course? Be specific if possible. Be sure to add, "My life is better without bulimia!" Life really is better without it.

MEDITATION & GOOD NIGHT

As mentioned in the short introduction to this program, set aside 10 to 20 minutes for a short meditation of some kind every night. (We won't remind you every night, you are expected to do this on your own.) Perhaps pick a time and place you can return to each night. To begin, repeat your intention for this course, and offer your blessings.

We know that today might have been hard for you. Even if we haven't met personally, we want you to know that we care about you and completely support your efforts. As you drift off to sleep tonight, recall that moment of happiness you wrote about earlier. Put yourself in that situation, and feel the warmth and joy. Somewhere nearby, we are there too, thinking of you as a wonderful, loving person. Sleep well.

DAY 2

Look for solutions, not problems.

Good morning! We hope you slept well and are excited about continuing this program. You may be used to avoiding your problems by bingeing, but bulimia only makes matters worse. Instead, look for solutions by thinking through situations and finding better ways to cope.

THOUGHT FOR THE DAY

I am confident and capable.

Even if you have trouble believing this affirmation, repeating it will help convince you that it is true. Start by concentrating on one or two specific ways in which you feel confidence and are capable.

MORNING WARM-UP

Take a long, hot shower or bath. While you're at it, sing at least part of one song out loud (maybe bring the lyrics in with you!). Gently stretch and massage yourself as you bathe. Think about the morning journal entry you will write and what will be acceptable for you to eat for breakfast.

MORNING JOURNAL ENTRY

Describe an incident from your life when you were able to fix something that was broken, did something particularly well, or solved a problem in an innovative way. Write about how that felt. What character traits made it possible for you to seek and find the solution you did?

TODAY'S THINGS TO DO INSTEAD OF BINGEING

1. Gather what might have been your binge food and soak it with water in the sink. Don't concern yourself with the waste; you would have wasted it by purging.

2. Pick up trash at a local park or beach.

3. Drink two glasses of water or eat a carrot slowly and feel the crunch when you chew.

4. Take a leisurely drive or go for a walk in a beautiful place.

5. If you have not already done so, destroy your home bathroom scale! A hammer will work just fine, though running over it with a car may be equally satisfying. You can write it a good-bye letter first, if you wish, but don't just throw it away—demolish it (and recycle the parts)! You don't need to be controlled by a number ever again.

HOMEWORK: DAY 2

1. Getting support is one way of looking for solutions, so begin compiling your *support list.* Make one list of all the people who already know about your bulimia. Make another of the people you want to tell, which should include almost everyone who is close to you. You do not have to contact anyone yet, so there will be some time to get used to this idea.

2. List five things that trigger your bulimia and brainstorm alternatives. Take particular note of the circumstances, such as the usual times or places you binge, friends who are negative influences, or rituals and habits that have you trapped. Then, list as many *different* ways of responding to each trigger as you can. For example: If you binge while driving to work, you can (a) take a bus or join a carpool, (b) avoid taking food with you on the drive, or (c) listen to a book on tape to change your routine.

3. When you begin to let go of the bulimia, you will need other activities, thoughts, and feelings to take its place. Today, begin thinking about something *new* you want to learn that will become part of your life and will continue beyond these two weeks. Some ideas: yoga, a musical instrument, a foreign language, a new computer program, figure drawing, or skydiving. We will ask you to spend some time on this learning project, so it should be something that you think you will enjoy.

MEDITATION & GOOD NIGHT

Sometimes, in the space of relaxation and meditation, solutions present themselves to a quiet mind. Take some time right now to appreciate any sense of joy and accomplishment you felt looking for solutions today. Or, if you felt frustrated and anxious, recognize that another day has passed—as will those feelings. Reaffirm that you will continue this program. You can do it! You *are* doing it! Sweet dreams.

DAY 3

Lighten up!
(This has nothing to do with your weight)

Everyone has a sense of humor, but sometimes life's pressures prevent us from having a good laugh. So, today is going to be a fun day, and it's going to feel great! Rearrange your schedule if necessary to get the most enjoyment out of today's assignments.

THOUGHT FOR THE DAY

I deserve to have fun!

People with bulimia tend to be serious and focused on the negative. Do you remember what it feels like to have a good belly laugh? Try to have a brighter outlook today, even if somber thoughts are lurking in the background. Force yourself to be more lighthearted and more at ease with the flow of the world around you.

MORNING WARM-UP

Bring a watch or timer into the bathroom with you and lock the door. Spend three minutes looking at your face in the mirror. Try not to look away. Make extended eye contact with yourself. Who is that? When was the last time you really looked at your face? Look at all of the colors in your eyes. How long has it been since you've noticed them? When you look at someone else, on what do you base your judgments? What kinds of judgments do you make about yourself? How about making some positive affirmations instead?

While you're at it, make dopey faces in the mirror. Stretch your face, wiggle your lips, squish your nose, and pull on your ears. Grunt, squeak, say, "Ho ho ho," "ha ha ha," and "hee hee hee." Laugh out loud, even if it's a phony laugh. Come on, lighten up and really get silly!

MORNING JOURNAL ENTRY

Write about something funny that you remember. It may be a story from childhood, something you or someone else said, or a story you read about or saw on a movie, TV, or computer screen. What made it funny? How does it feel to laugh?

TODAY'S THINGS TO DO INSTEAD OF BINGEING

1. Write affirmations in your journal 15 times each, such as: "I won't binge today," "Lighten up!" or "Every day, in every way, I'm getting better and better." As long as you are still tempted to binge, keep writing!

2. Look up your favorite comedian on the Web and read his or her biography. If possible, find clips to watch.

3. Tell someone a joke, even if it's really stupid. If you can't remember one, look online or try this one: "Why don't aliens eat clowns? They taste funny."

4. Draw a caricature of yourself.

HOMEWORK: DAY 3

1. Go online and watch clips from funny TV shows like *The Three Stooges*, *I Love Lucy*, or *Seinfeld*. Regardless of your age, these are timelessly hilarious. Give in to the silliness.

2. While you're at it, search for three funny jokes or clips. This might take awhile, because a lot of the stuff online isn't really that funny, but be persistent until you're laughing out loud. Tell these jokes or send the clip links to someone else today.

3. Get some washable markers or inexpensive stage makeup and draw on your face. Give yourself a mustache, glasses, or clown face. Looking like that, you can't possibly take yourself so seriously. Even though it might be embarrassing, allow yourself to be seen by some other people.

4. Begin to think seriously (as hard as that might be today) about how to get started on your new learning project, which was mentioned in yesterday's homework.

MEDITATION & GOOD NIGHT

Bulimia is no joke. There's nothing funny about it. However, recovery can sometimes be a lot of fun. Smile while you remember some of the amusing things you did today. We hope that it has been as enjoyable for you as it has been for us. We had a few good giggles conceiving it. Did you have a few laughs, as well?

DAY 4

Confront food fears.

You may have noticed that we haven't yet said much about food or eating. Today, we will. Whatever the causes of your bulimia—whether they are related to family, culture, chemical imbalance, karma, a desire to be thin, or anything else—you still need to eat. Don't wait to understand all your "why's" because that in itself will not stop you from bingeing. Begin to appreciate food for its taste and nourishment, and let go of your negative, obsessive thoughts.

THOUGHT FOR THE DAY

I can eat without fear.

Today, you will be facing food choices, preparation, and eating, and you will need to be more brave than you've been since your food issues started. Truly believing that you can eat without fear—day in and day out—may take time, but, for now, consciously keep repeating this affirmation, especially as you complete the food homework. Every time you say it, you will feel stronger.

MORNING WARM-UP

Do a short, five-minute stretch followed by some balance exercises. Stand on one foot for 20 seconds, then the other. Next, walk heel to toe in a straight line for about 30 feet. Finally, sit down and stand up five times without using your hands.

MORNING JOURNAL ENTRY

Identify one specific food item that you have been afraid to eat, but are willing to try today using the "Introducing New Foods" technique described in Chapter 6 on page 204. What is it about that particular food that frightens you? Have you ever had a positive experience eating it, perhaps before you were bulimic? Why did you pick this item for this exercise?

TODAY'S THINGS TO DO INSTEAD OF BINGEING

1. Remember a time when you did something brave. Write about how that felt.

2. Put binge food in bag. Drive over bag with car. Deposit bag in garbage can.

3. Ask yourself: What's the payoff to bingeing? How does that compare with the satisfaction of *not* bingeing? Make a list.

4. Take on a small, new responsibility. Buy a plant or new pet, such as a goldfish.

HOMEWORK: DAY 4

1. Pick a name or two from the support list you compiled on Day 2, and let them know about today's homework. You may need to call

someone for support if the food exposure tempts you to binge. You don't have to do these assignments alone.

2. Plan today's menu. Include breakfast, lunch, dinner, drinks, and snacks (adding dessert *only* if you feel okay about it), and be specific—you will go shopping for groceries later. Read pages 201–202 for guidelines. Don't forget the "fear food" from the morning journal entry. Your meals today should be balanced, tasty, and nonthreatening. Stick to this menu faithfully. This will give you the experience of using a meal plan.

3. Go grocery shopping. Using your detailed list, and only buy the food you need for the menu that you have prepared. *Do not buy anything that is not on your list.* Stick to your menu. You can do it!

4. Sometime today, ceremoniously eat the "fear food" you selected earlier. Afterward go for a walk. When you return, write about your feelings.

5. Plan one special meal today. For example, eat by candlelight and soft music, use good china, prepare a beautiful place setting, or picnic at a park. Perhaps start the meal with a blessing. Eat slowly, and with awareness. Put your utensil down between bites, taste your food, savor each morsel.

6. Write in your journal about your eating experiences today.

MEDITATION & GOOD NIGHT

Many people say that food is not the issue for bulimics. While we agree with this in principal, we still emphasize that reformed eating habits are crucial for recovery. The binge-purge behavior was learned, now it must be unlearned. You can eat without fear. Let your friends help you and believe in yourself. Begin introducing more "fear foods" to your menu, and you will discover a whole new world of taste and satisfaction. Thank you for all of your brave efforts today. Tomorrow will be easier.

DAY 5

Think lovely thoughts!

Your mind is a creative force. Whatever it thinks about is what is happening for you at that moment—abundance or scarcity, happiness or worry, self-hate or self-esteem. Today, notice your belittling thoughts and make an effort to replace them with positive ones. You are not unworthy; you just sometimes *think* you are. Changing your thoughts will actually change your experience. Today, look on the bright side.

THOUGHT FOR THE DAY

My life is good.

See positives in everyone and everything. If you begin to have a negative thought, stop and replace it with a positive one. Consciously and actively practice feelings of love, approval, and confidence.

MORNING WARM-UP

See yourself a little differently. Spend about 15–20 minutes doing this relaxation exercise. In a quiet place, lie on your back, eyes closed. Tense and then relax every part of your body. Start with your toes and feet, flexing them, holding the tension, and then releasing, allowing that area to gently relax. Follow this procedure up your calves, knees, thighs, buttocks, waist, chest, back, shoulders, arms, etc. Once you are in a completely relaxed state, spend a few minutes imagining yourself without judgment as: tremendously fat, skinny, tall, short, different races, the opposite sex, and pure light without form.

MORNING JOURNAL ENTRY

Write one sentence each about 5–10 things in your life that are positive. If this is too difficult, list 5–10 things for which you are grateful, and why.

TODAY'S THINGS TO DO INSTEAD OF BINGEING

1. Make a list of everyone you have ever loved.

2. Think about the ways in which your eating disorder has taken care of you. Then, write it a thank-you note, and tell it that you are saying goodbye.

3. Walk in a garden, art museum, or other lovely place.

4. Turn on a favorite love song and sing along.

HOMEWORK: DAY 5

1. Make a list of 25 favorite things. They can be activities, people, tangible items, events, places, or emotions.

2. Whenever you notice a negative thought today, write it down, then tear up the paper. Replace the thought with a positive one!

3. Review the plan for Day 9, when you will be going on an all-day excursion. You may have to do some rearranging of your schedule and planning ahead, so start today. Contact a friend to accompany you.

4. Allow yourself a small dessert tonight, even if it is just one bite. Do not obsess about it, merely select and eat it as a reward for your efforts to end bulimia. Do not count calories. If negative thoughts intrude, immediately stop what you are doing and write in your journal about the courage it takes to even attempt this kind of task.

MEDITATION & GOOD NIGHT

Words, whether spoken or thought, have tremendous power. The way that we verbalize something is how we perceive it. If negative words are used, negative feelings surface. You may have gotten used to thinking of yourself as worthless, unlovable, or unattractive. Purposefully change those words to worthy, lovable, and attractive—both inside and out—and see how that feels. You are *not "a bulimic,"* you are "*recovering from bulimia." Have sweet dreams.*

DAY 6

You are not alone.

Millions of people suffer from eating disorders. More than 150,000 throughout the world have read this book, and some are working through this program right now, at the same time as you! Although you are anonymous to one another—and we'll probably never meet in person either—understand that we all share a deep and meaningful connection. There is support out there even from people you don't know.

THOUGHT FOR THE DAY

I can accept support from others.

Getting support does not mean only having serious talks. A support relationship can be fun and fruitful for both people. By asking someone to help you in recovery, you are being honest, respecting that person's point-of-view, and deepening the bonds of friendship. What could be better than that? You are having many new experiences and thoughts as you do this two-week program. Share them!

MORNING WARM-UP

While in the shower or in front of a mirror, give a pep talk to an imagined dear one who is working on their recovery from bulimia. Reach into the heart of your own experience to get through to them. Tell them what you would want to hear from someone helping you. *Speak out loud!*

MORNING JOURNAL ENTRY

Write about someone who has overcome an obstacle. You might personally know them and their story or you can use a historical figure. Why did you select this person? Does their experience inspire you in any way?

TODAY'S THINGS TO DO INSTEAD OF BINGEING

1. Talk to a neighbor. Even casual conversation can distract you from bingeing.

2. Pamper your pet with fresh water, a bath, brush, or walk. Or pamper your plants!

3. Go to a nursery, buy something, and plant it!

4. Collect some of your most meaningful possessions and make a little "shrine" for yourself on a tabletop or shelf. Use seashells, letters, photos, candles, a book—anything that is indicative of your personality.

5. Tell someone you love them.

HOMEWORK: DAY 6

1. Tell someone new your entire bulimia story, especially the part about your recovery. They could be from your support list, a long lost friend or relative, or a therapist or dietitian.

2. Make a list of 5–10 myths and 5–10 rules that you may want to change. A myth might be something like, "Skinny people are happier." A rule might be something like, "I can't eat ice cream at night because I'll gain weight."

3. Make up an imaginary support group. Whom would you include and why? These can be real, imagined, fictitious, or historical people. What would you all talk about?

4. Make an effort to find a mentor, or order a book by someone who has recovered from an eating disorder, such as Jenni Schaefer or Geneen Roth.

MEDITATION & GOOD NIGHT

We hope you took the risk to reach out today. That's such an important step. If you didn't talk to someone today, you've got homework to do! We bet that you are a pretty likable person. Of the scores of people who have talked to us about their bulimia—we have often been the first ones told—each one has been sensitive, sincere, and had other great qualities. As you drift off to sleep tonight, feel the connection between your heart and the hearts of other recovering people out there in the world.

DAY 7

Take a Break!

Today you will finish the first week of this program to stop bingeing. Think about it for a moment. Have your binges decreased this week? Have you practiced new coping skills that you particularly like? Most of the course emphasis so far has been on getting to know yourself better and to start reaching out. Next week, we will encourage you to interact even more. However, today you deserve to take it a little easier.

THOUGHT FOR THE DAY

I deserve rest and relaxation.

Many bulimics are high-achievers and feel guilty if they are not being productive. Life is not a race or contest; everyone needs to take a break at times. If bingeing has been a way for you to unwind or be distracted, you need new ways to relax (see pages 145–148). You are not just a "human doing," you are also a "human being." Allow yourself to just relax and "be enough" in the moment.

MORNING WARM-UP

Use the progressive relaxation technique from Day 5. Today, though, when you are in that state of deep physical relaxation, visualize a special, safe, beautiful place. This can be somewhere you know well or an imaginary spot. Put yourself into the scene by seeing the sights, hearing the sounds, smelling the scents, and feeling your entire being in that restful spot.

MORNING JOURNAL ENTRY

Imagine, if you could go anywhere in the world for one day to relax, where would that be and what would you do?

TODAY'S THINGS TO DO INSTEAD OF BINGEING

1. Listen to or play soothing music.

2. Flush what would have been your binge food down the disposal. Do you see the irony?

3. Try gardening, taking a slow walk, joining a yoga class, or going for a drive just to see the sights.

4. Repeat this morning's relaxation and return to your special place, but do it outside in the fresh air.

HOMEWORK: DAY 7

1. Write or call someone you love. Perhaps seek out a person whom you have not seen for a long time but care for, such as a childhood friend or relative.

2. Today, speak less. Try to reflect more on your inner experience. Silence is golden!

3. Take a long, luxurious bath or a quiet time (with candles, music, etc.).

4. Catch up on unfinished homework from this week.

5. Read the plan for Day 9, and make any necessary preparations.

MEDITATION & GOOD NIGHT

Finding a balance between work, play, and rest feels nourishing on a very deep level. Enjoy that feeling because you have done it all this week! Get to bed early tonight and enjoy a long sleep. Congratulations on sticking to the program so far. That is an amazing feat! You're halfway there…

DAY 8

Love Day!

Today is "Love Day" and you're going to love it! Last week we concentrated on inner growth. This week we will expand our horizons to include people, places, and outside experiences. Incidentally, in the many letters we've received, this is often mentioned as a favorite day.

THOUGHT FOR THE DAY

I love me.

Love doesn't come from "out there;" it comes from within you. If you think no one loves you, that your parents didn't, your friends don't, and you're sure that the "right" guy or gal won't, how can you love yourself? You must realize that *you* are the source of love, that *you* can practice being in a state of love just by turning within.

MORNING WARM-UP

Take a sensual shower or hot bath. Don't just soak or wash but massage your muscles. Appreciate the sensuality of your skin. Touch yourself with a lover's embrace. If your situation permits, share this experience.

MORNING JOURNAL ENTRY

Write your definition of love. In what ways can you bring more love into your life?

TODAY'S THINGS TO DO INSTEAD OF BINGEING

1. Set a timer for ten minutes. Close your eyes, count your breaths, and relax.

2. Take a round-trip bus or train ride anywhere. Observe the people, and practice seeing each of them through loving eyes. Do not eat on this trip!

3. Compose a prayer.

4. Go to a lovely spot away from home, like a park, the beach, a hilltop with a beautiful view, or a particular tree or grove.

5. Make a list of the people, places, and things you love. Think about why you chose what you did.

HOMEWORK: DAY 8

1. Do a good deed—a random act of kindness. Some possibilities: visit a nursing home and give of yourself by talking to an elderly person; baby-sit for a friend with small children; visit someone and help them clean or cook; offer your services to a non-profit organization; give food or clothing to a homeless shelter. Don't just call or think about it. This is the main assignment today, so go somewhere and do it!

2. Tell someone you love them and why. This can be done in writing.

3. Have you lined up someone to join you tomorrow on Day 9?

4. Throughout the day, look at your reflection in different mirrors and windows. Does your mood depend on what you see? Think about it.

5. To elicit feelings of love, listen to a favorite old song or piece of music, look through a scrapbook or photo album, or watch a romantic movie.

MEDITATION & GOOD NIGHT

Everyday can be a "Love Day" if you practice. As we said before, love is not something that comes from outside of you. While we wrote this book, feelings of love generated the words. Doing good deeds, helping others, feeling positive about ourselves—these make us feel more "full" than food ever can.

DAY 9

It Takes All Kinds to Make a World.

Invite someone to join you in today's activities, which revolve around role playing. Most of the time, we get too caught up in our identities and our own particular roles, acting in ways to please our parents, bosses, teachers, and friends. What about you? Do you live for others with little regard for your own feelings? Do you want to be thin to please a lover, parent, or society? Who makes judgments about you? It's okay to be different from the norm! Don't be afraid of what people think; be fearless!

THOUGHT FOR THE DAY

It's all right to be different.

Today, you will be! Create a new identity for yourself and act it out! You don't have to be someone exotic—you can be what you consider to be a "normal" person. Obviously, continuing this masquerade all day can be difficult, but do your best. Be that person as much as possible, and use this "distance" to get to know yourself better. This can be fun as well as revealing. Of course, *you must choose not to be bulimic.*

MORNING WARM-UP

As you know by reading today's plan, you are going to pretend to be someone else today. Wash your hair and fix it how the other person would wear it—maybe with a scarf, curls, parted in the middle, or maybe you'll wear a hat. Dress as this person would dress. If you are usually casual, perhaps you'll wear more formal clothing. If you usually wear makeup, maybe this person won't. As you put on your "costume," begin to assume the new identity.

MORNING JOURNAL ENTRY

Write about the person you are pretending to be. What are your likes and dislikes? What's your background? What special talents do you have? What do you like to eat? Make your description interesting and complete.

TODAY'S THINGS TO DO INSTEAD OF BINGEING

1. The person you're pretending to be doesn't binge!

2. Use your support person.

3. Go to a busy intersection and people-watch. Notice how different everyone is.

4. Visit an animal shelter or zoo. Appreciate the biological diversity.

5. Write a letter from your new identity to the "real" you, explaining why stopping bulimia is a good thing.

HOMEWORK: DAY 9

1. Today you will be going on an all-day—or at least a few hours—excursion. If it is absolutely impossible for you to take the day off, then substitute this day for the earliest one possible.

2. You've been instructed to read today's lesson and to invite a friend to join you. If you are doing it with a friend, warn them in advance that you are going to be "in character" and he or she might want to be, too. It may sound crazy and you might be slightly embarrassed to suggest it, but both of you will have fun.

3. Leave your usual surroundings by going on an outing consistent with your new character. Maybe you are an artist and can visit a museum. Maybe you are a surfer and will hit the beach! Bring anything that the "pretend you" would bring. Even introduce yourself to people along the way as this other person. Go with it!

4. If your character is more reckless than you might usually be, still use good judgment.

5. When you return home, sit quietly for at least five minutes and

relax. As helpful as it is to get away, it is crucial to maintain your positive feelings and actions upon return.

6. Write a journal entry: What aspects of your make-believe character would you like to keep for yourself? Which aspects of the "real" you never changed?

MEDITATION & GOOD NIGHT

Wherever you go, you can carry your old baggage with you or leave it behind—your choice! You are not the same as anyone else, so celebrate what makes you unique!

DAY 10

Assert yourself!

Yesterday, you tried being someone else. Now it's time to enjoy being who you are. People with bulimia are often afraid to express their true selves. They hold back feelings and put the needs of others ahead of their own. Today, you will practice expressing yourself and your needs as you get to know yourself better.

THOUGHT FOR THE DAY

I can speak up for myself!

Expose your feelings, opinions, and real self. It's okay if people don't always agree with you or if you don't always agree with them. This may even mean choosing some different friends or living situations. The important thing is that you be true to yourself!

MORNING WARM-UP

Spend at least 5–10 minutes being active and aggressive. For instance, you can hammer nails, dance wildly, dig a hole, chop wood, rip up sheets of paper, or beat the stuffing out of a pillow. Be loud, and make noise!

MORNING JOURNAL ENTRY

Think back to a time when you didn't stand up for yourself. Write out what you wish you had said or done.

TODAY'S THINGS TO DO INSTEAD OF BINGEING

1. Express a strong opinion. For example, write a television network to complain about offensive programming or advertising.

2. Say "NO!" out loud to bulimia. Then leave the house and do an activity from your list.

3. Take cans of food from your pantry or old clothes from your closet and donate them to a homeless shelter or favorite charity. This is putting your beliefs to work.

4. Write down 25 times, "I am proud of myself for quitting bulimia!"

HOMEWORK: DAY 10

1. Write a short memoir entitled, "This Is Who I Am." Be authentic, but balanced, in your appraisal. In other words, add your positive qualities, but also accept that you've got weaknesses, too.

2. Draw a self-portrait. Use a photo of yourself or look in the mirror. It doesn't have to be a work of art!

3. Talk or write to a family member about your recovery from bulimia. This can be the same person you've spoken with before or someone new.

4. Make a list of ten ways in which you can say "no" to someone in different situations. Perhaps start with an "I" phrase, such as, "I'm feeling a little unsure how to put this, but I don't like what you are doing," or, "I hope you can understand my point of view, but I'd rather not go with you today." Practicing saying what you are feeling makes it easier when the situation presents itself.

5. Work on your learning project. This has been something we have not said much about, other than to do it. If you have pursued this project, it is already giving you great rewards.

MEDITATION & GOOD NIGHT

Expressing who you are to the world is a lot different than hiding in an eating disorder. It will take time to get comfortable being both visible and real with other people. Congratulate yourself on getting this far, regardless of whether or not you've binged. As you lie in bed, feel the tension drift out of your body. The more time you spend away from bulimia, the better you will feel.

DAY 11

Getting What You Want…

If wanting to binge has been your top priority, you have ignored a world of wonderful possibilities. Ask small children what they want to be when they grow up, and you might hear answers like astronaut, the richest person in the world, movie star, president, or professional athlete. No one says, "I want to be bulimic." Now that you have decided that *you don't* want to be bulimic, what *do* you want?

THOUGHT FOR THE DAY

I can get what I want.

We already know that you do not want to be bulimic anymore; but what *do* you want? There are "wants" of a physical nature: I want a new car, or I want to go on vacation. There are also "wants" of an inner nature: I want to be happy, or I want to love myself. Think about what *you* want.

MORNING WARM-UP

Go for a walk or gentle jog of about 15 minutes. Be sure to stretch first. Do not run a race!

MORNING JOURNAL ENTRY

Write about a time when you wanted something very much and were able to attain it either through your own efforts or the generosity of other people. How did that feel?

TODAY'S THINGS TO DO INSTEAD OF BINGEING

1. Have a meal with a support person, choosing foods that you really enjoy eating. Leave some on your plate and express thanks for the meal.

2. Go somewhere tourists go. Buy a souvenir you like.

3. Donate money you would have spent on bingeing to charity.

4. Write 20 times in your notebook, "I can recover from bulimia!"

3. Go somewhere to stare at flowing water. This can be a river, lake, fountain, etc. Spend at least 15 minutes listening to the sound of the water and let your mind wander. If negative thoughts arise, ease them away with an affirmation.

HOMEWORK: DAY 11

1. List 25 "I Want!" items including things you want to own, do, and feel. Separate them into short term (2–4 weeks), medium term (1–6 months), and long-term (6–24 months) goals. Be both general and specific. Pick three and make plans to work towards getting what you want.

2. Write an imaginary, heartfelt acceptance speech. It can be for something that exists, like an Academy Award or Most Valuable Player, or something you make up, for example Best Recovering Bulimic or Most Sensitive Person.

3. What have you learned so far in your study project? Reflect on your feelings about it, such as: a sense of accomplishment, intellectual fulfillment, or stimulation. If you haven't gotten into a study project, write about what other activities or hesitations have kept you from doing it.

MEDITATION & GOOD NIGHT

You've started to focus on some of your "wants." These are much healthier thoughts than obsessing about bingeing. Keep thinking about positive goals. Believe in yourself. You *can* get some of the things you want. For now, get a good night's sleep.

DAY 12

Improve Your Body Image.

Your body keeps changing from the time you are born through old age. As an infant, you have no concept of your body as anything more than something that eats, sleeps, and poops! You certainly don't make judgments about it. When did those begin? Why? Fat or thin, short or tall—your body is the vehicle for experiencing this mystery we call life. Accept it, take care of it, and above all, stop judging it!

THOUGHT FOR THE DAY

My goodness has nothing to do with my size or weight.

Who you are is more important than how you look. Thus far we have been encouraging you to love and trust your inner self. Now is the time to start accepting your *outer* self. Your worth is not based on a number on a scale. You can be loved and loving with a body of any size or shape. That is far more important than thinness.

MORNING WARM-UP

Do the exercise "Take a Mindful Look" on pages 170-171 that involves standing in front of a mirror and mindfully observing your body.

MORNING JOURNAL ENTRY

Complete the written part of "Take a Mindful Look" as your morning journal entry.

TODAY'S THINGS TO DO INSTEAD OF BINGEING

1. Do a gentle, stretching exercise followed by a quick-paced, short walk. Enjoy the feel of simple movement.

2. Make a list of 25 good things your body does for you, such as making it possible to dance, feel the warmth of a fire, or build a snowman.

3. Try fitting your body into a space that is too small, such as under a chair or desk. This is the type of prison you have made for yourself with bulimia.

4. Clean out your closet and donate what doesn't fit to a thrift store. Honor your body by going out and buying some clothes that fit to replace them.

5. Try standing on your head using a folded blanket to protect your neck, and a wall!

HOMEWORK: DAY 12

1. List some happy couples you know. Are they in love? Do you think they have a good relationship? Do they have "ideal" bodies?

2. Go to a busy, well-populated area—maybe the same place you're getting clothes that fit—and observe people. Does *anyone* have an "ideal" body? Do thinner people seem happier than larger people? Are people eating on the run? Do they seem happy? Record some observations and thoughts.

3. Throughout the day notice how you hold yourself. Stand more upright, smile more, look at people's eyes, etc. What do your body signs say about how you feel about yourself?

4. Carefully re-read pages 165–175 on "Improving Body Image"

5. Imagine that you have been reincarnated in different bodies throughout time. Obviously, you would not look the same from lifetime to lifetime. Describe what you might have looked like and done in three of these previous incarnations. Did your appearance matter?

MEDITATION & GOOD NIGHT

Many children in elementary school are already concerned about their weight and appearance, but there was an earlier time when they were joyful about their bodies. Think of a toddler thrilled at learning to walk, a baby sucking happily on its toes, or how fun it was to take a bubble bath. Remember the wonderful smell of baked cookies before you began to worry about calories. Get in touch with that innocent time of your life when you loved your body.

DAY 13

Be Here Now.

When you think too much about the future or the past, you miss your life as it is happening right now. Bulimia is a way of avoiding the present, because if you're not in the midst of a binge, you are either planning the next binge or feeling guilty about the last one. Make today a day of mindfulness, a quiet day of non-judgment. Observe silence as much as possible and avoid unnecessary external chatter, such as TV watching (except as explained in today's homework) or Internet browsing. Keep your contact with others to a minimum and fill the day with contemplation and the sound of your inner voice.

THOUGHT FOR THE DAY

I am alive in this moment!

Practice this idea by concentrating on what you are doing at all times. If you notice your mind wandering, bring it back to the present moment, much like in meditation. Engage your heart at the same time by appreciating that you are "alive in this moment" and able to offer your best effort.

MORNING WARM-UP

Observe your typical morning hygiene with mindful awareness. For example, as you wash your face, do it thoroughly using warm water, soap, and a washcloth. Scrub the pores deeply. Rinse completely, being sure to remove all of the soap. Gently pat dry with a clean, soft towel. Perform these tasks with a singular focus only on the task at hand.

MORNING JOURNAL ENTRY

Sit quietly with your eyes closed for about ten minutes. Afterward, write about what you noticed—thoughts, sounds, smells, bodily sensations, etc.

TODAY'S THINGS TO DO INSTEAD OF BINGEING

1. Listen to a piece of classical music and try to stay focused on particular instruments, like percussion or strings.
2. Pick up trash at a park or beach.
3. Slowly drink a large glass of water. Notice the way it feels in your mouth and going down your throat.
4. Draw a picture or write a detailed description of your physical setting.

HOMEWORK: DAY 13

1. Watch TV for 15 minutes, switching channels often. Every time you see an image that glorifies thinness in any way, moan out loud ("Oy," or "Eeww," or "No!") and switch to another channel.
2. Take note of the many kinds of feelings you have today (anger, wonderment, resentment, joy, etc.) and try to put a name to them as they occur. For example, if you are feeling angry, notice, "I'm feeling angry," and write down the word "anger." Note if you are also experiencing a physical sensation along with the emotion. Anger might feel like a tightness in your chest, and joy might make your heart sing. Later, list all the feelings and sensations you can remember in your journal and read

over the list at the end of the day.

3. Visit someone with small children or observe a day care center or schoolyard. Watch how kids are present in the moment. None are concerned with the past or future. Take a cue from them about how to live in the moment.

4. Do something fun today that requires your undivided attention, such as reading a novel, playing a musical instrument, painting a picture, or washing the dog. This activity should not involve any kind of screen (movie, TV, or computer).

MEDITATION & GOOD NIGHT

You can think about the past, but *right now* is what is real. This moment is what you're experiencing. Let go of the past; old concepts don't work anymore. Don't dwell on the future. We don't know what awaits—other than that there will be surprises. Make the most of every day.

DAY 14

Graduation Day!

Today is Graduation Day, and you should be quite proud of yourself. Hum "Pomp and Circumstance" (the graduation tune) to yourself all day. As with most educational endeavors, graduating means new challenges, independence, and some uncertainty. By doing this program, you have progressed far in your recovery, and now we ask you to reach even farther. Bulimia will get more and more distant from your thoughts and consciousness as long as you keep making an effort.

THOUGHT FOR THE DAY

I have accomplished something big!

Let's summarize some of the things that you have done in this course. You've set goals, taken initiative, examined feelings, laughed, learned something new, been honest and open with others, relaxed, identified wants, made affirmations, practiced eating without bingeing, and expressed love. Have pride; your horizons are limitless.

MORNING WARM-UP

Read through the past two weeks' Morning Warm-ups, and remember your experiences doing them. Do these kinds of activities every morning. Today, repeat one that you particularly liked.

MORNING JOURNAL ENTRY

Write feedback to us about the two-week program. You do not have to send it but may if you wish.

TODAY'S THINGS TO DO INSTEAD OF BINGEING

1. Visit a hospital newborn unit and watch the babies. You, too, are starting fresh.
2. Buy flowers or a plant in honor of your graduation.
3. Make a list of all the things you have done in the last two weeks to *not* binge.
4. Thank your support people and let them know about your graduation.

HOMEWORK: DAY 14

Did you think we wouldn't ask you do homework on graduation day? Well, maybe just a little...

1. One of life's great rewards is leaving a legacy, such as a work of art or an act of kindness, and everyone does that in one way or another. In fact, you have an effect on all of the people you meet without even realizing the significance of your interactions. Think about what you might want to leave behind for the benefit of others. What do you wish your legacy to be?

2. Review everything you've written in your journal during the last two weeks.

3. Write an intention for how you want to proceed with your "post-graduate" recovery.

4. Write a commencement speech as if you were addressing an entire class of people recovering from bulimia. Make it inspiring! Read it out loud.

MEDITATION & GOOD NIGHT

We're nostalgic writing this final message to you. We have shared ourselves, hoping that you will be motivated in your recovery. Think of us cheering you on while you continue making progress. With all our hearts, we wish you love, happiness, and freedom from bulimia.

Post-Graduate Studies

Your recovery is now in full swing, but you still have work to do. In the upcoming days, weeks, months, and years, you will continue to learn and grow. If you've gone through this two-week program, apparently you respond well to structure. Continue to meditate, write in your journal daily, and constantly repeat positive affirmations. Deepen your relationships, especially with the people who support you. Pursue professional therapy. Review the suggestions in Chapter 5 and the themes from the two-week program. Above all, believe in yourself.

We'd like to hear from you!

Nothing has given us greater satisfaction or has touched our hearts more than the beautiful letters we have received from people who have read our books. You can write to us in care of Gürze Books, PO. Box 2238, Carlsbad, CA 92018. At the time of publication, our email addresses are: Lindsey@gurze.net and Leigh@gurze.net.

Resources

EATING DISORDER RESOURCE CATALOGUE

Distributed by Gürze Books, this FREE annual catalogue contains the newest, most relevant books on eating disorders for both professionals and lay individuals, a list of national eating disorders organizations, a treatment directory, and short inspirational articles.

Gürze Books
PO Box 2238
Carlsbad, CA 92018
(800)756-7533
bulimia.com

BOOKS

Over 1,000 books about eating disorders and related topics have been published in the past 30 years. We know because we've been publishing, distributing, and collecting them! While a comprehensive selection of books on eating disorders and related topics is available at our website, *bulimia.com*, below are a few relevant titles to get you started.

For Individuals

Anorexics and Bulimics Anonymous: The Fellowship Details Its Program of Recovery for Anorexia and Bulimia by Anonymous. Anorexics and Bulimics Anonymous, 2002.

Beating Ana: How to Outsmart your Eating Disorder & Take Your Life Back by Shannon Cutts. Health Communications, Inc., 2009.

The Dialectical Behavior Therapy Skills Workbook for Bulimia by Ellen Astrachan-Fletcher and Michael Maslar. New Harbinger, 2009.

Eating in the Light of the Moon: How Women can Transform their Relationships with Food through Myths, Metaphors, and Storytelling by Anita Johnston. Gürze Books, 2000.

Finding Your Voice through Creativity: The Art and Journaling Workbook for Disordered Eating by Mindy Jacobson-Levy and Maureen Foy-Tornay. Gürze Books, 2009.

The Food and Feelings Workbook: A Full Course Meal on Emotional Health by Karen Koenig. Gürze Books, 2007.

Goodbye Ed, Hello Me by Jenni Schaefer. McGraw-Hill, 2009.

Hope, Help & Healing for Eating Disorders by Gregory Jantz. Random House, 2010.

Life Without Ed: How One Woman Declared Independence from Her Eating Disorder and How You Can Too by Jenni Schaefer. McGraw-Hill, 2004.

Making Weight: Healing Men's Conflicts with Food, Weight, Shape, and Appearance by Arnold Andersen, Leigh Cohn, and Thomas Holbrook. Gürze Books, 2000.

The Overcoming Bulimia Workbook by Randi E. McCabe, Traci L. McFarlane, and Marion P. Olmsted. New Harbinger, 2003.

The Rules of "Normal" Eating by Karen Koenig. Gürze Books, 2005.

For Families

Andrea's Voice: Her Story and Her Mother's Journey Through Grief Toward Understanding by Doris Smeltzer. Gürze Books, 2006.

The Body Betrayed: A Deeper Understanding of Women, Eating Disorders, and Treatment by Kathryn Zerbe. Gürze Books, 1993.

The Eating Disorder Sourcebook: A Comprehensive Guide to the Causes, Treatments, and Prevention of Eating Disorders–Third Edition by Carolyn Costin. McGraw-Hill, 2007.

Father Hunger: Fathers, Daughters, and the Pursuit of Thinness–Second Edition by Margo Maine. Gürze Books, 2004

Help Your Teenager Beat an Eating Disorder by James Lock and Daniel LeGrange. Guilford Press, 2004.

Off the C.U.F.F. A Parent Skills Book for the Management of Disordered Eating by Nancy Zucker. Duke University Medical Center, 2006.

The Parent's Guide to Eating Disorders by Marcia Herrin and Nancy Matsumoto. Gürze Books, 2007

Surviving an Eating Disorder: Strategies for Family and Friends–Third Edition by Michelle Siegel, Judith Brisman, and Margot Weinshel. HarperCollins, 2009.

Why She Feels Fat: Understanding Your Loved-One's Eating Disorder and How You Can Help by Johanna Marie McShane. Gurze Books, 2007.

WEBSITES

Websites with information on eating disorders vary in content and quality, so be a careful browser! Make sure the sites you frequent are focused on recovery, and are not triggering or pro-eating disorder. The following websites are sponsored and maintained by Gürze Books, where you can find links to many other reputable, eating disorder recovery sites.

Bulimia.com

Home website for Gürze Books, which specializes in eating disorder resources. Offers more than 150 annotated books on eating disorders and related topics, links to treatment facilities and non-profit organizations, a therapist directory, lists of support groups, links to other informational sites, a speaker's bureau, and much more.

EatingDisordersReview.com

Based on a clinical newsletter started in 1989 and edited by Joel Yager, MD, the website has a searchable database with hundreds of articles for eating disorders professionals. Also offers lay articles on recovery for individuals and families written by leading experts in the field.

EatingDisordersBlogs.com

A blog website with over a dozen active bloggers writing on a wide variety of eating disorder topics for both professional and lay readers.

NON-PROFIT ASSOCIATIONS

The following are major non-profit eating disorders associations in the United States and Canada. For a complete list, go to *bulimia.com.*

Academy for Eating Disorders (AED)
(847) 498-4274
aedweb.org
Global association for eating disorders professionals that promotes effective treatment, develops prevention initiatives, stimulates research, and sponsors an annual international conference. Also gives referrals.

Binge Eating Disorder Association (BEDA)
(443) 597-0066
bedaonline.com
Help for people who have binge eating disorder and their friends and family, as well as a resource for treatment professionals. Sponsors an annual conference.

Eating Disorders Anonymous (EDA)
EatingDisordersAnonymous.org
A fellowship of individuals devoted to recovery through free 12-Step meetings focused on balance, not abstinence.

Eating Disorders Coalition (EDC)
(202) 543-9570
EatingDisordersCoalition.org
A cooperative of professional and advocacy organizations working to advance the federal recognition of eating disorders as a public health priority through lobby days and other activities.

International Association of Eating Disorders Professionals (IAEDP)
(800) 800-8126
iaedp.com
A membership organization for professionals that offers certification, education, local chapters, a newsletter, and an annual symposium. Also gives referrals.

National Association of Anorexia Nervosa and Associated Disorders (ANAD)
(630) 577-1333
(630) 577-1330 - helpline
anad.org
Recovery support in a variety of forms including: a network of support groups, online discussion board, a referral list of therapists and treatment program, advocacy, research, and prevention efforts, and a helpline.

National Eating Disorders Association (NEDA)
(206) 382-3587
(800) 931-2237 - helpline
NationalEatingDisorders.org
The largest non-profit eating disorders organization in the United States, NEDA provides treatment referrals, and sponsors a toll-free helpline, an annual conference, and National Eating Disorders Awareness Week.

National Eating Disorder Information Centre (NEDIC)
(416) 340-4156
(866) 633-4220 - helpline
www.nedic.ca
Canadian organization that develops and disseminates information and resources on eating disorders and weight preoccupation through a variety of programs. Also offers a helpline.

Bibliography

American Psychiatric Association (APA). *Diagnostic and Statistical Manual of Mental Disorders (5th ed.)*. Washington, DC: APA, 2013 (in development).

American Psychiatric Association (APA). *Practice Guidelines for the Treatment of Patients with Eating Disorders*. Washington, DC: APA, 2006.

Andersen, Arnold; Cohn, Leigh; and Holbrook, Thomas. *Making Weight*. Carlsbad, CA: Gürze Books, 2000.

Bock, Linda. "Differential Diagnoses, Co-Morbidities, and Complications of Eating Disorders" in Lemberg, 1999.

Boskind-Lodahl and Sirlin, Joyce. "The Gorging-Purging Syndrome." *Psychology Today*, March 1977.

Broft, Allegra, et al. "Pharmacotherapy for Bulimia Nervosa." In Grilo, 2010.

Bulik, Cynthia. "Genetic Risk Factor for Eating Disorders." *Eating Disorders Recovery Today*, 5:4, 2007.

Cavanaugh, Carolyn. and Lemberg, Raymond. "What We Know About Eating Disorders: Facts and Statistics" in Lemberg, 1999.

Cutts, Shannon. *Beating Ana: How to Outsmart Your Eating Disorder and Take Your Life Back*. Deerfield Beach, FL: Health Communications, 2009.

Crow, Scott and Brandenburg, Beth. "Diagnosis, Assessment, and Treatment Planning for Bulimia Nervosa" in Grilo, 2010.

Crow, Scott, et al. "Increased Mortality in Bulimia Nervosa and Other Eating Disorders." *American Journal of Psychiatry*, 166:12, December, 2009.

Crowther, Janice, et al. "The Point Prevalence of Bulimic Disorders from 1990 to 2004." *International Journal of Eating Disorders*, 41:6 491-497, 2008.

Fairburn, Christopher. *Cognitive Behavioral Therapy and Eating Disorders.* New York: Guilford Press, 2008.

Fodor, Viola. *Desperately Seeking Self.* Carlsbad, CA: Gürze Books, 1997.

Frankl, Victor. *Man's Search for Meaning*. Boston, MA: Beacon Press, 2006.

Gaesser, Glenn. *Big Fat Lies.* Carlsbad, CA: Gürze Books, 2002.

Garner, David M. and Garfinkel, Paul E., eds. *Handbook of Treatment for Eating Disorders, Second Edition.* New York: Guilford Press, 1997.

Grilo, Carlos and Mitchell, James, eds. *The Treatment of Eating Disorders.* New York: Guilford Press, 2010.

Hall, Lindsey with Cohn, Leigh. *Eat Without Fear: A True Story of the Binge-Purge Syndrome.* Santa Barbara, CA: Gürze Books, 1980.

Hall, Lindsey with Cohn, Leigh. *Self-Esteem: Tools for Recovery.* Carlsbad, CA: Gürze Books, 1990.

Herrin, Marcia and Matsumoto, Nancy. *The Parentís Guide to Eating Disorders, Second Edition.* Carlsbad, CA: Gürze Books, 2007.

Hudson, James, et al. "Prevalence and Correlates of Eating Disorders in the National Comorbidity Survey Replication." *Biological Psychiatry*, 61:348-358, 2007.

Keddy, Diane. "Nutrition Hotline: Holiday Eating." *Eating Disorders Recovery Today. 5:4, Winter,* 2007.

Koenig, Karen. *Food & Feelings Workbook*. Carlsbad, CA: Gürze Books, 2007.

Koenig, Karen. *Rules of "Normal" Eating*. Carlsbad, CA: Gürze Books, 2005.

Le Grange, Daniel and Lock, James. *Treating Bulimia in Adolescents: A Family-Based Approach*. New York: Guilford Press, 2007.

Lelwica, Michelle. *The Religion of Thinness*. Carlsbad, CA: Gürze Books, 2010.

Maine, Margo. *Father Hunger*. Carlsbad, CA: Gürze Books, 2004.

Mehler, Philip and Andersen, Arnold. *Eating Disorders: A Guide to Medical Care and Complications (second edition)*. Baltimore: Johns Hopkins Press, 2010.

Mickley, Diane. "Medical Dangers of Anorexia Nervosa and Bulimia Nervosa" in Lemberg, 1999.

Mitchell, James, Specker, Sheila, and Edmonson, Karen. "Management of Substance Abuse and Dependence" in Garner, 1997.

Pearle, Catherine, Wack, Elizabeth & Tantleff-Dunn, Stacey. "Relapse Prevention: Once is Enough." *Eating Disorders Recovery Today. 5:2, Spring* 2007.

Piran, Niva. "A Feminist Perspective on Risk Factor Research and on the Prevention of Eating Disorders." *Eating Disorders: The Journal of Treatment and Prevention,* 18:3; May/June 2010.

Piran, Niva. "Prevention of Eating Disorders: The Struggle to Chart New Territories." *Eating Disorders: The Journal of Treatment and Prevention,* 6:4; Winter, 1998.

Powers, Pauline and Thompson, Ron. *The Exercise Balance.* Carlsbad, CA: Gürze Books, 2008.

Richards, P. Scott; Hardman, Randy K. & Berrett, Michael. *Spiritual Approaches in the Treatment of Women with Eating Disorders*. Washington, DC: American Psychological Association, 2007.

Richards, P. Scott, et al. "What Works for Treating Eating Disorders? Conclusions of 28 Outcome Reviews." *Eating Disorders: The Journal of Treatment and Prevention,* 8:3; Fall, 2000.

Russell, Gerald. "The History of Bulimia Nervosa" in Garner, 1997.

Safer, Debra, et al. *Dialectical Behavior Therapy for Binge Eating and Bulimia.* New York: Guilford Press, 2009.

Sánchez-Ortiz, Varinia C. and Schmidt, Ulrike. "Self-Help Approaches for Bulimia Nervosa and Binge-Eating Disorder." In Grilo, 2010.

Schwartz, Mark and Cohn, Leigh. *Sexual Abuse and Eating Disorders.* New York: Brunner/Mazel, 1996.

Schaefer, Jenni with Rutledge, Thom. *Life Without Ed.* New York: McGraw-Hill, 2004.

Tanofsky-Kraft and Wilfley, Denise. "Interpersonal Psychotherapy for Bulimia Nervosa and Binge Eating" in Grilo, 2010.

Thompson, Ron and Sherman, Roberta Trattner. *Eating Disorders in Sport.* New York: Routledge, 2010.

Wasson, Diane Hamilton. "A Qualitative Investigation of the Relapse Experiences of Women with Bulimia Nervosa." *Eating Disorders: The Journal of Treatment and Prevention,* 11:2; Summer 2003.

Woolsey, Monika. *Eating Disorders: A Clinical Guide to Counseling and Treatment.* Chicago, IL: American Dietetic Association, 2002.

Yager, Joel, ed. "Bulimia Nervosa: What 25 Years of Research Tells Us." *Eating Disorders Review. 21:1, January/February* 2010.

Yager, Joel, ed. "Eating Habits and Insulin Misuse among Young Adults with Diabetes." *Eating Disorders Review. 18:5, September/October* 2007a.

Yager, Joel, ed. "Improving Treatment and Awareness of Eating Disorders." *Eating Disorders Review. 19:1, January/February* 2008.

Yager, Joel, ed. "Major Adverse Perinatal Outcomes Reported in Women with Eating Disorders." *Eating Disorders Review. 18:4, July/August* 2007b.

Zerbe, Kathryn. *The Body Betrayed: A Deeper Understanding of Women, Eating Disorders, and Treatment.* Carlsbad, CA: Gürze Books, 1995.

Zerbe, Kathryn. "The Emerging Sexual Self of the Patient with an Eating Disorder: Implications for Treatment" in Schwartz, 1996.

Zerbe, Kathryn. *Integrated Treatment of Eating Disorders: Beyond the Body Betrayed.* New York: Guilford Publications, 2008.

Zerbe, Kathryn. "Psychodynamic Therapy for Eating Disorders" in Grilo, 2010.

Index

Q

R

S

T

About the Authors

Lindsey Hall and Leigh Cohn, who are married with two grown sons, have been working and writing together since they met in 1977. They are the founders and owners of Gürze Books.

Lindsey is a graduate of Stanford University with a B.A. in Psychology (1971) and was the first recovered bulimic to share her story on national television. In the late '70s, while in recovery from her eating disorder, she was a pioneer of the soft-sculpture art form, designing, manufacturing, and selling more than a half-million Gürze dolls throughout the world. She has co-authored or edited numerous books and articles on eating disorders and given presentations on self-esteem and recovery throughout the United States. From 1990-1992, she also served as volunteer Executive Director of Eating Disorders Awareness and Prevention (now NEDA).

Leigh, who received an M.A.T. from Northwestern University in English Education (1975), is the co-author of several books on eating disorders as well as the Editor-in-chief of *Eating Disorders: The Journal of Treatment and Prevention* (BrunnerRoutledge). He is a past-president of Independent Book Publishers of America (IBPA), a non-profit trade association of 3,000 publishing companies throughout the United States. He has been a featured speaker at universities and professional conferences throughout the United States, most recently on the topic of men and eating disorders.

Leigh and Lindsey are on the Founders Council of the National Eating Disorders Association (NEDA), and are members of the Academy of Eating Disorders (AED), the International Association of Eating Disorder Professionals (IAEDP), the Eating Disorders Coalition (EDC) and other related organizations. In 2005, they were presented with an Award for Service from the EDC, and in 2008, the Lori Irving Award for Excellence in Eating Disorders Prevention and Awareness from NEDA. Both have received honorary Certified Eating Disorders Specialist designations from IAEDP.

OTHER BOOKS BY LINDSEY HALL AND LEIGH COHN

Self-Esteem Tools for Recovery

Recoveries: True Stories of People Who Have Overcome Addictions and Compulsions

Dear Kids of Alcoholics

BY LINDSEY

Full Lives: Women Who Have Freed Themselves from Food & Weight Obsession

Anorexia: A Guide to Recovery (with Monika Ostroff)

BY LEIGH

Making Weight: Healing Men's Conflicts about Food, Weight, Shape, and Appearance (with Arnold Andersen, MD and Tom Holbrook, MD)

Self-Harm and Eating Disorders
(with John Levitt, Ph.D. and Randy Sansone, MD)

Eating Disorders: A Reference Sourcebook (with Ray Lemberg, PhD)

Sexual Abuse and Eating Disorders (with Mark Schwartz, ScD)

About Gürze Books

Since 1980, Gürze Books has been dedicated to providing quality information on topics related to eating disorders recovery, research, education, advocacy, and prevention. Thousands of professionals distribute our *Eating Disorders Resource Catalogue*, making it the most widely-used publication in this field. Gürze is also the publisher of quality books written by many highly respected authors, and maintains three helpful websites: *Bulimia.com*, *EatingDisordersBlogs.com*, and *EatingDisordersReview.com* for individuals who are suffering, their families, the professionals who treat them, and educators and activists who are working towards prevention.

ORIGIN OF "GÜRZE"

Gürze is a woman who came to Lindsey in a dream in 1976 at the end of her nine-year battle with bulimia. Waking up in the middle of the night, Lindsey wrote down the name, complete with the unusual "ü," and a quick sketch of the woman's appearance on the notepad she kept by her bed. Gürze's loveable face and long legs inspired Lindsey to make a life-sized doll, which was the beginning of a nationwide soft-sculpture business and an integral part of Lindsey's recovery. In a six-year period, over half a million hand-made dolls were sold!

People often ask what "Gürze" means. Although we don't know for sure, a student of Bavarian dialects once told us that it is a casual greeting, like "hello," which literally translates to, "I greet the God in you." We at Gürze Books like to think that this is true, and that our work inspires others to realize their own greatness.

To Order

This book is available from most booksellers or may be ordered directly from the publisher at *bulimia.com* or by calling (800) 756-7533. Quantity discounts are available.

For book trade distribution, contact Publishers Group West/Perseus Book Group: *pgw.com*.